Taxation in European Union

Pietro Boria

Taxation in European Union

Second Edition

G. Giappichelli Editore

Springer

Pietro Boria
Faculty of Law
Sapienza University of Rome
Rome, Italy

1st edition: © Giuffrè Editore 2014 with the original title "European Tax Law".

ISBN 978-3-319-53918-8 ISBN 978-3-319-53919-5 (eBook)
DOI 10.1007/978-3-319-53919-5

Library of Congress Control Number: 2017934921

Printed on acid-free paper

This Springer imprint is published by Springer Nature
The registered company is Springer International Publishing AG
The registered company address is: Gewerbestrasse 11, 6330 Cham, Switzerland

Introduction

The "European tax law" is a set of regulations issued by the EU institutions and designed to provide the control of tax matters over the tax legislations of the Member States.

However, the existence of EU rules aimed to regulate the procedures for taxation in the European Member States is not enough to identify an area of an independent and autonomous law.

In fact, if the tendency to profile the EU law is developing in the recent times, in order to valorize the regulatory provisions of specific areas of the legal system (giving a meaning to the definition of "European private law" or "European administrative law" or even "European trial law"), it must be considered that the identification of an autonomous sector of law requires the logic of a "legal system"; it basically implies the existence of principles and juridical values and the dynamic relationships between the norms.

Therefore, the existence of a set of general rules by EU institutions cannot be considered sufficient to identify a "European tax law"; if these rules compose a mere aggregate without a functional meaning, the element of the systematic unity would be lacking and there should not be an autonomous order of law.

In any case, there are several elements which lead to identify an independent and autonomous sector of law in the set of EU norms regarding the taxation law.

First of all, specific and peculiar sources of EU law may be detected, which clearly express the capacity of the European institutions to proceed independently in the regulation of tax laws over the legislative powers of the Member States.

Moreover, several principles, which are intended to set the basic values of the taxation procedure, would be defined at a primary axiological level and specifically in the Treaty of the European Union. Without anticipating topics that will be developed during this work, some juridical values may be certainly stated as the main guidelines of EU regulation: the removal of customs barriers, the protection of the fundamental economic freedoms in the common market, the principle of fiscal non-discrimination, the prohibition of the State aids, the preservation of national public finances and the tax harmonization.

In the EU derivative law, several specific tax disciplines are formulated on single taxes, where the principles set out in the Treaty are well executed. In this context, it is possible to find typical European regulations, meaning that the taxation models of national legislations are instrumentally coordinated to the goals of the European integration.

Sources, principles and regulations functionally connected to each other clearly indicate the existence of a systematic core which can appropriately stand as an autonomous legal sector; therefore they seem to justify the assertion of a *jus commune* of European impact concerning tax matters and liable to impose itself to all national tax legislations.

On the other hand, it must be noted that the fiscal discipline drawn up by the EU sharply drifts away from the developmental lines of the modern tax law.

In fact, the whole of the European fiscal regulations essentially meets the logic of the market integration on the basis of the principles of the trading free competition regardless of the nationality or the residence. Therefore, the tax system is free of its potential load of "obstruction" regarding the free movement of capitals, people, goods or services (the four freedoms of European tradition), in order to show up as a system of "neutral" rules compared to the market and the economic forces of a "free system".

There is a complete lack of the tradition of the European constitutional values which characterize the basic skills of the taxation phenomenon. Particularly, it can be observed as a lack of the "fiscal interest", intended as the general interest of the associates to the acquisition of tax resources in order to facilitate the social development, the institutional progress, the growth of the Welfare State and the essential equality of all the members of the civil community. Likewise, there is no trace of a reference to the ability to pay, an inescapable principle of distribution of tax burdens among the associates in order to ensure the concrete pursuit of a logic of the national wealth redistribution, which is at the same time a measure of guarantee and a safeguard of the individual sphere from the public administration excesses operated for the tax burden.

Therefore the function assumed by the EU taxation system is very different from that one assumed by the national tax legislations: it is a "negative" function, addressed to limit and to restrict the distortionary effects of the taxation system and not to affect "positively" the consistency of the national wealth and the redistribution process of the income among the members of a civil community.

The "negative" attitude of the EU taxation system clearly allows to highlight one of the features which tends to prefer noticeably the national system compared to the EU system.

In substance, the aim of fostering the process of the market integration brings the European institutions to develop principles and rules which determine the limitation of the power of the national systems without proposing alternative models of taxation. Therefore, EU regulations are set forth in order to contain the tax sovereignty of the Member States and not to replace this sovereignty, establishing a different level of values and rules.

Basically, a criterion of "negative integration" is established, which leads to the correction of the imperfections of the national taxation system through the deletion of all the divergent rules compared to the final neutralization of taxation towards the market and competitors. A new taxation system, which can replace the systems traditionally developed in the Member States, is not established.

In this regard, it can vividly refer to the attitude of the EU institutions to present themselves as an "anti-sovereign", which terminates the fiscal sovereignty of the other Member States without replacing it with a new sovereignty of their own, thus resulting in a sort of "land of no-one", which lacks the reference values.

This issue of the identification of a "European taxation law" appears so complex, since it may discover elements "for" and elements "against" such a nominalist choice.

Undoubtedly there exists a set of regulations which poses as a functional and systematic unit, suitable to be qualified as an autonomous legal system.

On the other hand, the lack of the essential values of the constitutional dialectic of the taxation phenomenon and the absence of a link with the sovereignty seem to testify a characterization of the regulatory system in a quite different way compared to tax law (as traditionally known).

In the awareness of such qualifying difficulty, some lexical doubts came out. In this regard, different nominalist choices have been proposed, such as "European Union tax law", essentially indicating the relevance of the tax regulations to the competence of the EU institutions; "taxation law in EU relations", in order to express the tendential supranational dimension of the EU tax system, primarily aimed at providing regulations for the Member States; or even "EU international law", in order to bring the taxation system of the European Union in the context of the international tax law, enhancing the pactional profile of such system.

However, while bringing the issue to an essentially formal and nominalist area, the choice of the expression "European tax law", as well as the great qualifying simplicity (and therefore a more didactic and classificatory assertiveness), contains an axiological impetus towards the establishment of the united Europe posing as a real federal State, which is indeed likely to overcome the conservative resistances and the particularities of the individual nation-States.

Therefore, the "European tax law" expresses a vital suggestion rather than a principled position: it is the wish for the actual development of the European integration process, which leads to the direction of an institutional organization of the European people according to the values that traditionally denote the tax law in the constitutions of the European countries.

This work is aimed primarily at those who are close to the tax matters for study purposes (university, specialization, professional qualification). Therefore, the text structure is imagined to provide an overall and systematic framework of the main topics of the "European tax law". The sequence of arguments answers to an institutional logic, and namely, it respects the progression usually addressed in the academic tradition of the tax law.

Basically, the book can be divided in two parts: the first one is devoted to the examination of the EU institutions for tax matters, and the second one is addressed to the analysis of the principles of EU taxation law.

Initially, the relevance of the taxation power in the European legal tradition is proposed following the main historical steps of the taxation relationship and highlighting similarities and differences that exist in the several European tax jurisdictions.

Subsequently, the general framework of the EU institutions is outlined, addressing special attention to the set of regulations regarding taxation, with particular reference to the stage of formation of EU rules and to the potential contrast with the national legal systems.

Then, the analysis of the European sources of law is carried out. First, the general principles of taxation set out in the Treaty of the European Union are examined. Second, the taxation system contained in the so-called derivative EU law is analysed (considering the rules formulated by regulations, directives and other regulatory tools). Finally, the case law of the Court of Justice, formed in order to address the main tax issues, is illustrated.

In the second part of the book, a particular attention is given to the general principles emerging from the European framework which typically involve the taxation system. This brings to a detailed examination of the fiscal importance of the customs Union, the European freedoms, the principle of tax non-discrimination, the balance between national interest and EU values, the tax harmonization, the State aids, the harmful tax competition and other general principles applicable in the tax jurisdiction.

Finally, an overall judgement about the development of the European integration process is proposed, with particular regard to the nexus between taxation power and sovereignty and to the values of taxation matters, in order to highlight the possible next stages of the evolution of "European tax law".

In the book, the European Union will be referred to as a community of 28 countries (qualified as Member States), as enforced at the date of the publishing. The exit of the United Kingdom (usually called "Brexit") is not considered because it is not currently effective.

Therefore, in the text, there is a continuous reference to the current number of 28 Member States.

My personal expectation is that this book can constitute a real contribution to the development of a European sensibility about a fundamental theme of the institutional framework of the common life: the tax relationship involves, indeed, some basic elements of the relation between the public power and the general interests of the social community, on one side, and the individual sphere of liberty and property of the single citizens, on the other side.

The European legal order is currently the fundamental framework within which the tax relationship should be determined and regulated and is going to become the point of reference of the taxation power.

Therefore, the analysis of principles and institutions of European tax law allows the formation of a solid background not only about the tax discipline but moreover about the dialectic of fundamental values of the social and civil life in the European territories.

I hope so that the European tax law can develop adequately in the national legal orders assuming the leading role of a common juridical basis for the definition of a unified and harmonized framework for the exercise of the taxation power in the current European democracies.

Contents

Part I The Institutions

1 The Tax Power in the Tradition of the European Legal Systems . . . 3

1.1 The Tax Power in the European Tradition . . . 3

1.1.1 The Tax Power as Distinctive Element of the Institutional Systems . . . 3

1.1.2 The Basic Features of the Tax Systems in Europe: Patterns of Affinity and Reason for Diversity . . . 4

1.1.3 The Balance Between Fiscal Interest and Protection of Individual Freedoms in the Formation of Modern Taxation Systems . . . 6

1.2 The Power of Taxation in the Modern European Constitutions . . . 10

1.2.1 The Age of the Constitution "Without Sovereignty". The Centrality of the Constitutional Values Involved in the Taxation Phenomenon . . . 10

1.2.2 The Adjustment of the Taxation Phenomenon in the Constitutional Charters of the European States . . . 12

1.3 The Coexistence of a Plurality of Taxation Systems and the Taxes Market . . . 15

1.3.1 The Crisis of the Taxation Function Resulting in the Fragmentation of the Taxation Systems . . . 15

1.3.2 The Coexistence of a Plurality of Taxation Systems: European Legal System, National Legal System and Regulations of the Minor Local Authorities . . . 15

1.3.3 The Horizontal Coordination of Different Systems . . . 17

1.3.4 The Crisis in the Ethical Consideration of the Taxation System . . . 18

1.3.5 The Market of Taxes . . . 20

2 The Role of Taxation in the EU Legal System . . . 23

2.1 The Legal System of European Union . . . 24

2.1.1 The Self-Limitation of Sovereignty of the National States About Taxation as Fundament of the International Taxation Law . . . 24

2.1.2 The Establishment of the EU Legal System 25
2.1.3 The European Constitution and the Treaty of Lisbon . . . 28
2.1.4 The Institutional Framework of the European Union: The Democratic Deficit and the Problems of the Sovereignty of the EU Institutions 30
2.2 The Regulation of Fiscal Policy in the EU 31
2.2.1 The Lack of a Proper Taxation System in the European Union 31
2.2.2 The Presence of EU Contributory Competences in Taxation and the Implementation of the Principle of Subsidiarity 34
2.2.3 The Procedures for Approval of EU Rules Related to Taxation 35
2.3 The Stability Pact and the Fiscal Compact 37
2.3.1 The Stability Pact 37
2.3.2 The Procedure for the Control and the Sanctions for the Violations to the Rules of the "Stability Pact" 38
2.3.3 The Fiscal Compact 40
2.4 The Relations Between European Union and National Legal Systems 41
2.4.1 The Orientation of the National Courts Tends to be Inspired by the Theory of the Separation of Legal Systems 41
2.4.2 In Particular, the Position of the Italian Constitutional Court 43
2.4.3 The "Monistic" Orientation of the Court of Justice . . . 45
2.4.4 The Dual Reconstructive Perspective Regarding the Transfer of Functions from the Member States to the European Union 47
2.5 The Conflicts Between the EU Legal System and the National Constitutional System 48
2.5.1 The Conflict Between the General Values of EU Law and the National Constitutional Values Concerning the Taxation System 48
2.5.2 The Limit on the Primacy of EU Law over the National Constitution: The Theory of Counter-Limits 49
2.5.3 The Violation of EU Obligations in the Field of Taxation by a Member State 50

3 The Sources of the European Taxation Law 53
3.1 The Fundamental Principles of the Taxation Law Expressed by the Treaties of the European Union 54
3.1.1 The System of the European Sources of Law and the Treaties of the European Union 54
3.1.2 The Discipline of Taxation Power in the Treaty as a Declination of the European Economic Constitution . . . 54

3.1.3 The Reduction of the Customs Duties and the Establishment of the Customs Union 56
3.1.4 The Principle of Taxation Non-Discrimination of Trade Among the Member States 57
3.1.5 The Discipline of the State Aids 58
3.1.6 The Containment of Public Monopolies 59
3.1.7 The Tax Harmonization 59
3.1.8 The Principle of Effectiveness and the Preservation of National Taxation Systems 61
3.1.9 The Recessive Scope of the Individual Rights with Comparison to the Phenomenon of Taxation 63
3.2 The Legislation of European Union 64
3.2.1 The Relief of Derivate EU Law in the Formation of the Processes of Fiscal Integration 64
3.2.2 The Regulations Relating to the Taxation Matters 64
3.2.3 The EU Directives on Taxation 66
3.2.4 The Use of the Instrument of the Multi-Lateral Agreement for the EU Discipline of Taxation 70
3.2.5 The Adoption of the Soft Law Instruments to Regulate the Taxation Matters 71
3.2.6 In Particular, the Package "Monti" and the Importance of the Issue of Harmful Tax Competition 74
3.2.7 The Translation of Soft Law in Binding Legislation by the EU Institutions 75
3.2.8 A Final Assessment Regarding the Use of Sources of EU Derivate Law 76

4 The Role of the Jurisprudence of the Court of Justice Within the EU Taxation Law 79
4.1 The Role of the Court of Justice Within the System of the EU Taxation Law 79
4.1.1 The Judicial Power in the European Union 79
4.1.2 The Role of the European Court of Justice in the System of Sources of the EU Taxation Law 81
4.1.3 Considerations on the Contribution of the Advocates General to the Formation of the Decisions of the Court of Justice 82
4.2 The Main Guidelines Followed by the European Jurisprudence on Taxation 83
4.2.1 The Essentially Acknowledging Attitude of the Court of Justice About the VAT 83
4.2.2 The Casuistic Attitude of the Court of Justice on Excises or Duties, as Well as on the State Aids 84

4.2.3 The Creative Jurisprudence in Relation to the Direct Taxes . . . 85
4.2.4 The Rule of Reason and the Balance of the European Interest with the National Interests . . . 86
4.2.5 Some Synthetic Observations on the Role of Court of Justice Relating to the Regulation of the European Taxation System . . . 87

Part II The Principles

5 The Customs Union . . . 91
5.1 The Abolition of the National Borders and the Customs Union as Founding Values of the European Common Market . . . 91
5.1.1 The Abolition of the National Borders in the Relationships Among the States . . . 91
5.1.2 The Institution of the Customs Union . . . 92
5.1.3 The European Customs Territory . . . 92
5.2 The Customs Union . . . 93
5.2.1 The Customs Union . . . 93
5.2.2 The General Principles for the Functioning of the Customs Union . . . 94
5.2.3 The Prohibition of Taxes with an Equivalent Effect . . . 95

6 The European Freedoms and the Principle of Non-restriction for Tax Purposes . . . 97
6.1 The Fundamental Role of the Freedoms of Movement Within the European Framework . . . 97
6.1.1 The Freedoms of Movement as Founding Value of the European Legal System . . . 97
6.1.2 The Principle of Non-restriction of the Freedoms of Movement for Tax Purposes . . . 98
6.1.3 The Judgment Concerning the Non-restriction in the European Jurisprudence . . . 99
6.2 The Free Movement of Goods . . . 100
6.3 The Freedom of Movement of Services . . . 102
6.4 The Free Movement of Capital . . . 102
6.4.1 The Free Movement of Capital for Tax Purposes . . . 102
6.4.2 The Exceptions to the Free Movement of Capital Expressly Provided by the Treaty . . . 103
6.4.3 A Derogation from the Principle of the Free Movement of Capital: The Judicial Clarification of the Concept of "Lucrative Rights" Provided by Directive no. 69/35 . . . 105
6.5 The Free Movement of People . . . 106
6.5.1 The Free Movement of Workers . . . 106
6.5.2 The Freedom of Establishment . . . 106

7 The Principle of Tax Non-discrimination . . . 109
7.1 The Principle of Tax Non-discrimination . . . 110
7.1.1 The Centrality of the Principle of Tax Non-discrimination Regarding the Trade Among the States in the EU Legal System . . . 110
7.1.2 The Types of the Principle of Non-discrimination . . . 111
7.1.3 The Judgment of Discrimination . . . 112
7.2 The Importance of the Principle of Non-discrimination in Direct Taxes . . . 113
7.2.1 The Judicial Clarification of the Principle of Non-discrimination Regarding Direct Taxes . . . 113
7.2.2 The Comparability of the Situations for the Purpose of Application of the Principle of Non-discrimination . . . 114
7.2.3 The Evolution of the European Jurisprudence Towards the Overcoming of the Principle of Non-discrimination Through the Application of the Principle of Restriction . . . 117
7.3 The Relevance of the Principle of Non-discrimination in the Regulation of Indirect Taxes . . . 117
7.3.1 The EU Regulations on the Principle of Non-discrimination for the Purpose of the Indirect Taxation . . . 117
7.3.2 The Prohibition of Discriminatory Internal Taxation on the Products of Other Member States . . . 118
7.3.3 The Distinction of the Non Discrimination Compared to the Prohibition of Taxes "with Equivalent Effect" to the Customs Duties . . . 121
7.3.4 The Implications of the Principle of Non-discrimination of Indirect Taxes and the Choice of the Country of Taxation . . . 122

8 The Tax Interest of the National States and the Balance with the European Values . . . 125
8.1 The Relevance of the Fiscal Interest of the National States in the European Order . . . 126
8.1.1 The Principle of the Efficiency and Preservation of the National Taxation Systems as Value of the EU Legal System . . . 126
8.1.2 The Dialectic Confrontation Between the Principle of the Efficiency of the National Public Finance and the EU Freedoms . . . 127
8.2 The Identification of the National Interests Qualified as Objective Causes of Justification with Respect to EU Values in the Jurisprudence of the Court of Justice . . . 128
8.2.1 The Creative Jurisprudence Regarding the Causes of Justification with Respect to the Application of EU Freedoms. The So-Called "Rule of Reason" . . . 128

8.2.2 The Emergence of the Overriding Reasons of General Interest as Cause of Justification with Respect to the Principles of Non-discrimination and Non-restriction: The Tax Coherence of the Internal Taxation Systems 129
8.2.3 The Jurisprudential Openings to the Principle of Territoriality 130
8.2.4 The Jurisprudential Appreciation of the Risk of International Tax Evasion or Tax Avoidance 131
8.2.5 The Protection of the Effectiveness of Tax Controls and Audits 132
8.3 The Balancing of the Court of Justice Between the EU Interest and the National Interest 133
8.3.1 The Use of the Principle of Reasonableness in the EU Jurisprudence as a Balancing Formula with Respect to the Principle of Tax Non-discrimination 133
8.3.2 The Recourse to the Principle of Proportionality as a Mechanism for the Mediation of the Possible Axiological Conflicts 134
8.3.3 Some Considerations About the Balancing of the National Tax Interest and the Individual Rights in the Jurisprudence of the European Court of Human Rights 135

9 The Tax Harmonization 137
9.1 Tax Harmonization in the European Legal System 137
9.1.1 The Notion of Tax Harmonization 137
9.1.2 The Implementation of Regulatory Instruments in the European Harmonization 139
9.2 The EU Harmonization of Indirect Taxes 139
9.2.1 The General Rules of the Harmonization of the Indirect Taxes 139
9.2.2 The Harmonization of VAT 140
9.2.3 The Harmonization of Excise Duties 142
9.2.4 The Harmonization of Customs Duties 144
9.3 The Harmonization of Direct Taxes 145
9.3.1 The General Rules of the Harmonization of Direct Taxes 145
9.3.2 The Policy of the Harmonization of Direct Taxes Followed by the European Union 146
9.4 The Regulatory Framework of the Principle of Tax Harmonization Within the EU 148
9.4.1 The Determination of Taxation Models as a Qualifying Result of the Process of Tax Harmonization 148
9.4.2 The Recessive Nature of the Principle of Harmonization in the EU Legal System 149

10 The State Aids 151
10.1 The General Framework Regarding the State Aids 151
10.1.1 The Prohibition of the State Aids as a Measure to Promote the Free Competition in the Common Market 151
10.1.2 Procedural Nature and Degree of Competence of the EU Guidelines on the State Aids 152
10.1.3 The Character of the State Aids Prohibited Under the EU Law 153
10.1.4 The Procedure for the Judgment on the EU Compatibility of the State Aids 154
10.1.5 A Progressive Perspective Regarding the Exceptions to the Prohibition of the State Aids 155
10.1.6 The Preventive Regulation for the Exceptions to the Prohibition of State Aids 158
10.1.7 The Eligibility of de minimis Aids 158
10.2 The Tax Relief as a Possible State Aid 159
10.2.1 The Qualification of Tax Relief as a State Aid 159
10.2.2 The Eligibility of Tax Incentives at a Regional or Local Level 160
10.2.3 The Urban Free Zones 162
10.3 The Recovery of the State Aids 162

11 The Harmful Tax Competition 165
11.1 The Harmful Tax Competition as an Emerging Value of the EU Legal System 165
11.1.1 The Notion of "Harmful Tax Competition" 165
11.1.2 The "Harmful Tax Competition" as a Paradigm of the Limitation of National Taxation 166
11.2 The Fight Against Harmful Tax Competition Within the EU Legal System 168
11.2.1 The "Monti Package" and the Introduction of the Code of Conduct 168
11.2.2 The Content of the Code of Conduct 169
11.2.3 The Effects of the Code of Conduct. The Assimilation to the State Aids 170

12 The General Principles of the European Law Applicable to the Taxation 173
12.1 The General Principles of the EU Law 173
12.2 The Principles of Legal Certainty and Legitimate Expectations . . . 175
12.3 The Principle of Effectiveness 176
12.4 The Principle of Proportionality 177
12.4.1 The Principle of Proportionality Within the EU Law . . . 177
12.4.2 The Applications of the Principle of Proportionality in Tax Matters 178

12.5 The Abuse of Law 180
12.5.1 The Abuse of the Law as a General Principle of the EU Law in the Elaboration of the Court of Justice 180
12.5.2 The Abuse of Law in Tax Matters 180
12.6 The Environmental Protection and the Principle "Who Pollutes Pays" 182
12.6.1 The Protection of the Environment as a Primary Value of the EU Legal Order; The Principle "Who Pollutes Pays" 182
12.6.2 The Environmental Taxes 183
12.6.3 The Tax Facilitations with an Environmental Purpose 184
12.6.4 The Principle of Differentiation and the Observation of other European Principles 185

Part III The Anti-Sovereign

13 The Relation Between Sovereignty and Taxation Power Within the European System: The Anti-Sovereign 189
13.1 The "Negative" Taxation as a Qualifying Feature of the EU Law 189
13.1.1 The Evaporation of the Taxation Power Within the EU Legal System: The "Negative" Taxation 189
13.1.2 The Cultural Background of the Discipline of Fiscal Power Lies in the Economic Doctrine Which Affirms the Principle of Neutrality 193
13.1.3 The Instrumentality of the Taxation Power to the Market in the EU Legal Order: The "Neutral" Taxation 195
13.2 The Anti-Sovereign 198
13.2.1 The Relationship Between Sovereignty and Power of Taxation in the European Union: The Anti-Sovereign 198
13.2.2 The Dangers of the Anti-Sovereign: The Risks of the Assumption of the Idea of "Market" as Paradigm of Taxation Power 199
13.3 The Remedies Against the Risks of the Anti-Sovereign 202
13.3.1 The European Constitution as a (Partial) Antidote to the Anti-Sovereign 202
13.3.2 The Formation of a European Financial Administration 203
13.3.3 The EU Taxation Law in the Transition Phase 205

Bibliography 207

Part I

The Institutions

The Tax Power in the Tradition of the European Legal Systems

1

Contents

1.1 The Tax Power in the European Tradition 3
  1.1.1 The Tax Power as Distinctive Element of the Institutional Systems 3
  1.1.2 The Basic Features of the Tax Systems in Europe: Patterns of Affinity and Reason for Diversity 4
  1.1.3 The Balance Between Fiscal Interest and Protection of Individual Freedoms in the Formation of Modern Taxation Systems 6
1.2 The Power of Taxation in the Modern European Constitutions 10
  1.2.1 The Age of the Constitution "Without Sovereignty". The Centrality of the Constitutional Values Involved in the Taxation Phenomenon 10
  1.2.2 The Adjustment of the Taxation Phenomenon in the Constitutional Charters of the European States 12
1.3 The Coexistence of a Plurality of Taxation Systems and the Taxes Market 15
  1.3.1 The Crisis of the Taxation Function Resulting in the Fragmentation of the Taxation Systems 15
  1.3.2 The Coexistence of a Plurality of Taxation Systems: European Legal System, National Legal System and Regulations of the Minor Local Authorities 15
  1.3.3 The Horizontal Coordination of Different Systems 17
  1.3.4 The Crisis in the Ethical Consideration of the Taxation System 18
  1.3.5 The Market of Taxes 20

1.1 The Tax Power in the European Tradition

1.1.1 The Tax Power as Distinctive Element of the Institutional Systems

Taxation—or more precisely the regulation of tax relations—is a distinctive feature of the institutional systems, since it is essential for the effective implementation of functions related to sovereignty. In fact only the actual availability of material resources—and specifically the financial resources—may help to achieve the purposes of government that the holder of sovereign power is required to seek. It

P. Boria, *Taxation in European Union*, DOI 10.1007/978-3-319-53919-5_1

seems so unquestionable in the general perception that the power of taxation is one of the closest features of the sovereignty, in order to make a decisive contribution to its own characterization under an ideological profile.

Indeed, the regulatory choices adopted for taxation in a legal system clearly show the core values and the beliefs about sovereignty in a social community. The relation between sovereignty and taxation is a distinctive feature of the constitutional arrangements of the European States, which is not expressed, however, according to uniform modules, but it takes many different forms and contents.

In this regard it is evident the contradiction between collective values, which address to the need for protection and development of the general community, and individual values, which refer to the protection and promotion of human rights and freedoms.

On one side, there is the public interest in the settlement of taxes in order to ensure the vitality and development of the community and to pursue the maximization of general goals, which can be called "*tax interest*" just to express the axiological connotation of the general value. On the other side, there are the protective values of the individual sphere, due both to the personal freedom (compared to the exercise of public power of taxation), and to the ability to pay.

The legal regulation of the power of taxation is thus shown as the fundamental transmission belt between the human wealth and freedoms and the care of the general interests and the developmental goals of the Welfare State, which is an evident index of the level of solidarity or individualism in the civil community, and, above all, an epiphenomenon of the fundamental relation between the "rulers" persons and the "ruled" persons.

This axiological relation, which is established between the collectivist and individual conflicting values, is the basic dialectic of the taxation system, according to which it can be identified the concrete unfolding of sovereignty in the several legal systems.

1.1.2 The Basic Features of the Tax Systems in Europe: Patterns of Affinity and Reason for Diversity

The power of taxation is the subject of legal regulation under several profiles. Firstly, a significant role is gained by the set of regulations regarding the taxation system and the implementation phase of the fiscal requirements (audits, collection, litigation, penalties) in which the general principles of taxation are customarily defined. In this regard it can refer to a *taxation macro-system*, indicating the collocation of the norms to an apical level of taxation directly into the Constitution or in constitutional laws (or in reinforced laws).

Secondly, the set of regulations that distinguishes the background structure of singles taxes is highlighted (with particular reference to the assumption, the taxpayers, the tax base and the tax rate). It is a set of rules which is placed intermediately between the macro-system (the set of principles and rules of general application) and the series of specific regulatory provisions relating to specific individual cases (which can be defined as regulatory micro-systems) and therefore it can be conventionally described as *taxation middle-system.* Unlike the macro-system, the middle-systems shows a lower degree of stability, not because of the use of ordinary legal sources (which therefore have not the regulatory protection of constitutional sources or reinforced laws), but especially for the functionalization that is necessary to the needs of the economic policy and of public finance.

Now, it should be noted that in the European countries it is to be found a common background about the main medium-tax systems. Indeed it is possible to verify obvious similarities in the underlying structure of the taxes which are the backbone of European public finances.

Direct taxes are articulated anywhere in the tax on personal income (basically a personal and progressive tax) and in the tax on corporate income (usually a flat tax); the relations between the two taxes are set, even though different ways, in order to prevent (or attenuate) the economic double taxation of corporate earnings.

Among the indirect taxes, the most important one is undoubtedly the value added tax (VAT), which has a regulatory legislation substantially similar in several jurisdictions (as it has been built on the same archetype). Other taxes, which come from the old European legal tradition (registration tax, stamp duty, inheritance tax), are characterized by a nearly homologous regulatory structure. Even the discipline of duties and excises is evidently similar in different countries (especially for the impulse of the EU).

The main differences are found within the local taxation systems, which are very heterogeneous and influenced by historical social matters that highlight the differences between the countries. In any case it can also be seen in this regulatory system how structurally homogeneous the various taxing jurisdictions are regarding the balanced comparison between central State taxes and regional (or local States) taxes.

In view of the similarities regarding the middle-systems, it appears on the contrary a significant differentiation among the European taxation systems regarding the connotation of the macro-system. In fact, not only significant differences can be registered in relation to the discipline of litigation and penalties, the powers of investigation of the financial administration and the protection of taxpayers rights, but also a different ideological position comes out about the comparison among the conflicting values referring to the alternative of "individual-community" which, as mentioned above, is the key element of the axiological matters that intrinsically permeates the taxation system since the evolutions of the modern State.

On one hand, the interest tax is imposed as a structural rule of the taxation system, legitimizing some invasive or at least strongly reductive regulatory requirements with respect to the freedom of the individual consociates. On the other hand, it gains great importance the liberal values which, in addition to measuring the position of the individual within the social community with regard to the needs of allocating taxation, allow to protect the minimal core of wealth and freedom of each citizen.

The dialectical relation between the fundamental values of the social community and those of the individual assumes a constitutional dimension which varies according to the transformation of the relations between "rulers" and "ruled", and especially to the degree of contrast between the individual sphere and the State sphere, so as to result a typical corollary of the general relations of public law.

1.1.3 The Balance Between Fiscal Interest and Protection of Individual Freedoms in the Formation of Modern Taxation Systems

The power of taxation is so the subject of a legal regulation which is different in several European taxing jurisdictions, because of the different constitutional systems and the changing of the axiological balance between the general interest and the individual interest. This diversity finds its clear basis in the legal traditions of the main European constitutional systems.

In the England of the seventeenth century, within the contrast between the royal authoritarianism and the instances of bourgeois pluralism expressed by the Parliament, it was outlined the antithesis between the public interest in the collection of taxes and the interest of the individual citizens to protect the individual rights of property and freedom. In particular, during the crucial period of the English constitutionalism it emerges the maturing of a dual conceptual shift. At first, a conflicting tension was formed between the taxing interest, intended as the interest of the sovereign to the pursuit of the common wealth, and the individual interest, resulting especially in the development of the sphere of freedom and property; the axiological opposition simply concerned the identification of the individual rights of freedom and property as limit of the sovereign power to impose taxes; it was not brought into question the sovereign right to apply taxes, but there was required a prior approval by the Parliament as representative body of individual interests in the civil community.

Later, with the rise of parliamentary power as inspiration for the second revolution of 1689, the inversion of the relationship of the axiological priority was marked, and the rights of freedom and property assumed a preponderant nature, such as natural attributes of the individual which are co-essential to the full development of human personality, while the position of the monarchical power is considered subordinate and instrumental. On the ideological premise that the individual had to be freed from the constraints produced by an intrusive public power and by an authoritarian public law, it was consolidated the belief that the core of the legal system was made up of the fundamental values of the individual sphere intended to ensure the protection of a space of action against an outside interference (according to the traditional model of negative freedoms), with respect to which the tax burden itself assumed a recessive position which required a constant mediation and balance. The individual interests corresponding to the values of freedom and property were placed in dialectical opposition to the interest of the social community to acquire the financial resources essential for the collective survival, so to terminate completely the connection of taxing rights with the control functions or the capital prerogatives of the sovereign-person.

Therefore, the position of the Parliament as the guarantor of the legitimacy of tax laws was considered essential to the full protection of the values of freedom and property, recognizing the role of sovereignty basically in the administration or in the executive function regarding the choices on taxes which had to be applied practically in a given situation. The tax interest was considered therefore a value belonging to the collective sphere, although it was more properly identified as connotation of the sovereign public authority, namely subjected to the proper values of the individual, which rose to a cardinal point of reference for the development of tax law.

There is a clear conceptual reversal that takes place in France on the assumption of the Enlightenment theories. First of all, it was stressed that taxes had to gain a positive role in the social organization, losing those unfavourable elements that had denoted their old history: the tax should no longer be represented as the right belonging to the sovereignty as co-owner of the land, or worse, as the capital effect of an inferior social condition, but it had rather to be judged as the consideration of the political rights; the citizen was asked to participate equally to the formulation of his country policies with his own vote and to the economic needs through his fiscal contribution. The ethic and political conception of taxation was completely renewed: "*the tax payment is placed as one of the citizen's highest duties; the equality of all citizens before the tax is stated; taxation is no longer looked upon as the attribute of the sovereignty, but as the needed tool of the State to provide public services*".

Natural corollary of this ideological approach was a significant transformation of the fundamental principles of the taxation. The interest to the perception of the taxes could not be identified any longer as a value belonging to the sovereignty sphere, which was in clear contrast with the interest of the consociates to the protection of the individual values (and especially to the guarantee of the rights of property and freedom). It was, instead, elevated to the level of the fundamental public interests, essential for the conservation and development of the civil community, in respect to which the position of the individual could only be in a position of subordination.

It was consolidating indeed the idea that the conflict itself between the public taxing interest and the individual interest substantially faded until they annulled each other. In fact the tax interest was based on a concept of sovereignty which was profoundly changed from its original notion: the sovereign power was no longer to be identified with the royal power or with the power given to rulers; on the contrary it was brought back to the general will of the civil community, emerging from all the individual wills. The individual, with his own political tools, joined to the formation of the general choices regarding taxation, and was forming and realizing his personal interest to the civil participation to the social community. Accordingly, this emphasis on the public nature of the taxation rules led to mark the traits of dutifulness of taxation, resulting in the recognition of a subjective interest of the consociates to the public power.

Secondly, in an apparent opposite direction, the bourgeois component of the Enlightenment led to an improvement of the individual interests. From the relation between the jus-naturalistic model and the bourgeois society descended the revaluation of the state of nature as a place for elementary relationships among the individuals, mostly presented as economical agents for the possession of primary goods. A higher level of importance was recognised to industrial instances and commercial aspirations of individuals regarding which the public interest had to withdraw, thus leaving space for private initiative; therefore, the discovery of the economic sphere represented the moment of emancipation of the bourgeois class, which was dominant in the production system, compared to the actual governing class. Consistently, it began to take shape the belief that legal criteria of the mandatory relations should be applied in the taxation system: also in relation to the theoretical contribution provided by the physiocrats school, taxes were classified as services rendered to the individuals in view of the enjoyment of public services issued by the State, as if there was a kind of market between sovereign and citizens regulated by the utilitarian settings.

The two conflicting theoretical lines—the presence of which is not surprising when compared with the alluvial production of the French Enlightenment—were found to coexist in the same general ideological context, expressing different settings even if they have a degree of complementarity. In essence, it began to be elaborated the idea of a compromise between individual consumers and general utility, between the ways of appropriation and transfer of property—the legal model of which could be found in the civil paradigm of the contractual relations—and the super-individual and almost metaphysical interest of the social community expressed by the regulations of the public law. The balance between conflicting public and private values was expressed in the search for a limit on the unconditional power of taxation, which was located in the principle of equality and in the bourgeois values of property and freedom of economic initiative, so that the distribution of the tax burden was traced back to the equal treatment of the consociates and to the abstention from producing a capital depletion, likely to limit significantly the sphere of the free initiative of the citizen. Thus, the mediation between the general interest to the perception of taxes and the protection of the individual values of bourgeois inspiration was realized through the setting of general regulatory parameters that would allow a reduction of taxing authority and, consequently, would lead to a protection of an individual area which would be impenetrable to the authoritative intrusions.

Tax interest, while remaining connected to the concept of sovereignty, was rebuilt within a different ideological context in relation to a different value of the community and not also to a value of monarchical power. In parallel, the individual interest lost considerable consistency, so that the values of freedom and property significantly faded at least in comparison with the fundamental values of the community (as opposed to the "*liberty and property clause*" of the English legal order). It has been suggested in this regard that the liberties of the Anglo-Saxon tradition would have been characterized as practical and effective rights to be compared to the French liberties, which were considered as abstract and subjective rights. This led in France to overcome the conflict between individual interests and general values (which remains, instead, well consistent in the English culture), from which the tax interest emerges as a reference point of the taxation powers, compared to which the individual rights were traced to a marginal and subordinate position.

To the French setting it has been reconnecting, however in a logic of further overcoming, the public law theory of German formation of the nineteenth century. On the theoretical premise that the interests of the civil society are reported in full to the needs of the State, according to the idealistic paradigm of "ethical totality", the individual values were recognized as entirely subordinate to the values of the social community; the power of the State, considered in its totality as the bearer of all the values and interests of the people, aimed to meet the interests and purposes of the civil community. In fact the will of the State—to be identified with the general will of the whole national community—limits the direction and the development of the ethical foundation of the collective sphere, and consequently could be designated as an expression of sovereignty.

In this theoretical context, the duty to participate to the public expenditure was considered as a typical manifestation of the general state of legal subjection of the citizens to the State-person, and therefore to the general community. In particular, the taxation lost its private character, that marked the original relationship between the State and the taxpayer, in order to acquire, in the modern era, the traits of a very general obligation founded on the ethical and legal relationship which linked citizens to the State. The tax contribution, as an essential moment in the life of the civil community, was considered as a fundamental value of the State sovereignty.

Therefore the taxation matter was so clearly brought back, in accordance with the ethical foundation of the Hegelian idealism, to an area of primary and general interests of the civil community in which the legal situation of the individual became blurred. The tax relations were qualified primarily in relation to the fiscal interest of the State and not to the individual rights of the consociate. The taxation duty (identified by Gerber as an organic duty which each citizen has got towards the State as a member of the general community) was classified under the general state of subjection that characterized the public law relation between the citizen and the State.

The public law theory of German enactment appeared, therefore, characterized by the absolute priority assigned to the taxation interest, intended as a general interest of the civil community, as assessed in an ethical and totalitarian sense compared to individual interests and rights. On the premise of the State "ethical totality", into which all the individual situations inevitably flowed, the community matrix of the taxation interest went strengthening to the point to ensure an axiological pre-eminence in the constitutional system of the values involved in taxation. The State was then considered, on one side, as the guarantor of the preservation and development of the human personality, as the place where freedom only can be realized objectively; on the other side, the individual sphere was subjected to a deconstruction process, being reduced to a mere point of abstract reference of the evolution guidelines of public law, and in essence losing the real and effective protection in the relationship with the public power; therefore, the position of individual was reduced to the mere obedience to the law and to the State jurisdiction.

Following the brief examination of those which can be considered the crucial moments of the developmental course of the European taxation systems, there can be explained two main different and opposed evolutionary directrixes: the first one connects to the idea of the prevalence of the individual rights on the power of taxation, and the second one, on the contrary, highlights the priority of the public power and the taxation interest compared to the individual sphere.

The first directrix (according to the doctrine expressed traditionally by John Locke) typically belongs to the Anglo-Saxon tradition, firmly oriented toward a pragmatic and utilitarian view of the public relations in which it is affirmed the logical prevalence of the individual sphere. This Anglo-Saxon tradition, inclined to recognize the self-regulation capability of the civil society, has always shown great care to avoid monist and centralist settings, making individual liberties the core of the jurisdiction. Therefore, the power of taxation will be judged as a declination of the essential term which recognizes and guarantees the liberty and property of the individual, and is placed in a serving position (or, at least, conceptually subordinate) to the individual rights.

The second directrix denotes instead the continental legal systems, in which the State and the general interest of the social community are identified as the supreme and totally prevalent values in an ethical and often transcending dimension. The public powers, as logical and legal tools of the general will of the civil community, are devoted to pursue the fundamental interests of the nation-State and to prevail over the individual rights. The taxation power, put in this context, is based on the fiscal interest and is destined to dominate over the individual interests.

1.2 The Power of Taxation in the Modern European Constitutions

1.2.1 The Age of the Constitution "Without Sovereignty". The Centrality of the Constitutional Values Involved in the Taxation Phenomenon

The legal and institutional evolution of the twentieth century has led to an exceeding of the notion of State sovereignty. Under the action of vigorous corrosive forces it has gradually been demolishing the superstructure of legal concepts that led to idealize the State as a model of political unity of a community.

On the one hand, there was the political pluralism, due to the formation of centres of power which were competitive and alternative to the State power, capable of operating in the fields of politics, industry, business, professions, culture and religion; on the other hand, there was the attribution of decision-making powers to supranational entities with respect to the regulatory framework of an increasingly wide range of circumstances, which led to a substantial attenuation of the State main function as holder of the monopoly of political decision.

The erosion of the principle of the political organization, represented by the loss of the predominant function of the State, has produced a transformation of the conceptual categories of public law.

In particular, a real starting platform for the identification of the developmental program of the common coexistence is traced in the Constitutions. In pluralistic societies, namely marked by interests, projects and ideologies highly differentiated and unable to be dominant factors compared to the State sovereignty (as it usually happened in the past), the Constitution presents itself as "the condition of possibility of life in common" and not as the bearer act of a pre-determined regulatory project of the community. Democratic pluralism thus imposes constitutional models in which rigid patterns are abandoned in favour of a "open" solutions of a possible coexistence (the "compromise of possibilities") which guarantee the spontaneity of social life.

In this perspective, the Constitution is no longer the corollary of the State sovereignty, from which all the regulations of legal system come as irradiation or automatic deduction, but it represents a developmental project of life in common with respect to which it is necessary to coordinate and to balance the system regulations according to the possible compromises.

Using a figurative formula, it can be defined as "*Constitution without sovereignty*" the historical period which modern institutional systems address in, indicating the shift from the State sovereignty to the "sovereignty of the Constitution", compared to which it is not detectable the presence of one or more material and political forces that could be able to assert themselves, if not unconditionally, at least in a decisive impact on decision-making rules.

The deep transformation of constitutional law, however, accompanies an historical change of the relationship between society and the State: unlike the Constitutions of liberal character, based on the principle of natural liberty, in which the main rule of distribution of social benefits was determined by the spontaneous breakdown of interest on the market while incorporated in the sovereign decision-making acts, in the current Constitutions the democratic and pluralist distribution of benefits and sacrifices among the associates is carried out according to the direction and control of the public authority in respect of the structure of values outlined in the constitutional level.

In the mono-class State the formation of the liberal legislative decision was designed to reflect the values substantially homogeneous shared by the ruling class, leading to a gap between the society in which it was drawn up from time to time the plot of the values and the State that limited to transpose uncritically the axiological choices made externally. In contrast, the presence of the multi-class State values—often heterogeneous expression of a the participation in political life of various classes and interest groups—determines the need to combine decisions and policies in a constant compromise between the majority and minorities, which is inspired and conducted according to the guidelines provided in the table of constitutional values.

The characteristic feature of the nineteenth century is the rule of law, namely the neutrality with respect to the values expressed by the civil society, which led to the recognition of the validity of the decision-making of the sovereign by the mere fact that there was a parliamentary majority, thus founding the famous equation legitimacy/legality; this feature is reversed in the modern pluralistic and democratic State where it is established a "valued legality" suitable to serve as a parameter for controlling the legitimacy of the legislative activity. From this reversal setup it follows that the distribution of resources and sacrifices of those belonging to a community, which constitutes one of the main forms of exercise of government, is carried out under the reserve of public action, in accordance with the core values expressed in the Constitution of the pluralistic and democratic society.

As part of this reconstruction, the tax interest, which is attributable to a higher redistributive requirement, can be understood as one of the key concepts of State sovereignty that arises directly in conflict with other values and interests. In the context of the plurality of values of the community the tax interest links with the principle of equality, with the principle of ability to pay, with the fundamental requirements of protection and development about the person and the dignity of the individual.

The necessary coexistence of a plurality of values leads to the need to seek combined solutions through which the potential of the constitutional values are not amputated, but amplified by harmonic cohesion. Common development and harmonious constitutional principles transpose the theme of the conflict of values on a positive fit to accentuate the reasons for the coexistence of diversity inevitably present in a pluralistic society.

This produces an important implication of methodology, namely the need to highlight the system of relationships that weave between the different constitutional values involved in the taxation phenomenon. Accordingly, the notion of any constitutional value called by taxation receives an "open" structure, that is not supported by the predominance of a single interest, affirmation of a particular hegemonic vision, but rather determined by compromise solutions resulting from the mediation with a plurality of values of constitutional significance.

Thus the relation between sovereignty and taxation power is developing in accordance with the axiological dialectic of the tributary phenomenon, highlighting the centrality of the values as an engine of the training process of the taxation system.

1.2.2 The Adjustment of the Taxation Phenomenon in the Constitutional Charters of the European States

The constitutional charters currently in force in the European States show a significant convergence in the regulation of the phenomenon of taxation.

In particular, in all the Constitutions it is regulated expressly the consent to taxation, as it is expressly enunciated the need for the use of a legislative instrument (and therefore the need to proceed to the involvement of the representative bodies of popular election) in order to establish and to modify the taxation discipline.

This rule (commonly referred to as a "reserve of law") is expressed in the various Constitutions in different ways: sometimes through the explicit formulation of the principle of the supremacy of law as a result of the assertion of the exclusive competence of the legislative act for the regulation of taxes (as happens, for example in the constitutions of Austria, art. 13; Denmark, art. 43; Finland, art. 81; France, art. 34 and art. 14 of the "Declaration of the Rights of 1789"; Greece, art. 78; Italy, art. 23; Luxembourg, art. 99; Holland, art. 104; Portugal, art. 103; Spain, art. 31 and 133; as well as in the Fundamental Law on the Swedish System of Government, chap. VIII, art. 5); sometimes through the enunciation of the legislative procedure adoptable for the promulgation of rules to the tax content (in the Constitutions of: Belgium, art. 170; Germany art. 105 and 106; and Ireland, art. 21 and 22); finally there is the case of the United Kingdom, notoriously lacking in a written constitutional text, in which, however, there are constitutional conventions that clearly show the centrality of the principle of consent to the taxes and the consequent involvement of Parliament (consider, in addition to the *Magna Charta* of 1206, especially the *Bill of Rights* of 1688, in which it is expressly forbidden to the executive power to impose taxes without the prior parliamentary consent; this document is believed to constitute the first formal enunciation of the principle of "*no taxation without representation*").

In the new context of pluralist democracy assumed by European Constitutions the maintaining of the centrality of parliamentary power seems possible due not so much to the Anglo-Saxon safeguarding function, nor to the need to enhance the authority of public power continental experience, but rather to the needs of a pluralistic society in which the parliamentary debate appears to be the most mature form of definition and weighting of collective values.

Indeed the participation of all the members—or at least a large and significant majority—of the social political and cultural community is able to ensure the functionality of the rules formed in the parliamentary procedure with respect to the collective interest with a higher grade than other procedures (even though constitutionally permissible), where there is only a majority government to formulate policy choices. The evaluative judgment referred to the taxation laws can only be usefully formulated taking into account the historical and cultural background or the economic situation of a national community which only an institutional structure with an articulate and representative composition (precisely as the parliament) can effectively represent. It should be added that the choices regarding financial matters, and in particular those concerning the moving the regulatory pendulum in the direction of the taxation interest rather than to the area of individual interests, are not likely to be entrusted to the impromptu regulatory procedures of the executive power (expressed by the government), whose speed is often marked by an approximation of the evaluative judgments; undoubtedly, at this regard, it shows greater adequacy the parliamentary process in which the appreciation of the different needs of individual and collective spheres is mediated through the work of parliamentary committees with the involvement of representative bodies, which allows a balanced assessment of the dialectic of the basic phenomenon of taxation.

In this perspective, it could be said that the principle of legality loses its formalist connotation, which had denoted the inclusion in the constitutional authoritarian contexts, to take the essential function of an unavoidable technique for the balancing of interests and values of the social community.

On the other hand, the link between the centrality of parliament and the formulation of tax laws is a further recognition of the constitutional provision that excludes a referendum on tax matters (in this sense you can explicitly see the Constitutions of Denmark, Art. 42; Ireland, art. 27; Italy, art. 75). It is obviously a provision that expresses a structural apprehension towards the adoption of direct democracy mechanisms in order to the delicate balancing of values to be operated in the taxation system, in the belief that the individual assessment appears to be strongly conditioned by the inevitable inclination to evade the depletion resulting from the application of taxes.

With reference to the discipline of legal sources it is to be mentioned the rule that excludes the retroactivity of taxation laws, which expresses a form of protection in the custody of the citizen (this rule is present in the Constitution of Greece, art. 78, and Portugal, art. 103).

It is less frequently posed in the constitutional texts a rule intended to regulate the substance of the balance of values in the taxation matters, and therefore the content of legislative decisions to be taken in the conformation of the tax system.

In some Constitutions, mostly in those ones dated longer ago, even reconnected to the texts issued in the full climate of the French Revolution, it is expressly prohibited the adoption of privileges in taxation, as if to specifically reiterate the application of the principle of equality to the taxation system (Constitutions of Belgium, art. 172; Luxembourg, art. 101; as well as the French Declaration of the Rights of 1789, art. 13 and 14).

More vigorously in the Constitutions of the Latin countries it is formulated a rule which establishes a criterion of ability to pay (or economic capacity) as a rule of redistribution of tax burdens among the associates, to be placed in opposition to the taxation interest (Constitution of Italy, art. 53; Portugal, art. 103; Spain, art. 31; and the French Declaration of Rights, art. 13). It is thus made explicit in the text of the Constitution the dialectic underlying basis of the taxation power, as if the axiological conflict in the definition of the regulatory institutions of a fiscal nature may find useful compositional criteria based on the expressed legal drafting. It is to point out that these rules take in the laws of the mentioned countries a strong legal weight as a result of the constant application of the courts from reviewing the legality of the regulatory choices made by the ordinary legislation.

Sporadically in the Constitutions there are further rules on the specific conformation of the tax system: this is sometimes enshrined in the progressivity of the taxation system (Constitution of Italy, art. 53; Spain, art. 31) or in the overall function of the conditions of individual taxes (Constitution of Portugal, art. 104).

1.3 The Coexistence of a Plurality of Taxation Systems and the Taxes Market

1.3.1 The Crisis of the Taxation Function Resulting in the Fragmentation of the Taxation Systems

The legal and institutional evolution of the twentieth century led to the overcoming of the usual rules of tax relations and especially to the idea of the coincidence of the taxation system with the national State. Under the action of vigorous corrosive forces it has been gradually demolishing the superstructure of legal concepts that led to idealize the State as a model of political unity of a social community.

The political pluralism due to the formation of competitive and alternative centres of power with respect to the State power, able to operate in the political, economic and industrial life, and the attribution of the decision powers to supranational entities regarding the regulatory framework of an increasingly wide range of circumstances have led to a substantial attenuation of the main function of the State as holder of the monopoly of political decision.

Democratic pluralism and the plurality of sources of law thus impose "open" models of legal system, namely where rigidly determined patterns are abandoned in favour of a flexible design of legal regulations, inspired by the logic of co-existence of the plurality of legal systems and capable of ensuring the spontaneity of social life and the variety of feasible solutions for policy decisions.

The taxation function, therefore, can no longer be identified with the centrality of the State, but it must also be attributed to a number of supranational jurisdictions (such as the European Union) or local jurisdictions (as that expressed by the local authorities minors).

The erosion of the principle of unity of the political organization, represented by the predominant function of the State, has so undetermined the unity of the same tax function resulting in the fragmentation of the taxation system in a plurality of systems, each corresponding to the list of values expressed by several legal systems. That was the transition from a monolithic State-like structure, which corresponds to a single tax system, to a pluralist structure characterized by the coexistence of multiple tax systems belonging to different forms of territorial an political community.

1.3.2 The Coexistence of a Plurality of Taxation Systems: European Legal System, National Legal System and Regulations of the Minor Local Authorities

In the current historical phase different legal systems related to different forms of territorial community coexist in the same context: the European Union legal system, the national legal system and the regulations of the minor local authorities.

Each of these legal systems is characterized primarily by a list of values assumed and shared by the social and political community which constitutes the referring macro-system and that assumes a conditioning role compared to the whole development of the vertical relationships between the different parts of the legal system.

With regard to tax matters, in the national Constitution it is evident a dialectic between the opposing values of ability to pay and taxation interest which expresses essentially the need to seek forms of balance of the values relating to the sphere of collective needs and the values corresponding to the protection and promotion of individual freedoms. Therefore, it must be identified the form of the distribution of tax burdens among the citizens in order to distribute over the entire national community the costs to be incurred for the development of the Welfare State. That produces an axiological tension innervating the legal system characterizing the substantial and procedural tax rules.

In local finance system, there are different needs. In the case of exponential institutions with a wide territorial base (as Regions) are pursued wide developmental aims that, despite not having the characteristics of the general purposes of the State, however, are related to the primary needs of a civil community (such as the protection of health or environment). Taxation is so essential for ensuring a relevant amount of revenues to be distributed among the associates according to general criteria for social redistribution. In this perspective it is noticeable that in the regional systems there are tax dimensions conceptually similar to those ones applicable to the State.

In the case of minor exponential institutions (such as Municipalities and Provinces) the expenditure functions shall be given, mainly, to the intervention for infrastructural or other local needs. This results in a smaller scale of financing needs and requires the adoption of criteria for the distribution of tax burdens centred around the commutative diagram of the exchange between tax and public services according to the principle of "benefit".

In the EU the taxation plays a very peculiar role: due to the pursuit of the four EU freedoms (free movement of goods, persons, services and capital) and to the fundamental aim of promoting market liberalization and competition among enterprises, the use of tax leverage is considered as a possible obstacle likely to produce distortions and impediments; so the taxation is concerned with distrust by EU institutions, as a bearer of a load of potential obstruction with respect to the free action of business and to the natural capacity of the market to be adjusted around the natural balance of economic forces. The EU rules demonstrate a notion of "negative" taxation, to alleviate the taxation power of the national States in order to avoid discriminatory or protectionist use of national tax rules.

The diversity of macro-systems inevitably means that the consequent variation of the tax laws is distinct and specific for each system of law, in response to a juridical logic (or rather, to a system of vertical relationships) which is self-centred and inherent to the principles and to the basic values of the social community. Therefore, it is not applicable an interpretative procedure or the analogy that lead to export institutions or legal categories from a system of law to another legal system.

Evidently, the sources of law tend to take significantly different connotations for each jurisdiction, by reason of the attribution rules of regulatory powers to the various institutional centres. Just the comparison of rules generated from sources belonging to different legal orders determines the problem of establishing the diriment criterion of possible conflicts and, therefore, the logic of coexistence of the plurality of legal orders.

1.3.3 The Horizontal Coordination of Different Systems

The relations between the different legal systems are inspired by the research of a combination of regulatory solutions through which the systems can develop forms of harmony or at least harmonious coexistence of the different tables of values. In terms of positive law, the conflict between the various legal systems must be solved through forms of legal relations that allow the coexistence of diversities.

In a structure characterized by the equal ordination of the various systems it is not possible to find a rule of higher grade (a sort of "meta-norm") that governs the contrast between the rules belonging to different systems—and thus the conflict of sources of law—in accordance with a hierarchical criterion. Deductive logic, which requires solving the contrasts according to the principle of the superiority of a source with respect to the other, is in fact only applicable in systems of the vertical type, namely where it is established the dependency of a legal system with respect to another one.

Therefore it is necessary to find a criterion of horizontal coordination that allows to resolve any conflict of regulations without penalizing a type of source than the others and consequently allows to maintain the integrity of each legal system. This criterion seems to be identified typically in the "principle of competence", under which each legal system (and therefore each corresponding type of source of law) has an area of relevance to be managed in exclusive form without permitting the interfering of other sources relating to other legal systems.

However, where the principle of competence does not remedy the overlapping of various regulatory authorities, producing some regulatory "grey areas", the conflict resolution should be sought by the dialectic of values and interests, according to a model of coexistence typical of the regulatory framework inspired to the pluralism. The axiological antinomy represents an inevitable corollary of the power imbalances arising from the free play of social forces and uncertainties determined by the spontaneous mechanisms of the market, and generates an instability of the structure of the values bound to grow as a result of the acceleration of cultural dynamics, economic and policies found in pluralist democracies. In a pluralistic society in which it has failed the sovereignty of a single dominant political and legal centre (that is, the nation-State), interests and values underlying the rules no longer represent the sedimentation of the principles of universal significance, as if it were transcendental conditions of living in common, but they express the volatility and instability of the social system according to the game of political and economic forces.

Therefore it seems essential to find solutions to these contradictions that contribute to building a harmonious order through compositions and combinations of conflicting rules with the purpose of finding equilibrium points, changeable and unstable, but still oriented to allow the preservation of legal systems.

Inevitably abandoned the option to formalistic and deductive models, the solution of conflicts between norms moves to the sensitivity of the interpreters and practitioners of law (judges, directors, professionals, taxpayers) with the aim to identify the possible combinations suitable to preserve the coexistence of diversities. The classical legal thought has to be deconstructed in order to permit "open" solutions feasible for appropriate regulatory compromises to mediate conflicting interests and values depending on the historical circumstances and economic situation. It is therefore necessary to abandon the rigid and bivalent logic of "true/false" in order to adopt the logic of "possible", "likely", "reasonable" and to bring out the mediation and the balance as possible forms of solution of the conflicts between the legal orders.

1.3.4 The Crisis in the Ethical Consideration of the Taxation System

In the older public law models, the coincidence of the taxation system with the State entails that the tax function is typically controlled by the pursuit of the general interest taken as the reference basis for the development of the national community without other ideological elements may be involved in the determination of the conditions of use of taxation.

The State, considered in its entirety as the bearer of all the values and interests of the people, becomes the linchpin of the development of civil society posing as entity in which the affiliates get to enhance all ethical forces for the common good. The decision-making capacity of the State is thus its limits and the direction of the ethical foundation of their being (that is to say the identification with the will of the general community).

In this context, the duty to participate in the contribution to the public expenditure is considered as a typical manifestation of the general state of subjection of the citizens from the State-community, founded precisely on the ethical and legal relationship of belonging to the State. Thus, the payment of taxes, saved by the remote connotation of prejudice and discrimination, is regarded as a fundamental obligation of citizenship necessary for the survival of the civil community.

Therefore, on the premise of the ethical foundation of the State, even the tax system suffers from this ethical connotation, taking on a leading role in the constitutional order of a State. The tribute comes as an instrument to achieve the fundamental goals of the State and to pursue the protection and the growth of the community of citizens.

The slippage of fiscal sovereignty by the State to a plurality of territorial entities has led to a deep transformation of the ethical concept of the taxation system: as compared to the plurality of jurisdictions, it is no longer possible to detect the presence of one or more material forces and policies that are able to impose itself predominantly on regulatory choices.

In the mono-class State the formation of liberal legislative decision was designed to reflect the values substantially homogeneous shared by the ruling class, leading to a deep gap between the civil society, in which it was drawn up from time to time the plot of the values, and the State, which was limited to transpose uncritically the axiological choices made externally.

On the contrary, in the modern multi-class State the presence of heterogeneous values, which is expression of a broadening of participation in political life for various classes and groups, determines the need to combine decision-makers in a constant compromise between majorities and minorities, which is inspired and conducted according to the guidelines provided in the table of the constitutional values.

The characteristic of the State in nineteenth-century—consisting of the neutrality with respect to the values expressed by civil society that led to the recognition of the validity of the decision-making by the mere fact of the existence of a parliamentary majority, according to the famous equation "legitimacy/legality"—is reversed in modern democratic and pluralist community which states a "legality for values" suitable to be a criterion for the judgement of legislative activity.

The taxation system of the liberal State really represented, like other sectors of the legal system, a legal instrument to achieve the purposes assumed by the ruling class and therefore arose as a means to serve the ideological beliefs of the civil society. This required, as mentioned, an ethical conception of the taxation system as a factor of institutional aid and support to the ideas and the needs of the society.

In the modern era we are witnesses to a cancellation of this ethical conception of the taxation: the crushing in a plurality of legal systems undermines the correspondence between the tax system and the ideological and axiological background, making clear that the tax instrument can be adopted at a flexible manner for a wide number of purposes and collective aims.

The tax system thus becomes one of the institutional factors, fundamental for the implementation of the values expressed by each legal system, according to a relation of instrumentality that highlights the "neutrality" of the tax with regard to ideological beliefs of a civil society, enhancing the correlation with the values of the constitutional order of a community. It emerges therefore the "neutralization" of the ethical function of the taxation system, as part of a process of disclosing the many instances coming from an ontologically pluralist society.

Consistent with the transformation of the general framework, the notion of the taxation receives an "open" conformation, that is not supported by the pre-eminence of values from one social class (and therefore, by a particularistic and hegemonic vision of society), but rather determined by compromised solutions resulting from the political and social mediation of a plurality of instances emerging from the civil community.

The crushing of the unique taxation system in the various "taxation systems" thus produces an ideological deconstruction consentaneous to the dynamic situation of a pluralistic society, not ossified around dominant ideas, but oriented toward forms of harmonious coexistence of the values of civil society.

1.3.5 The Market of Taxes

The spread of globalization and the harmonization of markets have determined a significant impact on the mechanisms for defining the taxing choices by the States. Indeed, the tax burden becomes an important factor in the competition between enterprises, because it affects directly or indirectly on the criteria of price formation, as well as it determines the position in relation to the demand curve formulated by the market.

Therefore, decisions about the shape of the tax system and the incidence of the tax burden on economic activities are crucial to facilitate the localization of the initiatives of enterprises and the production plants in some States than others. So, it can be argued that the reductive manoeuvre of taxation represents an element of attraction of foreign investments in the national territories.

It follows that, in addition to the typical function of collecting the revenue for the maintenance and the development of the national community, the tax becomes a tool for encouraging the allocation of foreign investment.

In this context, it is possible to recognise a logic of competition between States measured on the basis of the attractiveness of taxation, namely the ability to define a level of overall taxation that is attractive to foreign companies in order to favour a location of productive initiatives in the State.

This establishes a real "market of taxes" in which the offer of a reduced tax burden is the "commodity" for attracting the settlement of the business in the country.

The lack of regulatory mechanisms for the heteronomous processes of globalization and the serious risk that tax competition assumes the characters of the wild contest between the States with the aim to mark down the tax burden led to a general rethinking about the existence of an indiscriminate freedom to conform the taxation system exclusively according to the reasons of the particular convenience of the single State.

Particularly in the European Union it has been hollowing out the conviction about the importance of greater coordination of tax policies for the countries in order to avoid that the Member States could issue legal regulations whose main effect consists in the erosion of the tax base in other States. The fiscal bleeding, coming from the erosion of the tax national base, has increased the awareness that tax competition between States not only alienates the EU integration, but also hampers the identification of a balance of taxation, creating situations of "fiscal crisis of the State".

Therefore, a solicitation to the transformation of the taxation system may be identified as a result produced by the changes generated by other taxation systems because of the processes of tax competition, according to a logic of osmosis of the international standards. The research of a calibrated level of taxation for the attraction (or even just the maintaining) of the substrate business within the territory of the State is a brake and a limit for the identification of a standard tax at the European level.

So, it can be argued that the taxation system is the result of a competition of a plurality of sources, placed at the State, sub-State and international level, which produces pulses of opposite sign, and sometimes divergent, whose balance is the point of arrival, contingent and changeable, for the regulatory process.

The Role of Taxation in the EU Legal System 2

Contents

2.1 The Legal System of European Union ... 24
  2.1.1 The Self-Limitation of Sovereignty of the National States About Taxation as Fundament of the International Taxation Law ... 24
  2.1.2 The Establishment of the EU Legal System ... 25
  2.1.3 The European Constitution and the Treaty of Lisbon ... 28
  2.1.4 The Institutional Framework of the European Union: The Democratic Deficit and the Problems of the Sovereignty of the EU Institutions ... 30
2.2 The Regulation of Fiscal Policy in the EU ... 31
  2.2.1 The Lack of a Proper Taxation System in the European Union ... 31
  2.2.2 The Presence of EU Contributory Competences in Taxation and the Implementation of the Principle of Subsidiarity ... 34
  2.2.3 The Procedures for Approval of EU Rules Related to Taxation ... 35
2.3 The Stability Pact and the Fiscal Compact ... 37
  2.3.1 The Stability Pact ... 37
  2.3.2 The Procedure for the Control and the Sanctions for the Violations to the Rules of the "Stability Pact" ... 38
  2.3.3 The Fiscal Compact ... 40
2.4 The Relations Between European Union and National Legal Systems ... 41
  2.4.1 The Orientation of the National Courts Tends to be Inspired by the Theory of the Separation of Legal Systems ... 41
  2.4.2 In Particular, the Position of the Italian Constitutional Court ... 43
  2.4.3 The "Monistic" Orientation of the Court of Justice ... 45
  2.4.4 The Dual Reconstructive Perspective Regarding the Transfer of Functions from the Member States to the European Union ... 47
2.5 The Conflicts Between the EU Legal System and the National Constitutional System . 48
  2.5.1 The Conflict Between the General Values of EU Law and the National Constitutional Values Concerning the Taxation System ... 48
  2.5.2 The Limit on the Primacy of EU Law over the National Constitution: The Theory of Counter-Limits ... 49
  2.5.3 The Violation of EU Obligations in the Field of Taxation by a Member State . 50

P. Boria, *Taxation in European Union*, DOI 10.1007/978-3-319-53919-5_2

2.1 The Legal System of European Union

2.1.1 The Self-Limitation of Sovereignty of the National States About Taxation as Fundament of the International Taxation Law

The formation of an international taxation law designed to regulate the competition of the prescriptive authority of two or more States in order to define the tax relationships, is evidently to be referred to a supranational legal framework, typically characterized by a "negative" element: the absence a superordinate authority entitled to act as a legal regulator (according to the well-known internationalist principle *superiorem non recognoscens*).

In fact, even in taxation (like other areas of international law) the relationships between States are established on the basis of various agreements (conventions, treaties, pacts multilateral etc.), inspired by the principle of mutual consent between subjects who "recognize" each other to be placed on an equal level. Therefore there is not the typical act of production of the rules of a modern legal system, namely the legislation, as a corollary of the lack of a supranational sovereignty that legitimizes the exercise of legislative power.

It should also be verified whether the individual State, by reason of membership in an international community, is subject to the limits and the constraints of a legal nature regarding to the tax rules, and hence whether those restrictions affect the national sovereignty in taxation matters in connection with elements of strangeness with the territory of the State (covering the taxation of foreign entities or taxation of citizens and residents for events that occurred abroad).

The traditional doctrine excluded the possibility of limits of international law to the taxing power of the State, as this power could not operate for the actual implementation of national rules on foreign territory (for the obvious inability to exert a coercive force in the territory of another State).

On the other hand, it subsequently went overshadowing the conviction about the existence of a rule of customary international law that precluded the taxation of foreign events which did not show a reasonable connection with the territory of the State (the theory of *reasonable link*). In this assumption, the need for a link with the territory of the State derives not so much from a rule of international law, but rather by the constitutional provision of the ability to pay generally accepted in the various legal systems (explicitly dictated art. 53 of the Italian Constitution and, although with different nuances, in the constitutional jurisprudence of the main European countries).

Another international limitation to the taxing power of the State was found in the principle of equal treatment of foreigners compared to the citizen. In this case the strong objections raised in the literature concern the international character of the norm, which has to be identified in the constitutional principle of equality. The constant practice of including in explicit form in the various international treaties the rule of equal treatment between residents and non-residents clearly expresses the non-existence of a rule of customary international law. Moreover, there is not a general principle of international law that requires equal treatment of foreigners of different nationalities with respect to the imposition of a State, precisely because of the widespread practice of introducing differentiated taxation systems according to the various agreements concluded bilaterally between the different States.

Therefore, it is quite possible to argue that the only international constraint to fiscal sovereignty of a State arising from the international agreements entered into with other States shall be identified basically in a covenantal and conventional dimension. This essentially confirms that the principles and norms of international taxation law are due to a non-authoritarian nor hetero-conditioned legal framework, but are rather determined by choices of self-limitation by the individual States.

The centrality of the pactional dimension clearly puts in prominence the Treaties establishing the European economic community as the primary expression of the self-limitation of fiscal sovereignty by the European states.

2.1.2 The Establishment of the EU Legal System

The process of European integration has been historically determined following a very long and articulated path. Wanting to leave out the relevant references while the appropriateness of a European federal aggregation in the culture of the nineteenth century (it may be cited in this regard, the Mazzini's brilliant intuitions), it is already in the twenties of the twentieth century that some forms of European co-operation appear with the aim to promote the marketing of steel products (trust between the owners of the mines of coal and iron of Lorraine in France, the owners of the mines of Borinage in Belgium and steel industry of the Ruhr, Germany).

The destruction which followed the Second World War clearly puts the historical conditions to revamp, with renewed vigour, a process of integration of European countries. Exemplary of such ideological climate is the speech given by Winston Churchill on 09/19/1946 at the University of Zurich in which it was argued the need to create, through a gradual process, the United States of Europe.

On the practical level the first fundamental step was the proposal for the establishment of a High Authority for the control of the production of steel and coal (essential materials for the production of armaments), which was accepted since the beginning by France, Germany, Italy, Belgium, Netherlands and Luxembourg. The project, formulated by the French Minister for Foreign Affairs, R. Schumann, had for objective to lay the foundations for a real European federation: "*by putting the entire Franco-German production under a common High Authority, within the framework of an organization open to the participation of the other European countries, it will be carried out, with simple means, the fusion of interests required for the establishment of an economic community, and it will be the catalyst for a wider and deeper community of countries opposed by bloody divisions*". In these few words it is evidently contained the germ of the European

Union: the integration of European States must be realised around a core of economic interests, in order to initiate the establishment of an "economic community", which can be intended as the first step of a process of a political integration.

On April 18th 1951 the Treaty establishing the European Coal and Steel Community (so-called ECSC) was signed in Paris among the six countries mentioned above. That was the first concrete act which resulted in a limitation of sovereignty for the individual nation-States in favour of a supranational body of matrix typically European.

In 1954, on the initiative of the Netherlands, it was presented a memorandum explaining the reasons for a widening of the scope of supervision of the supranational. In 1956 it was approved in the Venice Conference a report given by a committee chaired by the Belgian Minister Spaak (the so-called "Spaak Report") regarding the establishing a common European market. On March 25th 1957 were signed in Rome two other treaties concerning the establishment of the European Atomic Energy Community (EAEC) and, above all, the European Economic Community (EEC).

While not containing an explicit statement of principles in the regulatory text, the Treaty allowed to single out the purposes of the aggregation supranational, especially through the indication of purposes and means essentially attributable to the economic order: first, the establishment of a common European market, which could guarantee certain fundamental economic freedoms; and secondly, the progressive approximation of the economic policies pursued by individual national States. Accordingly, the main rules of the Treaty were to protect and to promote fundamental freedoms regarding in general a competitive structure of the market and particularly:

a) the free movement of goods;
b) the free movement of people;
c) the right of establishment and the free movement of services;
d) the free movement of capitals.

The limitation of sovereignty of each Member State was the abdication about the power to deal independently with the issues implied by the four freedoms, entrusting the European institutions the power to regulate by legislation the related matters.

During the eighties of the twentieth century it was progressively strengthened the process of European integration. With the Single European Act, signed on February 14th 1986 it was initiated the completion of the single market, overcoming the uncertain implementation of the first phase of integration with greater completeness and redefining the text of the Treaties. Furthermore, in a series of international conferences the expansion of Community powers was addressed beyond the economic functions provided for by the Treaty. This ferment came, finally, in the signing of the Treaty of Maastricht on February 7th 1992 by which the Member States (which meanwhile reached the number of fifteen) undertook to pursue two additional purposes in addition to those originating in the European Community, namely the beginning of a political union and, above all, the establishment of an effective monetary union.

The structure of the European Union, as outlined in the Maastricht Treaty, is based on the three pillars that make up the symbolic temple of the Union:

a) the Community dimension, governed by the provisions contained in the Treaties establishing the European Communities (so-called first pillar);
b) the Common Foreign and Security Policy (CFSP) governed by Title V of the Treaty on European Union (so-called second pillar);
c) cooperation in the fields of justice and home affairs (CJHA) covered by Title VI of the Treaty, which has become, following the amendments to the Treaty of Amsterdam, police cooperation in criminal matters (so-called third pillar).

In particular, the amendments to the EEC Treaty represent the most innovative part of the whole Treaty of Maastricht, starting with high symbolic value attributed to the provision that replaces the name "*European Economic Community*" by "*European Community*" throughout the Treaty of Rome in 1957, making evident even in formal terms the transition from a functional conception of Europe to the European Union. Further amendments made to the Treaty of Rome appear substantial and relate in particular to the institutional structures, to the decision-making and especially to the extension of the areas of European competence.

In this latter regard, it should be noted that the Community is expressly entrusted the task to promote and ensure: a) the balanced development of economic activities, respecting the environment (according to the criterion of sustainable growth), b) the convergence of economic performance; c) the pursuit of high employment and social protection; d) improving the quality of life and social cohesion, to the advantage of the least favoured regions; e) solidarity between Member States, including through mechanisms for the financial contribution for the less developed regions. Just the list of the additional tasks conferred upon the EU (all contents are basically economic) makes clear that the purpose of a political and social integration continues to be prefigured essentially through a process of cooperation to achieve in terms of economic development. It is correctly noted, in this regard, as the Maastricht Treaty, while achieving the nominal passage from the European Economic Community to the European Union, does not create a federal union in actual sense, remaining always the original character of a community of States aimed at seeking forms of coordination and cohesion of an economic nature.

To confirm the centrality of economic functions in the process of European integration it can also be mentioned the last phase, at least in order of time, namely the establishment of the monetary union among all the member countries through the replacement of national currencies by a single European currency (euro). This phase resulted in the substantial abdication of the national States about monetary policy with respect to the transfer of all powers connected (and primarily the management of the discount rate) in favour of a European institution, the

European Central Bank. Even in this case the reduction of the sphere of national sovereignty—and the consequent transfer of functions to the European Union—has typically involved a competence of economic order.

Finally, it should be noted that on 04/16/2003 some treaties were signed in Athens in order to fix the extension of the number of the countries belonging to the European Union through the acceptance of ten Member States from May 1st 2004. Later agreements were finalised that have allowed the entry of two other Member States since January 1st 2007 and one Member State since January 1st 2015. Currently, therefore, the European Union consists of twenty-eight member countries.

2.1.3 The European Constitution and the Treaty of Lisbon

In December 2001, it was published the "*Declaration of Laecken on the future of Europe*" in order to clarify the goals for the European Union in the medium and long term and particularly:

1. the simplification of the legislative instruments adopted by the EU;
2. the redefinition of competences between the Union and the Member States;
3. rethinking the role of the EU institutions with the aim to pursue greater efficiency, transparency and democracy.

To achieve the goals set in the "Declaration of Laecken" it was recognized the opportunity to develop a true "European constitution". At this purpose, it has been established the "Convention on the Future of Europe", chaired by Valerie Giscard d'Estaing, with the task of examining and resolving various legal and institutional issues related to the provision of a European constitution.

The work of the Convention have been divided into a number of working groups, addressed to specific issues (in particular, with respect to the issues raised by taxation, it was formed the Working Group VI—economic *governance*) and subsequently defined in plenary sessions coordinated by the *Praesidium* (in essence, the Presidency of the Convention with functions of pulse and direction).

As a result of this work it was issued a draft European Constitution, which was approved by the European Council on June 18th 2004 and therefore assumed the character of an act legally binding for the Member States, however without absorbing it into the national laws. Moreover, these procedures have not produced a positive result, for several Member (also as a result of specific resolutions referendum) and therefore it was decided not to adopt the European Constitution.

The European Constitution draft has thus stalled, failing the required unanimity for final approval of the regulatory text in the European Union.

Subsequently, a treaty which incorporates the fundamental lines of the European Constitution has been approved in Lisbon on 12/13/2007 by the 27 Member States that made up the EU at that time, making not relevant changes to the previous version as a result of a new political agreement between Member States (so-called *Lisbon Treaty*). The procedures for implementation of the Lisbon Treaty in the various countries have been completed successfully and the Treaty entered into force on 12/01/2009.

The Treaty of Lisbon preserves the basic structure of the framework of the European Union by the regulations currently in force, while producing some significant changes:

- removal of a distinction between the various European economic communities and devoting themselves to the uniqueness of the European Union;
- expansion of the powers and spheres of action of the EU, surpassing the theory of so-called "Three pillars";
- redefinition of the system of sources of law with an adjustment of the functions of the EU institutions and legislative instruments;
- inclusion of the rules and principles on fundamental human rights elaborated in the Charter of Nice.

With regard to taxation the existing rules in the Treaty were essentially maintained, in many cases with a restatement of the full regulatory text foresight. Some adjustments have been made to the discipline of legislative procedures regarding the enactment of tax rules, without any distortion of the regulatory system currently in force.

The approval of the European Constitution, at first, and of the Lisbon Treaty, at second, has been a critical step in the consolidation of the European architecture, opening up new spaces for the development of the European integration so as to ensure the attainment of the purpose of political and social unification in addition to economic and business integration. Indeed, the expansion of the sphere of competence of the EU institutions beyond the horizon of the specific freedoms and competitive single market has been one of the issues of greatest significance to the European Constitution, almost in the direction of unification of an effective federal State.

On the other hand, not all expectations of renewal originally entrusted to the Convention seem to have paid off, as the conservative demands of many countries and the inevitable tendency to seek compromises imposed combined solutions that essentially have marginalized many of the innovative interventions on the role and functioning of the EU institutions.

In this perspective, the enactment of the Treaty of Lisbon does not seem to be able to be still considered as the final stage of the integration process, but rather as an evolutionary step, hopefully a stepping stone towards a European federal State, which will have to be followed by further steps and actions in order to ensure the assignment of powers and more effective functions to the European institutional bodies.

2.1.4 The Institutional Framework of the European Union: The Democratic Deficit and the Problems of the Sovereignty of the EU Institutions

In the Treaties of the European Communities different institutions are involved for the decision-making policy and for the administrative powers recognized by European law.

The regulatory power with the primary character is essentially recognized to the Council, a body made up by a representative of each Member State, authorized to commit the government of that State. The Commission, made up of 28 members chosen by the Member States, holds a restricted power on legislation, although it has broad powers to adopt implementing rules of Council acts (delegated by the latter); it also holds significant powers of an administrative nature, especially in relation to the task of monitoring the compliance with the obligations under EU laws by the Member States. The Parliament approves the EU budget and performs a control function, mainly of a political nature (without actual binding instruments) compared to the work of the Commission; contrary to what happens in the modern institutional arrangements, the Parliament does not exert the regulatory function in a direct manner, but basically performs a function of advisory support to the Council.

Just this characterization of the institutional architecture of the European institutions poses a significant problem in relation to the first dimension of sovereignty attributed to the European Union.

The European institutions were not designed with a sort of democratic character, with the aim to ensure compliance with the fundamental principle of popular representation, but they were conceptualized rather as an inter-governmental organization, in which the distribution of powers between the various bodies favours in substance the decisions taken by the executive power of single nation-States.

In fact, in the communitarian form of government for the decision of the regulatory choices the protagonist is undoubtedly represented by the Council, the body having a typical executive nature, while to the Parliament it is essentially attributed a marginal role, without concrete decision-making powers. While in recent times the powers of the Parliament were expanded, the fact stands that such a representative body remains today without the legitimacy of any legislative power, assuming essentially an advisory role in order to the regulatory procedure (role which can assume the form of consultation, coordination, cooperation or co-decision).

So, the atrophy of the parliamentary power causes a severe discomfort of functioning of EU institutions, at least in terms of basic values metabolised by European constitutions; indeed, the lack of democratic legitimacy, due to the lack of implementation of the principle of popular representation, marks a significant distance with respect to the parliamentary democracies of the European States and, in some way, is to induce a sense of distrust for the decisions taken at the European level.

The democratic *deficit* thus leads to undermine the very foundations of European sovereignty, introducing a more substantial doubt about the legitimacy of the EU institutions to take the place, in a complete (or at least, significant) way, instead of the nation-States in the regulation of matters that affect the fundamental rights of citizens.

Moreover, the problem of the functioning of the EU institutions—and in particular of the Council—is further accentuated by the unanimity rule that is frequently imposed on relevant matters (and for the extension of EU competence under art. 352 TFEU), in order to determine the criteria for approval of collegial resolutions (although with the temperament that the abstention is not considered to prevent the adoption of the resolution). The acceptance of the unanimity principle clearly entails the assignment of a "veto power" to each State, which in fact reduces strongly the decision-making power of the Council. In this perspective, the adoptable options for the collegial resolutions need the basis of a significant prior mediation among the Member States.

In the design of the Lisbon Treaty it is expected that the legislative power is exercised jointly by the Parliament and the Council, on a proposal coming from the Commission, according to a certain legislative procedure. In this context, the Council could decide in principle by recourse to the criterion of a qualified majority of Member States representing at least three fifths of the total population of the European Union. It is a rule (which is not applicable to the taxation, as it will be seen later) that to some extent, though not in a decisive manner, can produce an attenuation of the democratic deficit of the EU institutions.

2.2 The Regulation of Fiscal Policy in the EU

2.2.1 The Lack of a Proper Taxation System in the European Union

Compared to the formative process of the European integration, the adjustment of tax legislation takes on a special importance as it is presented as one of the most important index detectors of the idea of sovereignty that is attributed to the EU institutions.

Indeed, according to the lines of evolution of the European tradition (as emerging from the above analysis, Chap. 1) it should be clear that taxation constitutes one of the most "intimate" attributes of sovereign power, contributing in a decisive way to the characterization of the same power under an ideological profile. Therefore, it is quite possible to examine the options adopted in European legislation about the taxation in order to recognise the fundamental values and the underlying beliefs with regard to the sovereignty of the European Union.

It should be noted, first of all, that a peculiar feature of the European Union is to be considered the system of institutional financing; the public finance is placed in a kind of median area between the mechanism of contribution to be paid by the Member States, which typically denotes the international organizations, and the mechanism of collecting own resources, constituting one of the typical features of the nation-States.

Originally, the Treaties for the EEC and EAEC established that the operating budget was covered by financial contributions distributed among the single States because of an eminently political criteria (namely connected to the role that each State had in the composition of the organs and in the voting procedure). The provisional nature of this financial structure was also demonstrated by a rule of the EEC Treaty (Article 269), where it was assigned to the Commission the task of studying forms and procedures for the replacement of the financial aid system with a system based on own resources, mainly taken by the Common Customs Tariff.

In 1969 in The Hague, based on proposals put forward precisely by the Commission, the Member States started and concluded negotiations aimed at establishing guidelines for the system of self-financing of the European Communities. In 1970 a treaty was signed in Luxembourg which amended the rules on the formation of the Communities budget and established the use of its own resources in replacement of the financial contributions from Member States. Subsequently, by the Council Decision of 05/24/1988, against the risk of the small size of its own resources, the funding system has been overhauled with a broadening of the types and mechanisms of computation of income payable directly to the Community.

Indeed, currently (according to art. 311 TFEU), the European Union holds its own financial resources mainly due to four types of revenue:

- customs duties collected at the borders of the European Union;
- withdrawals and contributions from agricultural activities;
- profit-sharing in the revenue of VAT applied by the Member States (to an extent that may not exceed 1%);
- and finally a contribution (in principle determined as oscillating around 1% of GDP) imposed each year by the EU to the individual Member States.

These financial resources are annually based on the results of the budget drawn up by the EU and are allocated among the Member States in relation to economic data and budget. In this case, the sharing of VAT revenue is to be determined by reference to an abstract evaluation of the general data of the national accounts in order to determine the overall tax base of VAT on a uniform basis throughout the European Union (and not, therefore, in relation to the effective and real progress on economic transactions subject to VAT). The total amount of own resources can not in any case exceed a certain quantitative threshold, calculated as a percentage of GDP of each country (now in an amount equal to 1.27% of the total gross domestic product).

Therefore, these fiscal resources may not (with the exception of customs duties) be attributed to a direct exercise of taxing powers, but on the contrary to the revenues transferred to the European Union by individual Member national; therefore, this income can be classified mainly in terms of derivate taxation. Indeed, although these resources are defined as a result of an autonomous decision-making process of the European Union, and consequently they are classified precisely as own resources, they do not consist in the application of taxation criteria on taxpayers, but in contribution rates applied to the individual States on the basis of existing taxes and other macro-economic indices.

It should also be noted that, in quantitative terms, these resources appear significantly distant from the volumes of the taxing flows generated by the individual States, reaching very small percentage compared to the wealth produced in the EU territories; that indicates, so vividly, as the actual financing system of the European Union has a marginal size compared to the public finance of the national States, posing as a "primordial" system which may not be adaptable to the public finance systems of the modern State.

It should be added that the EU lacks an administrative power in respect of the management of the tax flows, as the collection of taxes is entrusted exclusively to the tax authorities of the individual Member States (also for customs duties) which then uses to deposit into an account that the European Union has opened in each State. Moreover, a percentage of the revenues (currently 25%) is retained by the Member as compensation for the collection service (as set out in the Council Decision of 29.9.2000).

As mentioned, the financing scheme expresses to some extent the idea of overcoming the logic of purely aggregative supranational unions, indicating a shift towards an integration to be joined conceptually to an association (and thus to an autonomous State, with its own resources). On the other hand, it also indicates the incompleteness of such a switch, given the lack of qualitative and quantitative elements that can be ascribed to a proper taxation (as a manifestation of a taxing powers exercised directly on the consociates). That confirms the transitional nature of the current stage of the evolutionary process of the European Union, and in particular the institutional placement in a sort of grey area where it is not yet perfected the "leap forward" from the inter-governmental union to the federal model.

The lack of a substantial proper taxation evidently affects on the constitutional definition of power tax: in fact it appears irrelevant to regulate the basic dialectics of the taxation phenomenon, given that there is no need to acquire tax resources (and thus to introduce the principle of *taxation interest*), nor to distribute the tax burdens over the consociates (and therefore to establish distribution criteria following the principle of the *ability to pay*, or at least the principle of equality). It felt so clearly the axiological distance of the European fiscal system compared to the national tax system, because of a difference of significance of the values associated with the regulation of the taxation phenomenon.

In the context of the European Constitution it has developed a significant debate regarding the appropriateness of including explicitly a rule that would allow the European Union to adopt "own taxes" (with alternative formula—or at least additional—than the traditional phrase "own resources"). The majority of Convention members insisted on the inclusion of such a reference, but the intransigence of the British position has prompted the presidency of Giscard d'Estaing to seek a compromise solution: the regulatory change has not been approved, but in the work of the Convention it is formulated the belief that the current legal basis—provided in the rules of the EU Treaty—still allows the creation of new European Union own financial resources, including specifically the tax revenues and own taxes.

2.2.2 The Presence of EU Contributory Competences in Taxation and the Implementation of the Principle of Subsidiarity

In contrast to what is stated in most of the Constitutions of the federal States (or in those ones characterized by a strong regionalism), in the Treaties there are not rules that clarify the overall architecture of the relations between the European Union and the Member States with regard to the exercise of taxation power. In particular, while some basic principles are fixed on the fiscal responsibilities of the European Union, are entirely absent rules that seek to preserve a core of tax competencies for the Member States. It must therefore proceed on the basis of interpretation for the reconstruction of the general framework of relations between the EU and individual States in order to control the phenomenon of tax.

The lack of a own taxation makes clear that the European Union may not claim any exclusive competence in matters of taxation, assuming essentially a role of coordination and adjustment of fiscal policies implemented by Member States.

Moreover, the EU institutions do not have a particular interest in the collection of large tax flows, whereas the general aims of the European Union—with respect to which the taxes are placed in a teleological relationship—are typically pursued by national States. It must be highlighted that the competence with respect to social welfare programs and income redistribution (and usually to the demands of the *Welfare State*), which is the inevitable *pendant* of the exercise of the power of taxation, is established and jealously defended by the individual Member States, making it one of the fundamental determinants of political relations between "rulers" and "ruled" in each national community.

Thus the principle of subsidiarity finds application to the taxation phenomenon, whereby the legislative power around certain subjects is secured to the level of government that is the best able to assess and to accommodate the interests of all stakeholders involved. Indeed, the link "tributes/public expenses" leads the centre of gravity of the tax power basically at the national level, relegating the EU competence to a marginal role.

In particular, the European Union is interested in the phenomenon mainly to avoid the taxation determined by the rules laid down in national tax legislation which may result in appreciable obstacles to the freedom of market competition, negatively interfering with the process of economic integration which, as mentioned, is the engine of the substantial European integration. The EU competence in tax matters resolved, therefore, in a concurrent jurisdiction with respect to the national States (except in the case of customs legislation where there is an exclusive competence of the European Union, for obvious reasons of safeguarding the functioning of the common market). Therefore, the EU institutions have the burden of proving that a particular legislative action on taxation matters at European level is more effective than an action realised directly by the individual States (or than the sum of the regulatory actions of the Member States).

In this regard, it can be argued that the EU taxation is a typical example of a "superstructure", namely lacking a positive content and directed rather to define the framework within which the "positive" taxation ordered by the national States can be developed. Therefore, it is a "second level" taxation, and its object is basically made up not so much of the definition of tax relations, but rather of the regulation of the tax powers executed by the national authorities.

From these basic structural elements it seems that the phenomenon of tax is set in European Union not in "positive" terms, with the aim to regulate the dynamics of constitutional and basic values of taxation, but rather in "negative" terms, with the purpose to contain and to circumscribe the typical power of individual States where appropriate to interfere with the fundamental freedoms of the European market.

2.2.3 The Procedures for Approval of EU Rules Related to Taxation

In line with the institutional structure of the European Union, the rules related to taxation are decided by the Council.

In this regard, there are specific sessions of the Council composed of the ministers of finance and economic interests of the Member States (often referred to as the European Economic advice: so-called ECOFIN). In general it is up to the ECOFIN to define the economic guidelines in order to ensure the coordination of national economic policies, to decide the recommendations to be sent to the States in default or otherwise misaligned with respect to the common policy, and finally to ensure the compliance with the parameters of public finance agreed at European level (especially to guarantee the stability of the European currency).

The tax matters, as well as other matters that are crucial for the national "security", are the subject of deliberations by the Council adopted, in principle, by unanimity of the members. The principle of qualified majority for the taxation deliberations of the Council is provided sporadically by EU legislation (e.g. regarding the fixation of taxing exemptions to exportation or countervailing taxes on imports in accordance with Art. 112 TFEU).

In particular, in terms of harmonization it is planned the recourse to the criterion of unanimity for directives for the approximation of direct taxes in accordance with art. 115 TFEU. Moreover, where it is found a difference in legislative or administrative provisions among the various member countries liable to distort competition in the common market, the Council—pursuant to art. 116 TFEU—may issue directives on the basis of decisions taken by a qualified majority; however, that is sporadic, even considering the provision of a particular procedure law (in this case the Commission must give prior consultations with the State in order to verify hypothesis of agreements leading to the elimination of distortion).

Also the reference to Art. 352 as a legal basis to allow for EU action in the field of taxation—if necessary to achieve one of the European goals (and therefore also the "non-fiscal" use of taxation regulations as a means to encourage the pursuit of non-fiscal goals such as the economic development, environmental protection, etc.)—assumes the decision of the Council acting unanimously.

The Commission plays a function of the address of the Council, through the examination of the various legal and institutional structures and the investigation about the effects produced in concrete by EU legislation and/or national laws. Only in the area of State aids it performs a primary function of a legislative nature in order to identify the protectionist measures of the individual Member States incompatible with EU law.

The Parliament is called upon to decide only on a consultative basis, delivering not binding opinions to the Council to be taken into account. Moreover, this parliamentary consultation is mandatory only where it is expressly provided for by the EU legislation (as the case of the harmonization of indirect taxes pursuant to art. 113 TFEU).

Even the setting of fiscal policy in the European Union is so entrusted to complex regulatory procedures that confirm the data of the lack of democratic legitimacy in the phase of creation of the norms. Therefore, it may be observed a clear disconnect between the attribution of the choice of fiscal policy to an executive branch and the legal effects that reverberate inevitably on EU citizens. This seems to confirm the democratic deficit that is seen typically to characterize the institutional system of the European Union, showing the inadequacy of the institutional bodies to take decisions on tax matters that are substantiated by a level of popular representation.

This structure is a further confirmation even after the approval of the Lisbon Treaty as the ordinary legislative procedure—which involves the co-decision of the European Parliament and the Council—does not apply to tax matters. The Council continues to decide unanimously after consulting the European Parliament and the Economic and Social Committee (Art. 311 TFEU). However, if the Council determines—through a resolution approved unanimously—that some fiscal measures relate to administrative cooperation or to combating fraud or tax avoidance, it may take decisions through qualified majority. Similarly, if the Council finds—always through a resolution passed unanimously on a proposal from the Commission—that some regulations on the corporate tax are functional to ensure the functioning of the internal market and to avoid distortions of competition or are addressed to fight tax evasion or tax avoidance or even to promote cooperation between the tax authorities, it has the right to adopt a resolution by a qualified majority, after consultation with Parliament and the Economic and Social Committee. The so-called "toll bridges" introduce a very marginal derogation from the principle of unanimity, intended to be applied in some cases that remain limited and sporadic.

It does not still find any space in the Lisbon Treaty with regard to the tax provisions the rule about the approximation of the laws, which is laid down for other subjects (art. 111 TFEU).

Finally, it should be noted that in the context of the Lisbon Treaty there is the possibility of having recourse to the mechanism of "enhanced cooperation", namely a form of collaboration made on a contractual basis between a plurality (and not the totality) of the Member States. This mechanism may play a central role in the taxation, as a development opportunity of tax integration for some regulations which have not yet been approved by the unanimous vote of the member countries, but which are recognized as useful from a large number of States, so that they are willing to start their concrete implementation in their own taxation systems.

2.3 The Stability Pact and the Fiscal Compact

2.3.1 The Stability Pact

The EU legal order contains some rules devoted to contrast the national debt of the member States and, consequently, to preserve the financial integrity of the European Union. Although these rules do not concern directly the tax discipline, they are usually referred to the fiscal policy because they impact evidently over the public finance of the member States and impose some constraints over the tax policy to be adopted in order to pursue the European integration.

Since the Treaty of Maastricht emerged clearly the basic logic of the European Union: the protection of the public finance of the national States is considered the necessary guarantee for the functioning of the common market, especially in the perspective of the monetary integration (due to the introduction of the euro); only solid national economic systems may permit a good working of the European freedoms. To avoid the crisis of the single nation State is the assumption for increasing the grade of efficiency and reliability of the common market, according to an overall global economy characterised by strict connections of the national economic systems.

In this perspective, the principle of efficiency of the national public finance assumes a remarkable relevance in order to the values of the European legal order, contributing to favourable conditions for the stability of the prices, for the increasing employment and for the economic growth.

At this purpose, the rule of art. 104 TFEU (already contained in the art. 104 of the Treaty of Maastricht) establishes the general principle according to which the member States must avoid an excessive deficit. This principle is related to the aim of promoting "healthy public finance and healthy monetary conditions" (as expressed by the art. 119, par. 3 TFEU).

So, the Commission is entitled to execute the power of control about the development of the national public deficit and the general situation of the national debt in order to verify serious violations by the member States. Particularly, the Commission may verify the correctness of the public finance under two main criteria:

i. evaluation of the mathematical relationship between the public deficit, estimated or effective, and the gross domestic product of the State in comparison with a general parameter; the overcoming of this general parameter is admitted if the relationship shows a trend of continuous and substantial decreasing and it is reaching a level close to the parameter; or, alternatively, if the overcoming of the parameter is to be considered exceptional and transitory and the relationship is close to the parameter;

ii. evaluation of the mathematical relationship between the public debt and the gross domestic product of the State in comparison with a general parameter; also in this case, the overcoming of this general parameter is admitted if this relationship is decreasing substantially and is reaching a level close to the parameter.

The general parameters to be considered for the above mentioned criteria are specified in the Protocol about the procedure for the excessive deficit attached to the Treaty (art. 126 par. 2). Particularly the parameter for the evaluation of the relationship between the public deficit and the gross domestic product has been established in the amount of 3% (three per cent) of the GDP in the document called "Pact about stability and growth" [1]. This is a very remarkable act which is devoted to address the outlines of the virtuous development of the member States in order to pursue the aim of the "healthy public finance" as expressed by the Treaty.

2.3.2 The Procedure for the Control and the Sanctions for the Violations to the Rules of the "Stability Pact"

The procedure for the execution of the rules contained in the "stability pact" is distributed in two phases: the control and the surveillance about the European constraints to the public finance; the procedure for the return from the situation of crisis (and especially by the excessive deficit).

At first, an articulated procedure is established for the control about the behaviours assumed by the member States (including the local governments) and for the verification of the conditions expressed by the "stability pact" in order to the relationship between the public deficit and the gross domestic product.

The Commission verifies periodically the financial statement and the document of financial forecast produced by the member States related to their public finance; if the Commission ascertains that a member State does not respect the conditions expressed by the "stability pact" (or however considers well possible the risk of an excessive deficit), it prepares a report for the examination of the specific position of the public finance of this member State; in this report the Commission:

i. ascertains the relationship between the public deficit and the gross domestic product;

[1] The "Pact about European stability and growth" is contained in the Regulations of 7.7.1997 n. 1466/97 and n. 1467/97 (as modified by the Regulations of 27.6.2005 n. 1055 and n. 1056) and in the Resolution of the European Council of 17.6.1997.

ii. evaluates some other reasons for the overcoming of the general parameter established by the "stability pact";
iii. considers the general position of the public finance of the member State in a middle term.

The economic and financial Committee (ECOFIN) formulates an opinion about the above mentioned report of the Commission.

If the Commission considers that an excessive deficit of a member State exists or may exist concretely in the future, it transmits the report to the government of the member State and inform the Council.

The Council is called to express about the recommendation of the Commission, after having heard the observation by the government of the member State; therefore, the Council expresses his deliberation about the excessive deficit (or other violations) according to a general evaluation of the position of the public finance of the member State.

If the Council deliberates that an excessive deficit has been produced by the member State, it formulates some recommendation to the member State in order to terminate the existing violations within a determinate term. This recommendation is to be considered confidential and cannot be disclosed. If the recommendation is not adequately followed by the member State, the Council may disclose the recommendation itself.

If the member State continues in the violation and does not follow adequately the recommendation, the Council may summon to the member State to adopt the behaviour necessary for reducing the deficit; in this case the Council may require to the member State to present periodical reports about the trend of the restructuring of the public finance according to a specific timetable.

As long the member State does not comply with the decisions assumed according to the described procedure, the Council may decide to apply or to increase one or more of the following actions:

- to require that the member State disclose additional information to be specified by the Council, before the issue of bond;
- to invite the European Investment Bank to modify his policy of loan towards the member State;
- to require that the member State settles a non interest bearing deposit of an adequate amount in the European Union until the excessive deficit is not reduced according to the opinion of the Council;
- to impose monetary sanctions of an adequate amount.

The decisions of the Council are assumed with a qualified majority (55% of the member of the Council and 65% of the European population; art. 238 par. 3 lett. a TFEU), without considering the vote of the member State under evaluation.

On the basis of this articulate procedure for the surveillance and the possible sanctions, the constraints to the public finance deriving from the European integration are to be considered as well as "procedural rules", devoted to fix terms and conditions to the decisions of the member States in the financial matters, and not as well as "substantial rules" addressed to define the content and the substance of the choices of public finance.

At this purpose, it must observe that the European rules impose a procedure for the surveillance very articulated for the verification of the excessive deficit and establish light sanctions (and not easy to be applied) for the violations of the member States. It means that these rules do not represent a significant deterrent to the excessive deficit by the member States and, therefore, they appear ineffective in order to the pursuit of the aim of stability of the European public finance.

2.3.3 The Fiscal Compact

As mentioned before, the monitoring procedure about the public balance of the Member States, established by the art. 126 TFEU, is typically focused over the verification of the excessive deficit (and less over the control of the dimension of the public debt). Evidently, the main preoccupation of the EU bodies is to ensure a management of the current activity of the Member State that complies with the European parameters.

Recently, it has began a phase of deep review of the rules and procedures addressed to the principle of efficiency of the national public finance. Particularly, it has been discussed the conviction that the European protection should be referred basically the excessive deficit and not also the dimension of the public debt. Indeed, the serious recent economic crisis induced the EU bodies to keep a more severe behaviour in front of the public debt of each Member State.

Firstly, some rules have been approved in order to favour a redefinition of the EU discipline regarding the national public finance. Especially, on 4th October 2011, the Council has issued a series of measures, called *Six pack* (containing five Regulations and one Directive), with the aim to introduce some European constraints for the coordination of the EU economic policy, for the surveillance of the national public finance and for the measuring of the public balance of the Member States.

Secondly, on the 9th December 2011, the 17 States belonging to the Euro area, resuming the matters contained in the *Six pack*, has agreed, on a the outlines of the "Treaty of fiscal stability" (so called "*Fiscal compact*") which stiffens the parameter of the relationship between public debt and gross domestic product (and strengthens the parameter of the relationship between deficit and gross domestic product), and at the same time provide for automatic penalties for the State which does not comply with the mentioned parameters. The *Fiscal compact* must be qualified as an international agreement, and therefore it is to be considered as a tool of the international legal order and not as an institution of the EU legal order. In any case this treaty reveals a remarkable symbolic value in the European integration process, since it defines the virtuous route to be followed in order to pursue a general context of healthy national public finance as required by the aim of growth and development of European economics.

Particularly, the *Fiscal compact* establishes the following rules about the public finance of the Member States:

1. the structural deficit does not have to exceed the 0.5% of the gross domestic debt (GDP); for the Member States whose public debt is higher than 60% of the GDP, the structural deficit does not have to exceed the 1% of the GDP;
2. in any case, the deficit must remain every year beneath the level of 3% of the GDP (as established by the Stability Pact); if this level is exceeded, some automatic penalties shall be applied;
3. Member States with a public debt exceeding the level of 60% of the GDP must reduce their debt within 20 years, on the basis of a trend of one twentieth (corresponding to 5%) per year;
4. any Member State must guarantee automatic corrections to the public finance if it does not achieve the targets agreed with the EU bodies;
5. there must be established specific rules about the balanced budget of the public finance in the legal order of the Member States (preferably in the constitutional charters).

It should be observed that the rules contained in the *Fiscal compact* are intended to assume a relevant impact over the public finance of the Member States: not only the deficit should be contained within a determined level, consistent with the conviction of a healthy public finance, but moreover the public debt should be reduced consistently in order to achieve the level of 60% of the GDP, which is considered a sustainable level for the current stage of the international economics.

The *Fiscal compact* has been approved by the Council (with a contrary vote of United Kingdom and Czech Republic) on 30th January 2012 and will be in force after the formal approval by 12 member States. Every Member State should establish specific rules about the balanced budget of the public finance in its legal order; only after the approval of these rules, the State shall be able to receive loans by the European mechanism of stability.

2.4 The Relations Between European Union and National Legal Systems

2.4.1 The Orientation of the National Courts Tends to be Inspired by the Theory of the Separation of Legal Systems

It seems consolidated the idea that the European Union constitutes an independent and autonomous legal system, structured as a set of legal norms provided by its own sources, and organized on the basis of organs, procedures and mechanisms capable of permitting the interpretation, the application and the execution of the same norms.

It appears, in this regard, the very delicate topic of the relations that are being established with the national legal systems, in order to define the degree of integration and, consequently, the effectiveness of the European law in relation to the internal rules. Evidently this is the fundamental legal step to define the concept of sovereignty referring to the European Union or, rather, to clarify the scope of the transfer of sovereignty it by the nation States.

In the various systems of the Member States it has progressively defined a line of interpretation that leads the relationship with EU law to the principle of separation of legal systems (so-called "dualist" thesis); it is a theoretical reconstruction of typical internationalist inspiration, which basically is based on the recognition of a real separation between the domestic law and the European legal order, whose integration process is entrusted to the logic of liaison and coordination that occurs precisely in international organizations.

In Germany as well, the legal basis for the transposition of Community rules, even before art. 23 of the Constitution (newly formulated and designed to contain the explicit reference to the European Union), was found in art. 24 of the Constitution which regulates the transfer of sovereign rights to supranational bodies, where it is established the principle that the transfer is designed to achieve a lasting peaceful order in Europe (besides "among the peoples of the world"). This is clearly a clause which allows easy insertion of rules of international roots within the internal order. In this regard it should be noted that, after a significant theoretical debate, during which it was fervently supported the thesis of the primacy of the domestic provision due to parliamentary sovereignty, it seems to have finally stabilized, especially in constitutional jurisprudence, a setting of openness towards the EU law although still characterized by the belief of the separation of legal systems: the integration process must be pursued recognizing the prevalence of the rule of EU law, provided that in each case it is secured the respect of fundamental rights and the principles underlying the national Constitution. Emblematic in this regard is the well-known decision of the German Constitutional Court of 10/12/1993 in which it is explicitly stated that Member States are to be considered as "masters of the Treaties", as the national parliaments must still preserve the substantial and primary legal functions, including the decision on the implementation of the EU Treaty.

In France, despite the presence of a strong legal tradition of monistic type, it is dominant the dualist approach, based on the principle of separation of the legal systems; however, it has spread the conviction that, on the basis of constitutional requirements, the sovereignty may not be transferred, even partially, to supranational bodies, but it is possible to individuate an original competence in favour of the EU bodies in order to regulate matters that are beyond the national jurisdiction.

In the United Kingdom the EU Treaties were implemented through an analytical legislative regulation of the effects; in the national cultural background it is clear the idea that the parliamentary sovereignty does not lend itself to being compressed or limited by exercising a concurrent power, although coming from a supranational body.

In Spain, the Constitutional Court has adopted the principle that the rule of EU law must be judged prevalent than the rule of national law, being able to exert a direct effect in national law.

2.4.2 In Particular, the Position of the Italian Constitutional Court

Also the Italian Constitutional Court has gone by placing essentially on the same theory mentioned above, assuming a typical dualist approach.

Initially, adopting a clear set of internationalist derivation, the Constitutional Court (judgment no. 14/1964) found that the application of European law arises from the implementation of international treaties by the order of execution contained in an ordinary domestic law: the art. 11 of the Italian Constitution, according to the Court, upon the occurrence of certain conditions, makes possible to conclude international treaties by which the limitations of sovereignty can be assumed and carry without causing any deviation from the rules in force regarding effectiveness in law. This constitutional rule, expressly considered by the Court as "permissive provision", does not render the ordinary law, which executes the Treaty, more effective than a typical source of law. On the basis of this approach it was considered, therefore, that the contrast between domestic law and EU law went resolved according to the usual criteria (the succession of laws in time).

A significant change of trend can be seen when the Constitutional Court (by the sentence no. 183/1973) stated that the fundamental requirements of equality and legal certainty postulate that the EU rules have to be fully mandatory and, in some cases, to produce a direct application in all the Member States in order to enter into force at the same time and to get equal and uniform application to all the recipients.

It is, therefore, recognized the primacy of European law over domestic law and, simultaneously, it is abandoned the idea that national law must exercise direct control over EU acts through the required implementation by the internal law.

The Court, according to the dualistic approach, also noted that the legal basis of the execution law is to identify in the art. 11 of the Italian Constitution which, recognizing the limitations of sovereignty by reason of the accession to international treaties that promote the pursuit of a peaceful system, offers a "constitutional cover" for the ordinary law that allows to give effect to conventional provisions able to produce an impact on constitutional requirements.

In this perspective, the internal legal system is posed in terms of autonomy and separateness from the European legal system, keeping the need of a functional coordination in order to achieve the aims set by the accession to the EU treaties.

In this regard, the Court stated further that "*basing on art. 11 of the Constitution, limitations of sovereignty were permitted only to achieve the purposes specified therein; therefore it must be excluded that such limitations... may still lead the bodies of the EEC to an unacceptable power to violate the fundamental principles of our constitutional system or the inalienable rights of the human person. And it is obvious that if [the rules of the Treaties] were given such an aberrant interpretation, than it would always be assured the guarantee of jurisdictional syndicate of this Court on the compatibility of the Treaty with the fundamental principles mentioned above*".

On this conceptual line there is a series of decisions of the Court in the seventies that, on the assumption of the prevalence and the direct effect of EU rules, established the illegality of internal laws that were incompatible with the EU regulations (judgment no. 232/1975). However, this position did not even led to recognize the power of the internal court to disapply the internal laws incompatible with the rule of EU law, being provided in this case the judgment of the constitutional legitimacy of the internal regulation, which is considered to be violating the Art. 11 of the Constitution. Otherwise, it was believed that the EU regulation implicitly would abrogate the incompatible internal laws previously in force, according to the chronological order.

The final composition of the relationship between EU law and national law is finally realised by the Decision No. 170/1984 in which the Court has recognized the competence of the national court to give full and immediate application to the EU rule through the non-application of the internal norm which is considered to be in conflict with the European regulation.

The system of primacy of EU law over national law is characterized by the fact that conflicting domestic law, while remaining intact and valid (being neither repealed nor cancelled), is irrelevant to the outcome of the dispute before the national court. This mechanism of automatic prevalence occurs only when the European legislation is complete and immediately applicable (namely, when it puts clear, precise and unconditional obligations on Member States) and not when the same is in conflict with the fundamental principles of fundamental human rights (the so-called *counter-limits*).

However, it is significant that, in this context, the Constitutional Court explicitly states, as founding premise of their argument, that "*the EU and the national systems are different but interconnected (by means of the Treaties) and that the EU regulation is produced by a European source, namely a distinct, coordinated legal system, compared to the State system*". Despite being enshrined in a substantial change compared to the internationalist origin (by some considered as a real "peaceful revolution" of the relationship between EU law and national law), constitutional case law preserves the conceptual background of dualist thesis, namely the separation and the independence of the two legal systems.

Finally, a further opening of the Constitutional Court with European law is found in a subsequent decision (judgment no. 168/1991), in which, expanding the "category" of EU acts directly applicable, it recognizes the primacy over the law of the so-called *detailed directives*; these are the directives which, despite their failure to transpose into national law, are given immediate applicability in the Member State under certain conditions; in particular, according to the constitutional jurisprudence, they required the existence of three elements: a) clarity, accuracy and completeness of the European rules; b) absence of any condition to their effectiveness; c) expiration of the time limit for the transposition at national level. In making this "openness", the Court should also observe that the EU "prevalent" rule does not make disapplicable the conflicting domestic norm, but it makes indeed "not applicable".

This clarification is intended to emphasize again that the contrast among the norms does not imply any defect of the national rule and, consequently, attempts to preserve even the dualist theory of the relationships between national law and EU law. The disapplication of the national rule, in fact, leads to bring down the primacy of European law from the application of hierarchical criterion for the sources of law, indicating a reconstruction of the relationships between the EU legal system and the national legal system according to a predominantly monist theory. Differently, the use of the institution of "non-application" leads to delineate distinct areas of application of the two norms, recognizing the operation of the principle of specialty and, thus, safeguarding the opportunity to reconstruct the relationship between the internal rule and the EU rule according to the dualistic theory.

Subsequently, the Constitutional Court, acknowledging the findings made by the EU institutions, has recognized that the national Parliament is entitled to make the necessary amendments to the internal law in order to eliminate the incompatible national rules or to disapply them in an appropriate manner so as to ensure the effective primacy of European law and the principle of legal certainty.

2.4.3 The "Monistic" Orientation of the Court of Justice

In contrast to the jurisprudence of the constitutional courts of the Member States, the European Court of Justice has taken a jurisprudence decidedly oriented in favour of the "monistic" theory.

In a first fundamental decision (Van Gend & Loos in 1963, significantly concerning a tax issue), the Court notes that "*the European Economic Community constitutes a new legal system in the field of international law generally in favour of whom the Member States have dropped, albeit within limited fields, their sovereignty which not only Member States, but also their citizens are subject to*".

In a second, equally important, decision (the sentence Costa, 1964), the Court continues to assert the same principle, tracing the line of distinction from the traditional internationalist approach: "*in contrast with ordinary international treaties, the EEC Treaty has created its own legal system, which is integrated into the legal systems of the Member States before the entry into force of the Treaty and which the national courts are required to observe... By setting up a European Community of unlimited duration, having its own institutions, personality, legal capacity, capacity of representation on an international level, and in particular, real powers stemming from a limitation of sovereignty or a transfer of powers from the States to the Community, these have limited, albeit in limited ways, their sovereignty, and then created a set of rules binding for their citizens and for themselves*". And moreover "*the transfer by the States in favour of the EU legal system, the rights and obligations corresponding to the provisions of the Treaty, implies a definitive limitation of their sovereign power*" and, accordingly, "*the obligation imposed on Member States by the EEC Treaty ... is integrated into the legal system of the Member States, it has an imperative value and directly affects their citizens, who are attributed individual rights which national courts must protect*".

It is significant the use of the term "*transfer*" in relation to the passage of powers from the States to the European Union as it indicates that the EU powers retain the same character and the same nature as those previously belonging to the national States, and must accordingly being considered as "sovereign rights".

The position expressed by the Court of Justice in the two decisions above mentioned has remained essentially unchanged over time. Indeed, some steps have been taken up and developed: thus it has been argued explicitly that "*the foundation and the persuasiveness of this rule (of the superiority of EU law) emerges from the principle of unity and functional capacity of EU law. The validity of EU law may be judged only according to EU law, as created by the Treaty, so resulting from an autonomous source of law it may not be omitted by a regulation of internal law, if the legal foundation of the Community shall not be questioned*" (judgment of the *International Handelgesellschaft*, 1970).

The Court comes, therefore, to state expressly the superiority of the European legislation on the internal law, whether it is pre-existing or rear, considering that the primacy of EU law is a prerequisite for the feasibility and, for some aspects, for the existence itself, of the European Communities.

In line with this approach, the Court of Justice went even further to qualify the Treaty of Rome as a "*basic Constitutional Charter*" suitable to found a community of law autonomous and independent from the legal systems of the Member States (judgment *Le verts*, 1986).

The actual automatic recognition of the prevalence of the EU rules on incompatible domestic law, without the need of a receptive act and even the repeal or the annulment of conflicting national rules, has been a result of the statement by the Court itself that " *... the national court, which is called upon, within its jurisdiction, to apply provisions of EU law, has the obligation to give full effect to those provisions, if necessary, refusing of its own initiative any provision in conflict with the national law, without having to request or await its prior cancelation by legislative or other constitutional means*" (judgment *Simmenthal* 1978).

Evidently pursuing the goal of eliminating national barriers to the uniform application of common rules in a truly integrated European law, the Court of Justice makes clear that it disagrees with the position taken by the Constitutional Court, with an emphasis on "*the defects*" of the mechanisms for resolving contradictions between EU legislation and domestic legislation proposed so far by the latter and, above all, emphasizing the inability to ensure the immediate application of EU law.

In a later development, the EU Court has held, however, the failure of the non-application of the national rules conflicting with the EU law and the obligation imposed on the Member States to abrogate the same internal rules, observing that "*in the legal system of a Member State, to maintain unchanged an incompatible rule with the provisions of the Treaty, which is even directly applicable in the legal system of the Member State, creates an ambiguous situation as it keeps the parties in a state of uncertainty about the possibility of appeal to the EU law*". Therefore, such retention of the incompatible norm constitutes for the State a transgression of the obligations imposed by the Treaty that "*can be finally remedied only by internal binding provisions which have the same legal force as those to be changed*" (case 10/15/1986, C-168/85).

2.4.4 The Dual Reconstructive Perspective Regarding the Transfer of Functions from the Member States to the European Union

According to the guidelines set out, it should be clear that around the nucleus of sovereignty attributed to the EU bodies stirs a debate not yet resolved.

On the one hand, the constitutional jurisprudence of the Member States has acquired the conviction that the European Union is entrusted with some regulatory powers, even exclusive, delegated by the Member States, which have to be implemented through legislative measures in order to be integrated into the national law; in this perspective, the EU legal order operates as a separate and distinct legal system compared to the national legal order (according to the typical postulates of the "dualistic" theory), and acts essentially as a real limit to the legislative power of each State.

On the other hand, in the case law of the Court of Justice it has developed, since the beginning, the idea that the EU legal order represents a constituent part of a single legal order together with the national law; in this perspective, the European Union is not as a mere custodian of delegated legislative powers, but rather is a subject (preferably a combination of institutions and organs) which has the power to issue rules that make up immediately the unique legal system ("monistic" theory).

Now, if the distance between the two different logical reconstructions has been largely reduced, as it was recognized in the constitutional jurisprudence about the immediate effectiveness of EU rules and the non-application of conflicting national rules (so that it shows the substantial coincidence of the effects of the "dualistic" theory with respect to the "monistic" theory), it is equally true that the conceptual background remarks a considerable distance to separate the two theoretical approaches.

Indeed, the basic belief underlying the "dualistic" theory can be traced in the affirmation of the sovereignty of the nation-States that does not disappear, but rather is defined and limited in reason of the regulatory powers delegated to the European Union; therefore it is not registered a transfer of sovereignty to a third party, but rather a self-determined limitation of the original regulatory power by the individual owner (the nation-State), which can be reconstituted in terms of a "self-limitation".

On the contrary, in the "monistic" perspective by virtue of the establishment of a unified (and unique) system of law, the sovereignty of the States is, albeit partially, divided and attributed to the European Union, which takes the typical connotation of the subject holder of an original regulatory power.

Obviously, the distinction between the two theoretical approaches is the identification of the legal logic that determines the allocation of regulatory powers in the hands of the European Union: in the "dualist" thesis the prevailing view is that the State is "stripped" of its skills regulations to be assigned to the European Union, while in the "monistic" thesis the European Union is recognized originally entitled to the exercise of regulatory powers. In one case the transfer of regulatory powers to the European Union posed itself as a sort of "proxy" and thus implies the "self-limiting" will of the State, that can be defined as a " second-degree sovereignty" and indicates the derived character of sovereignty to the supranational bodies. In the other case, the transfer of powers and responsibilities to the EU is the result of the establishment of a new (and unique) legal order, in which, since the beginning, it is defined a new logic of regulatory powers of sovereignty; in this perspective, the European Union is shown equipped with a "first-degree" sovereignty, as entirely comparable to that accorded to the national States.

Therefore it is opportune to understand, in both perspectives indicated, what is the dimension of the sovereignty attributed to the European Union, given the special nature of the assigned powers and the lack of some of the distinctive and characteristic features of sovereignty (at least in the traditional sense).

It is interesting, at this purpose, to examine the principles and the rules existing in the European law in the area of taxation power also in order to verify what could be a reconstruction line of the relations between the Member States and the European institutions regarding the transfer of powers from one side to the other side and, consequently, how it can be configured conceptually the sovereignty of the European Union.

2.5 The Conflicts Between the EU Legal System and the National Constitutional System

2.5.1 The Conflict Between the General Values of EU Law and the National Constitutional Values Concerning the Taxation System

In the substantially (although not exclusively) liberal context which constitutes the framework of the values protected by the EU do not seem to find space the typical values of the basic dialectic of the taxation phenomenon (namely the ability to pay and the general interest to taxation).

With regard to the first value there is no trace in the EU legal order about directions provided to the Member States on the criteria for the allocation of the tax burden among the citizens, as this matter is considered a typical attribution of the national legislature. The inclusion in a supranational level presents some criteria of distribution of the tax burden which are competitors with the ability to pay, in order to pursue the economic and social targets assumed by the European Union: in particular, the European integration usually suggests the acceptance of different criteria than the ability to pay taxes such as the tax relief in the face of volatile wealth (such as financial income) and in any case the appreciation of fiscal measures designed to create jobs or to attract investment.

Regarding the general interest to taxation, intended as a collective interest in acquiring tax revenues, EU rules do not show elements that allow to presume a significant role in the context of the European values. Probably the lack of a proper tax system, oriented to provide the resources for the functioning of the European Union, significantly reduces the interest to ensure the effectiveness of the tax claim, entrusting this need to the competence of the Member States. Moreover, the same fiscal interest of the European Union poses as a substantially different value from the general interest to taxation of the national States, turning to supranational purposes which are typically the unified and convergent development of the wealth and the proper application of the tax systems of the Member States.

Therefore, the contrast between constitutional values and European values assume a concrete consistence, resulting in a quite possible collision between the EU sources of law inspired to the liberal logic and the national sources of law directed to the pursuit of the ability to pay and the general interest to taxation. In other words, there may be a development of the national tax system that follows the guidelines represented by the general interest to taxation and by the ability to pay tax, which leads to conflicting and divergent regulatory frameworks with respect to the principles and the legal order developed by the EU.

2.5.2 The Limit on the Primacy of EU Law over the National Constitution: The Theory of Counter-Limits

At this point, it must be analysed how it can be composed the potential conflict between the EU values and the values ordering the national tax in the constitutional framework.

Considering the primacy of the EU law, the main point of the matter is represented by the conflict of EU legislation in the area of taxation with the fundamental principles expressed in the national Constitution. It is known, in this regard, that the case law of the Constitutional Court and the doctrine have developed the theory of "counter-limits", by virtue of which it is required that the EU rule does not arise ever at odds with the basic principles of the democratic community expressed by the national Constitution (which represent, precisely, the so-called "counter-limits") because this contrast would call into question the same reasons underlying the accession of the State to the European Union.

Therefore, it has to be verified if in the category of the "counter-limits" to the effectiveness of the EU rules it can be included the values regarding tax matters.

In a large part of the doctrine it is widespread the conviction that both the ability to pay taxes and the general interest to taxation are to be included as part of the fundamental principles of the Constitution, as expressive of the core values necessary for the vitality of the democratic community. Consequently, the two fundamental values of the constitutional dialectic of taxation law seem to belong to the axiological and indispensable set of the democratic legal system, involving the same existence of the social community, or at least the maintenance of the project of development of the national community in the basic terms outlined in the Constitution.

In any case it does not appear easy to draw with confidence the conclusion that the ability to pay tax and the general interest to taxation constitute impassable "counter-limits" compared to the EU regulatory power.

This issue indeed shows a remarkable complexity, involving the reasons of the European integration and the general evolution of jurisprudential thought, with regard to the degree of the axiological prevalence that assumes the level of values formulated in Europe. In particular, where it is spreading the idea that it is necessary to identify a "table of EU values" with constitutional force—regardless of formalization in a special statutory text—suitable to serve as a reference centre for the legislative evolution of the legal system of the Member States, it appears not probable that tax matters, although the fundamental role of taxation is recognized within the framework of the relations between public institutions and citizens, may assume an axiological meaning in order to lead to the general judgment of illegality of the accession of the State to the Treaty.

Under this profile it seems preferable to believe that the constitutional values of the ability to pay tax and the general interest of taxation are to be referred to a typically axiological national scope, although of primary grade, and are unable to be considered "counter-limits" to the normative power carried out by the European Union.

Probably, only the value of tax equality can be included as part of the fundamental principles of the democratic community nationwide. It is indeed a principle of distributive justice that is considered to indicate an inescapable ideal of democratic community that may not go back even in front of the needs of the European liberties.

However, it must be mentioned the recent literature which highlights the usefulness of carrying out a dynamic integration between the axiological meaning enunciated in the Constitution and the values expressed by the EU through the typical patterns of the balance values. On the assumption, in fact, that the constitutional cover may not be parcelled out, nor it may be acknowledged in a purely formalistic perspective, and that the fundamental relations of communal life and society should be remitted to the unitary vision, it follows that the axiological dimension concerning the same relationships is composed and recomposed dynamically through a process of osmosis between the constitutional values and the European values.

Therefore it is quite possible that the axiological value attributed to the internal rule could be recognized as a relevant standard over the provision of EU law, without any affection about the legitimacy of the entire EU Treaty. It is clear, following this theoretical orientation, that the fundamental values of the democratic community outlined in the Constitution—and among them undoubtedly the general interest to taxation and the ability to pay tax—can find a space of axiological relevance also in front of the same European values, through a relation of combination and complementarity.

2.5.3 The Violation of EU Obligations in the Field of Taxation by a Member State

The contrast between the internal regulations and the EU legislation does not constitute a merely hypothetical event, traceable to a sporadic extent and therefore regarding primarily a discussion of theoretical and academic scope.

Indeed, the national States often show a reluctance to the implementation of the EU obligations in tax matters, which is repeatedly stigmatized by the institutions of the European Union. In particular, the Court of Justice has pronounced a great number of convictions for the non-compliance with the tax rules laid down by the EU law.

On tax matters it can be outlined some mostly homogeneous groups of violations:

- internal regulations incompatible with the principles of the Treaty about tax matters, and in particular with the prohibition of fiscal discrimination and with the prohibition of taxes having equivalent effect to the duties;
- failure to implement the EU directives, or failing to properly implement them within the national territory;
- discrepancies of internal discipline in the area of VAT compliance with EU rules;
- failure to discharge internal standards judged as State aid that are incompatible with EU law.

It should also be noted that the failure to comply with EU rules, in addition to take an emblematic significance of the European position of a Member State—and thus to constitute the basis for disapproval of the political and institutional policy—can lead to a legal responsibility of the Member State: and in fact, the State is obliged to compensate the damage that might be produced as a result of the failure to the EU rules. In application of the principle of loyal cooperation enshrined in the art. 4 TEU, the States have the duty to implement in good faith their obligations under EU law, so that when there is a breach of this duty and there are certain damages to resident citizens in the European Union, the defaulting Member State is considered to be responsible for the damages.

In particular, the Court of Justice pointed out that the purpose of such responsibilities must be a direct causal link between the breach of EU obligations perpetrated by a State and the injury of a single individual (case 19.11.1991, C-6/90 e C-9/90, *Francovich*). On the other hand, it is further stated that not every breach is likely to determine the financial liability of the State, but it is necessary a serious breach of the EU obligations which entails a real passing over the area of discretion allowed to the Member States by the EU law (case 5.3.1996, C-46/93, *Brasserie du pecheur*).

At this purpose, it is well known that the responsibility of the Member States can also regard tax matters; in this case the State can be sued by the injured person with the aim to compensate the suffered damage for the violation to the EU tax law.

The Sources of the European Taxation Law 3

Contents

3.1 The Fundamental Principles of the Taxation Law Expressed by the Treaties of the European Union ... 54
3.1.1 The System of the European Sources of Law and the Treaties of the European Union ... 54
3.1.2 The Discipline of Taxation Power in the Treaty as a Declination of the European Economic Constitution ... 54
3.1.3 The Reduction of the Customs Duties and the Establishment of the Customs Union ... 56
3.1.4 The Principle of Taxation Non-Discrimination of Trade Among the Member States ... 57
3.1.5 The Discipline of the State Aids ... 58
3.1.6 The Containment of Public Monopolies ... 59
3.1.7 The Tax Harmonization ... 59
3.1.8 The Principle of Effectiveness and the Preservation of National Taxation Systems ... 61
3.1.9 The Recessive Scope of the Individual Rights with Comparison to the Phenomenon of Taxation ... 63
3.2 The Legislation of European Union ... 64
3.2.1 The Relief of Derivate EU Law in the Formation of the Processes of Fiscal Integration ... 64
3.2.2 The Regulations Relating to the Taxation Matters ... 64
3.2.3 The EU Directives on Taxation ... 66
3.2.4 The Use of the Instrument of the Multi-Lateral Agreement for the EU Discipline of Taxation ... 70
3.2.5 The Adoption of the Soft Law Instruments to Regulate the Taxation Matters ... 71
3.2.6 In Particular, the Package "Monti" and the Importance of the Issue of Harmful Tax Competition ... 74
3.2.7 The Translation of Soft Law in Binding Legislation by the EU Institutions ... 75
3.2.8 A Final Assessment Regarding the Use of Sources of EU Derivate Law ... 76

P. Boria, *Taxation in European Union*, DOI 10.1007/978-3-319-53919-5_3

3.1 The Fundamental Principles of the Taxation Law Expressed by the Treaties of the European Union

3.1.1 The System of the European Sources of Law and the Treaties of the European Union

The sources of European law can be distinguished essentially in two basic types:

i) the primary law established in the Treaty of the European Union;
ii) the derivate legislation, defined in legal acts issued by the EU institutions (and thus typically in the regulations and the directives, as well as in the so-called *soft law*).

In particular, the Treaty on the European Union (TEU) and the Treaty on the Functioning of the European Union (TFEU), signed in Lisbon in the year 2007, constitute the real "Constitutional chart" of the European Union, devoted to establish the qualifying principles and the fundamental values of the process of integration of the Member States and to express the primary legal logic of the EU.

Consequently, the axiological framework of taxation of the European Union can be properly identified through an analysis of the EU framework at the first level (the primary law), namely the general rules and principles formulated by the Treaties and likely to contribute to the realization of the fundamental purposes of the European Union.

In the following paragraphs it will be outlined a review of the rules laid down in the Treaties of the European Union in relation to the tax matters.

3.1.2 The Discipline of Taxation Power in the Treaty as a Declination of the European Economic Constitution

It is well known that the basis of the European Union should be sought, at least according to the original inspiration, in the European economic constitution, that is the order of principles and standards devoted to regulate the market and the economic activities, which informs the regulated structure of the European common area.

The founding values of the EU are to be found around the core of the principle of "unity of the market" and the four fundamental freedoms (freedom of circulation of persons, goods, services and capital) traditionally regarded as the basic reasons of the adherence to the process of supranational unification.

The "unity of the market" refers to the need to ensure a levelling of the subjects who are confronted on the stage of the market, eliminating the distortion factors of inequality in the belief that the "equal starting conditions" (equality of *chances*) constitutes the only acceptable premise of the market in the perspective of a free competition. It produces, therefore, as a natural corollary, the need to avoid discrimination of economic operators related to legal frameworks and legislative choices made by the single nation States.

The freedom of movement, in its fourfold partition, ensures the effective pursuit of the target of the European integration, according to an obvious instrumental relation to the principle of "unity of the market", to the point that in its absence the existence of a common market would be compromised. Furthermore, the centrality of this value is also highlighted by the recognition of juridical subjective situations in favour of the citizens, as well as by obligations of the States.

The mentioned values evidently express the need to promote a reduction of the physical barriers and of the legal restrictions that mark the division between the national States in order to promote an integration primarily, and essentially, economic and commercial. In this regard it is suggested to consider the European economic constitution not as much as the epicedium of a liberal policy, but rather as the beginning of a process of integration between the various political and constitutional States, which begins with a "deconstruction" of the national sovereignty through the first (and fundamental) reduction of the trade and protectionist barriers.

However, the appreciation of taxation looks like a variation of the plot of the values assumed in the European economic constitution. It appears, in fact, common ground that the tax is an essential tool to achieve the process of the European integration and, in particular, to ensure the removal of the protectionist barriers in the national laws, showing as an indispensable instrument to ensure the effective implementation of the four freedoms fundamental.

Already in this perspective some typifying sections of the legal significance of taxation may be recognised within the European framework.

In particular, it appears the atypical nature of the tax regulations for EU action in relation to the phenomenon of taxation in general: considering the peculiarities of the system of financing the European Union, taxation is not framed as a tool for collecting essential financial resources for the subsistence and the development of a democratic community, with the consequent need to identify some criteria for a fair and reasonable allocation of the tax burden among the citizens, as it is typical in the constitutional arrangements of the nation-States; on the contrary, taxation is measured in a "negative" perspective, possibly as a factor of distorting competition, which should be limited and possibly eliminated in line with the axiological postulates resulting from the European economic constitution.

Therefore, it can be argued that the EU regulation of the taxation power essentially relates to the pursuit of the purposes of non-discrimination of competition and equalizing of the conditions of all operators in the market, according to its own definition of a "negative taxation".

3.1.3 The Reduction of the Customs Duties and the Establishment of the Customs Union

The banning of customs duties or charges having equivalent effect on goods entering and leaving the State is a fundamental rule of the European legal order, which is enunciated in the art. 3 point a) TEU.

This rule establishes clearly the fundamental standard for the establishment of a common market, namely the removal of customs borders with the aim to allow the free movement of goods or services within the territories of the Member States. The conceptual core of this principle has been identified precisely in the existence of an instrumental link with the freedom of movement of goods. The axiological centrality of this rule emerges even from a formal basis, considering the classification of the prohibition on the use of customs duties as the first of the fundamental actions of the European Union, set out as a general rule in art. 3 of the Treaty, which should preferably be pursued for the attainment of the common market.

Moreover, there is the consolidation of the theoretical belief that this rule constitutes an unavoidable step of the process of European integration: and indeed, in the economic doctrine the removal of customs barriers, and the creation of an area of free movement of goods, is considered as the first regulatory instrument to be taken in order to facilitate the establishment of a supranational common market.

The acceptance of this principle constitutes a significant element of the first axiological framework of the European Union: the removal of customs barriers is, in fact, a natural corollary of the "negative taxation" in European Union, as a rule applied to deleting an appropriate factor to discourage or, however, to alter the neutrality of the decisions regarding the allocation of the productive resources in the various nation-States.

This value is then connected to the principle of the Customs Union, which provides for the establishment of a unified tariff of customs to be applied to all goods coming from outside countries; this is clearly a further step than the abatement of the customs borders (and thus the establishment of the free trade zone), because it indicates a higher level of integration of the Member States in the trade relations with the foreign (extra EU) countries.

However, it is significant that this criterion, expressive somehow of a positive integration (since it determines the coordination and the harmonization of the national customs legislations), has not been explicitly transposed at the level of the primary EU law. It means how the main goal of the EU integration, at least at the level of the general principles, may be recognized in the elimination of the internal barriers (according to the "negative" taxation) and not also in the definition of a common adjustment (according to the dictates of the "positive" taxation).

3.1.4 The Principle of Taxation Non-Discrimination of Trade Among the Member States

A second general principle applicable to fiscal matters can be easily inferred from the regulatory provisions formulated with the art. 110, 111 and 112 TFEU.

The norm of art. 110 (previously enunciated in the art. 90 Treaty of Maastricht and art. 95 of the Treaty of Rome) prohibits Member States from applying domestic taxation to the products of other Member States in excess of the charges applied to similar domestic products, and prohibits in any case to have recourse to an internal tax designed to protect domestic goods over foreign products.

The norm of art. 111 (ex art. 90 Treaty of Maastricht and art. 96 Treaty of Rome) precludes the use of internal tax rebates in excess of the taxes actually levied for the goods exported to the EU countries, so as to avoid forms of tax shelter designed to promote exports to other Member States.

And finally the art. 112 (ex art. 92 Treaty of Maastricht and art. 98 Treaty of Rome) states that for the taxes different from indirect taxes it can be applied remission and repayment to the exports and introduced compensation fees (applicable to imports from the Member States), provided that it is expressly formulated the approval of the EU bodies (and in particular the Council by a qualified majority on a proposal from the Commission) and that these internal provisions cover a limited period of time.

Evidently these provisions of the Treaty express the same need to ensure a neutral treatment to the commercial transactions carried out within the common market, excluding that the Member States may take protectionist or interventionist positions oriented to encourage and to protect the domestic production or, otherwise, to contribute to the elevation of tax barriers equivalent to the customs duties which are evidently contrary to the European target of the free movement of persons, capital, goods and services.

Thus, the mentioned rules can be considered as the expression of a perspective essentially "negative", since they are devoted to prescribe a number of foreclosures over the adoption of tax laws which are discriminatory between residents and non-residents, and not also to define a "positive" content to the tax treatment of the national tax systems. And indeed it is not fixed any obligation to ensure equal taxation between domestic and foreign products, according to a criterion of a positive integration, but only it is forbidden to adopt a less favourable tax treatment of foreign products (emerging clearly the distinction of the European principle of non-discrimination with respect to the constitutional principle of equality). Otherwise, if it is missing a similar production in the internal territory, the State can establish levies on the export virtually without any limitation, only with the general attention to avoid that taxation takes an incidence so high to compromise the free movement of goods within the common market.

The legal value around which are to be coordinated the mentioned regulations of the Treaty, usually referred to as the "principle of tax non-discrimination", assumed a fundamental consideration for the process of development of the European Union as it is sufficient to preclude the formation of tax barriers that might seriously endanger the primary purpose of free movement of factors of production and economic products. In this respect it is correctly observed that this principle is an instrumental rule to the pursuit of the four fundamental freedoms of EU law.

3.1.5 The Discipline of the State Aids

One of the issues with respect to which is more important the problem of resolving conflicts between national law and EU law is represented by the provision of financially differentiated and preferential treatment for certain categories of domestic enterprises.

The establishment of a common market presupposes the settlement and the working of a unified economic space in which the exchange of products and services, and in general the commercial transactions can take place under the same conditions as those applying in the domestic market. So it is necessary not only that the barriers and the obstacles to the free movement of goods and services are removed, but also that the competition between the enterprises resident in the territory of the European Union is not distorted by the financial measures taken by the Member States which are destined to generate an economic benefit limited to a narrow audience of national subjects.

At this purpose it must be reconciled two requirements and especially: i) to avoid that the most favourable national legislation may collide with the freedoms on which it is founded the common European market; and, at the same time, ii) to allow the Member States to maintain their margins of autonomy in the decision-making policies with regard to the economic choices and to the internal taxation. The point of balance between the two conflicting demands, European and national, can be essentially identified in the line of distinction between "permitted standards" and "prohibited standards".

In this context it can be inserted the art 107 TFEU (formerly art. 87 of the Treaty of Maastricht, and art. 92 of the Treaty of Rome) that prohibits the granting of State aids which, by favouring certain enterprises or certain products, may affect trade so as to distort (or threaten to distort) the system of free competition; the benefit, to be considered legal and allowed by EU regulation, must necessarily be selective, revealing that is suitable to benefit specific and limited enterprises (or market sectors) and not even the totality (or the majority) of the enterprises (in which case there would not be a State aid, but rather a questionable measure of support to the national enterprises, to be considered possibly incompatible with respect to the principle of non-discrimination). Just the selectivity of the measure devoted to produce a business support is the guiding principle in the verification of the compatibility of the State aid with the EU law.

This rule has been referred to the area of the reserve of powers in favour of the EU institutions: and indeed, the rules laid down in the art. 107 essentially provides that, through a complex procedure, the Commission should start a "formal investigation", basically with a preventive nature, about the compatibility with the EU law of the internal measures oriented to give a support to domestic enterprises in order to issue the relevant authorization. Therefore, it is not established the principle of the absolute and automatic inadmissibility of the State aids, but rather it is defined the jurisdiction of the EU institutions (and especially of the Commission) with regard to the assessment of compatibility of more favourable national rules to the principles and rules of EU law.

Now, it can certainly be included in the area of the State aids the tax regulations devoted to produce tax benefits or tax relief to the domestic enterprises (or to the products generated in the national territory) as rules which can distort the competition in the same way of the expenditures or the spending measures: in fact, the tax concessions, resulting in more favourable treatment to the beneficiaries, are likely to reduce the cost of production and thus to be detrimental to the common competition. Differently, for the "purpose taxes" or the special contributions the judgment of compatibility with the EU law does not apply to the tax structure, but rather to the financial effect and primarily to the bond of destination (and therefore to the expenditure made as a result of the tax revenue).

3.1.6 The Containment of Public Monopolies

The art. 37 TFUE introduces a number of limitations with regard to the fiscal monopolies. This norm requires to initiate a gradual reduction of the existing monopolies, as well as to refrain from establishing new monopolies compared to the existing ones (so-called *standstill* clause).

In the line of the harmonization of the fiscal monopolies it is also established that the EU institutions will issue recommendations to the Member States aimed at promoting the progressive abolition of the public monopolies.

This rule clearly expresses the belief that fiscal monopolies are an unnatural restriction of the competitive order, due to an undue presence of the government (or the State authorities) in the market, capable of distorting the normal dialectic of the competition regime and, therefore, to alter the framework of the fundamental freedoms recognized by the EU law.

3.1.7 The Tax Harmonization

A further general principle of European order can be enucleated under the art. 113 TFEU (formerly art. 97 of the Treaty of Maastricht and art. 99 of the Treaty of Rome), which defines the target of the harmonization of the laws of the Member States with regard to the turnover tax, consumption tax and other indirect taxes, to the extent that harmonization is necessary to ensure the establishment and functioning of the common market.

This rule is clearly intended to achieve a regulatory framework which tends to a homogeneous architecture of the tax systems of the various Member States, reducing the national autonomy to specific aspects or details of the discipline, in order to avoid that the national legislation can alter or affect the structure and the function of harmonized taxes. In this perspective the harmonization can be considered so as to identify a methodological decisive criterion for the European integration.

The principle of harmonization seems to envisage a configuration of the fiscal discipline of the Member States which is compatible with the unitary and integrated models defined at the EU level. Therefore, it is presented as a general principle with a "positive" content, namely intended to establish a rule of gradual integration of national taxation systems and not a mere delimitation and foreclosure.

About the rulemaking procedure it is expressly stated the use of the method of the prior consultation of the Parliament, which is mandatory but not binding on the Council. Evidently, in the belief of the EU legislature, the tax harmonization is a very important phase of the integration process that calls into question some main characters of national sovereignty and therefore it may not be entrusted solely to the judgment of an executive and intergovernmental branch, which is impregnated by assessments often connoted by the only economic opportunities, but it has to pass, even if only on a consultative basis, through the parliamentary debate, which undoubtedly has the capability to the weighting of the values at stake.

Moreover, it should be noted that, under a procedural point of view, the scope of the principle of harmonization (as envisaged by the EU Treaty) appears unsatisfactory overall, because is not included the adoption of the principle of qualified majority being on the contrary required the unanimity in the decision of the Council. The Commission itself (in the *White Paper on completing the internal market*) found that the harmonization of indirect taxes, which is essential for the completion of the process of economic and trade integration, must accelerate its procedural standpoint, identifying in the principle of unanimity an obstacle which is often insurmountable.

In particular, in the field of indirect taxation the harmonization is qualified as a primary value of the European unification process, since it is likely to have a decisive influence on the degree of functioning of the internal market. It is clear, in fact, as a disparity of taxes on commercial transactions and affairs between the different Member States should be to affect a regulatory framework where the economic sensitivity is most acute and, therefore, could easily lead to harmful tax competition, capable of leading to competitive mechanisms driven so as to accentuate the centrifugal tendencies within the European community. Therefore, the attention of EU bodies has been focused primarily on the area of indirect taxation, with specific reference to the turnover taxes, excise duties and other indirect taxes, given the suitability of these forms of taxation to change the price of goods or services to the consumer, thus altering the competitive neutrality of the market.

For the process of harmonization of direct taxes it is no longer applied the art. 293 of the Treaty of Maastricht (formerly art. 220 of the Treaty of Rome) which has been repealed by the Treaty of Lisbon. This rule established that negotiations had to take place between the Member States with the aim to ensure the abolition of double taxation within the European Union. Therefore the process of harmonization of direct taxes, involving key aspects of fiscal sovereignty of the nation-States, is not explicitly set by the EU rules; at the same way it is not admitted the implementation of this process by the dense network of bilateral (or multilateral) international agreements between the various Member States. The harmonization process for the direct taxes must be executed through the ordinary procedure, and therefore by the application of the unanimity principle of the decisions. However, the loss of decision-making authority on portions of the national taxable matters in favour of arrangements defined by the EU and the consequent weakening of the choices of economic policy constitute an event that is considered not readily absorbed by the Governments of the Member States.

Evidently it is applicable to the harmonization of direct taxes, the general rule laid down by the art. 115 TFEU (ex art. 94 of the Treaty of Maastricht and art. 100 of the Treaty of Rome), by virtue of which it is possible to approximate the national legislation to the extent that is necessary, or at least useful, for the process of establishment of the common market. This rule has been interpreted as the axiological foundation of the use of recommendations and other forms of soft law addressed to Member States concerning the progressive approach of the provisions relating to the taxation of income (and especially to the taxation of business and savings). This is, basically, a level of approximation of national legislations that assumes a lower grade than the harmonization of indirect taxes (for which it was formulated the figurative definition of "elastic convergence").

Finally, it was pointed out in the literature as the harmonization constitutes a mechanism to search for an uniform taxation model only for the common taxes of the Member States, with the consequent inapplicability to the special or atypical taxes of each State (subject to these taxes are not considered as charges having equivalent effect). Similarly, because of the general protection of the European market which is the founding value of the principle, it was excluded the applicability of harmonization to the local taxes, which are territorially confined to a restricted community and thus appear overall to be unsuitable to affect the freedom of movement protected by the EU law.

3.1.8 The Principle of Effectiveness and the Preservation of National Taxation Systems

An important relief takes on the general interest pursued by the European Union to the proper application and functioning of the various tax systems, which is to be considered with precedence over the mere national interest and the interests of individual groups or categories of traders.

This principle is explicitly stated in the art. 119 par. 3 TFEU, where it is expected that the aims of economic policy (especially monetary policy) of the European Union demand, among other essential requirements, "healthy public finances". This principle seems, also, easily deduced by the rules set out in the art. 121 TFEU—where it is declared that the Member States should regard their economic policies as a "matter of common interest"—and in the art. 126 TFEU—where it is expected that the States must avoid excessive public deficit based on predetermined parameters (and in particular in relation to the ratio of public debt compared to the GDP, gross domestic product).

Natural corollary of this principle is that the European Union must ensure, to the level of the EU legal system, the establishment of appropriate regulatory mechanisms to allow the individual Member States the research for the target of efficient public finances, even (and perhaps mainly) in terms of the proper functioning of the tax system.

In this perspective, the principle of effectiveness of national public finance plays a dialectical, and often conflicting, role as compared to other values of European inspiration, functionally correlated with economic freedoms forming the basis of the common market. The preservation of a "strong" nucleus of sovereignty about the taxation power in each Member State poses, in fact, as a real contrast with the needs of non-discrimination and harmonization of national legislation, likely to lead to tensions in the axiological declination of EU legislation.

However it must be said that the conceptual basis of these principles is to be found in the same underlying logic of EU law: the protection of national public finances should never be understood in a conservative way, like a desire of the nation-State to resist to the process of European integration, but rather it must be intended as the necessary protection of the fundamental mechanisms of the common market, which are based on the single national economic systems. In order to prevent, or at least to contain, the "fiscal crisis" of the nation-State it seems necessary to increase the degree of efficiency and soundness of the common market, according to a consolidated logic of a globalized economy, in which close interdependencies are developed constantly and progressively among the national economic systems.

In this regard, it can point out two different lines of regulatory intervention teleologically related to the principle of efficiency and preservation of national taxation systems.

At first, the European Union must ensure the concrete pursuit of the general interest to taxation of the national State as a determining factor for the achievement of the flow of tax revenues needed for the optimization of the public budget; in particular this involves the recognition of the legitimacy of national standards established to cover the tax obligation through the limitation of the phenomena of tax evasion and avoidance, even when in conflict with other rules of EU inspiration. Indeed, the value of consistency and integrity of national tax systems may well collide with the demands of non-tax and abatement of fiscal frontiers, if it determines obligations for non-resident taxpayers (including those resident in other Member States) identified as "fiscally dangerous"; therefore, in this context there is a balancing of values, having to weight the liberal principle of "openness" of borders, and the consequent elimination of the factors generating fiscal discrimination, with the principle of the integrity of national public finances.

At second, there is a need to ensure full assistance to the tax administrations of the Member States, mainly through information exchange and cooperative mechanisms, in order to ensure constant monitoring and, consequently, a greater degree of efficiency in the supervision and control of the conduct of taxpayers. Evidently, this responds to the idea that the cooperation of the Member States under the administrative procedure is able to provide practical effect to the obligations of the national taxation, increasing the level of deterrence with respect to the evasive or elusive conducts and, in any event, reaching a greater functionality of the national tax systems.

On the other hand, it is not explicitly stated in the Treaty the principle of the "danger of tax evasion" as a possible limit to object to the general execution of the fundamental EU freedoms. The only exception in this regard is provided by a specific rule about the freedom of movement of capital (namely art. 65, par. 1 TFEU) where it is determined that the Member States have the option of applying the national tax provisions in order to distinguish among the taxpayers according to the place of residence or allocation of invested capital, and they have the right to take all necessary measures to prevent violations of the tax laws.

3.1.9 The Recessive Scope of the Individual Rights with Comparison to the Phenomenon of Taxation

Within the general framework of EU law it is well known that a central role plays the recognition and the promotion of fundamental rights of the individual sphere, which are considered as a irrevocable and irreplaceable kit of the human biological unity and represent a crucial criterion for the same assessment of eligibility of the Member State to join the European Union.

It is also important to consider the absence of specific rules on the potential conflict of individual rights with respect to the power of taxation: if this "empty" regulation could be justified simply as a mere reference to the general rules, it is equally true that the specificity of the conflict between the powers of the State and the individual rights, and especially the compression of the capital freedom and the personal freedoms determined by the exercise of the function of taxation, suggests that the Treaty did not intend to take a position on this issue, consecrating the inviolability of the choices made at the national level.

This idea seems to be confirmed also by the European Convention for the Protection of Human Rights, where it is established that the protection of the right to the enjoyment of property and the individual heritage, presented as a fundamental attribute of the person, strictly functional to the freedom and dignity, can be compressed by the execution of the fiscal needs of the nation-State.

It seems to emerge a recession of the axiological classification of the individual rights in the dialectical confrontation with the power to tax, coherent with the above mentioned principle regarding the need to ensure the preservation of national public finances as a crucial milestone to the functioning of the market common.

However, also this lack of legislative regulation on a fundamental step of the fiscal dialectic can be judged as an additional character of the "negative" taxation within the EU legal order.

3.2 The Legislation of European Union

3.2.1 The Relief of Derivate EU Law in the Formation of the Processes of Fiscal Integration

In addition to the principles and rules elaborated in the Treaty, belonging to the so-called primary tax law, tax matters are also regulated by the rules set out in the regulatory measures adopted by the EU institutions. It will obviously refer to the Regulations and to the Directives, as well as to the rules contained in programmatic acts which are essentially the recommendations (and in general all the acts belonging to the so-called European *soft law*).

In this regard, usually the doctrine designates this complex legislation such as *derivate taxation law* to indicate precisely the nature of rules which do not originate with respect to the establishment of the European community in the Treaties, but "derived" from the choices made by the EU bodies.

This structural feature is to be considered in order to assign a specific weight to these standards in the integration of the tax systems of the various Member States: indeed, although these rules do not take the primary axiological relief among the principles emerging from the plot of the Treaty, they apply to connote deeply the European tax law, since they express the convictions achieved gradually by the institutions of the European Union with regard to the tax regulations.

It should be noted, in this regard, that the implementation of the principle of unanimity in taxation matters (as indeed in many other sectors of the EU legal system) leads to the necessary involvement of each State belonging to the EU in the decision-making policy; therefore, if this principle generates procedural difficulties, with possible obstructions for the individual Member States with regard to the decisions on tax matters, resulting in delays or blocks to the legislative phase, on the other hand it implies a high symbolic value to be given to each adopted tax rule, as due not to an impromptu or cyclical game of alliances (as it occurs in majoritarian systems), but rather to a metabolised process of decision-making underlying the statutory provision.

3.2.2 The Regulations Relating to the Taxation Matters

As part of the sources of EU law the legal instrument adopted with greater prescriptive intensity is undoubtedly represented by the Regulation, whose main characteristics are represented by the general and abstract regulatory effect and by the direct applicability of the rule.

The general regulatory effect indicates that the sphere of the recipients of the regulation is made up of all subjects in the EU legal order—and thus as by the Member States as by individuals and entities or companies resident in the European Union—while the abstractness expresses the applicability of the Regulation to all cases attributable to the provision of law.

The rule stated by the Regulation is to be considered mandatory for the Member States, that means the subordination of the nation-States with respect to the EU source of law: the Regulation, in fact, cannot be waived nor objected by the internal discipline, even through the call to any reservations expressed during the preparatory work or accompanying report. The obligatory character affects the entire legal content of the Regulation and clearly distinguishes this source of law by the Directives (where the compulsory effect only affects the scope and the purposes of the measure).

The direct applicability to the Member States means that the Regulation produces automatically changes to the national legal order, without the need for any legislative act of transposition (therefore it is characterized as self-executing act). Moreover, the same Court of Justice has condemned the practice of some States to reproduce the normative content of the EU Regulations in specific national legislative acts, as potentially liable to "compromise the simultaneous and uniform application throughout the European Community" (case C-39/72) and in any case to subtract the interpretation of the rule to the EU jurisprudence in favour of the internal jurisprudence. So the Member States may proceed with the issuance of the implementing rules of Regulation only where they are authorized by the same EU legal framework.

The EU Regulations become effective on the date provided in the same provision or by the twentieth day following its publication in the EU Official Journal.

For the purposes of tax matters the Regulations have been used sporadically. Particularly, it must be distinguished two sets of measures.

Firstly, there are the Regulations concerning customs duties; it can be found a very significant number of provisions since the late sixties which have defined substantial and procedural aspects of the customs rules. Among them it may be mentioned:

- the establishment of the Common Customs Tariff: Reg. 68/950;
- the definition of the origin of goods; Reg. 68/802;
- the establishment of customs duties; Reg. 69/1544;
- the EU system of shipments; Reg. 77/222
- the discipline of repayments and repetition of duties: Reg. 79/1430 and 79/1697;
- the document for the definition of the single tariff; Reg. 85/678 and n. 85/679;
- the revision of the Common Customs Tariff and the definition of tariff nomenclature; Reg. 87/2658;
- the discipline of the tariff; Reg. 90/1715;
- the revision of the document single tariff; Reg. 91/717;
- the introduction of the Community Customs Code: Reg. 93/2913 of 12.10.1992;
- the implementation of the Community Customs Code: Reg. no. 92/2454, 19.10.1992;
- the mutual assistance between the administrative authorities of the Member States to ensure the correct application of customs legislation: Reg. 97/115.

These measures are essentially referred to the profile of the customs union, that is the passage of trade European integration which is not explicitly set out in the primary legislation (namely in the establishing Treaty). Therefore, the above mentioned EU Regulations constitute a source that integrates the primary EU legislation, expressing a position taken by the European Union after the original institution. In this perspective, it can be argued that the derivate EU law arises in function completely complementary to the primary EU law.

Then, must be considered separately the Regulations that affect other areas of fiscal discipline. In this regard it may indicate five regulations:

- the establishment of an EEIG (regulation of the economic group of European interest, as a form of organic understanding between companies from different European countries); Reg. 2137/85 of 25.7.1985;
- the definition of the Intrastat system (creation of a permanent system of collecting statistical data related to the implementation of VAT intra-Community); Reg. 3330/91 of 7.11.1991;
- the regulation of the exchange of information (preparation of a computerized system of administrative cooperation between Member States in relation to the supervision and control of direct taxes); Reg. 218/92 of 1992;
- the implementation of exchange of information (preparation of a computerized system of administrative cooperation between Member States in order to control the movement of goods and services with particular reference to VAT); Reg. 3046/1992 1992;
- integration of the discipline of the exchange of information with particular reference to e-commerce: Reg. 2002/792 2002.

These Regulations are devoted to regulate aspects not central in the structure of the tax relation. In particular, four of these Regulations relate to purely procedural aspects, namely the phase of control and supervision of the proper implementation of tax obligations, and particularly the cooperation between the tax authorities through the procedures for the exchange of information. The other Regulation, in regulating the establishment of an innovative type of legal entity (precisely the EEIG), contains a variety of provisions of law of a civil (not fiscal) nature and only a marginal and supplementary rule pursuant to a fiscal nature.

Ultimately, it is possible to detect that the Regulations relating to the establishment and implementation of the EU customs code, and those that generally govern customs matters, represent the main example of use of this source of law for the regulation of an entire sector of taxation.

3.2.3 The EU Directives on Taxation

The main legislative instrument for the formation of EU law in tax matters is certainly made by the Directives issued by the Council. As it is well known, these acts produce a binding effect for the Member States relating to the setting of the aims, general or detailed, to be achieved in a certain period of time, compared to which the States are free to choose the most appropriate forms and methods for the practical implementation into the national legislation (subject to the compliance with the requirements and the limits imposed by EU Directive).

Unlike the Regulation, this source of law does not have a general nor a direct applicability, as it exclusively imposes to the Member States to assume a regulatory framework compliant with the European rules and principles. The Directives can be considered, therefore, as regulatory instruments with greater elasticity and flexibility compared to the Regulations and so they may produce a less contrast with the internal discipline.

The enactment of the Directive determines a procedure in two steps: at first, the Member State is dependent on the achievement of the result set by the EU provision with the obligation in good faith to avoid the production of internal rules that are conflicting with the rules of the EU Directive (so-called *standstill* clause); at second, by the transposition of the Directive in a legislative act of the State, the rule of EU inspiration assumes a general and abstract effectiveness than the rule belonging to the national legal system.

The Directive thus provides a source of a programmatic nature, whose effectiveness is basically mediated through the legislative measures taken by the national transposition. It should however be noted that, as a result of the jurisprudential inputs, it has been consolidated the belief that the Directives containing detailed and unconditional rules, when it is over the deadline for their implementation by the national transposition, produce direct, immediate and mandatory legal effects (so-called *self-executing* Directives). In this case, the individuals assume those rights which can be enforced in front of the national courts against the defaulting States (so-called "vertical effect"), but also against other European citizens (so-called "horizontal effect").

The Directives become effective on the date provided for in the provision or since the twentieth day following its publication in the EU Official Journal.

With regard to the tax regulation it can be identified numerous Directives concerning various areas of taxation.

First, it is relevant the discipline of the value-added tax (VAT), which is intended to regulate the taxation of trade at national and European level. The EU rules have led to the replacement of the previous regime for the taxation of business transactions, essentially entrusted to a cumulative multi-stage tax (so-called "cascading" tax), through a set of innovative character which ensures respect for the neutrality in the relations among the enterprises. In this regard different phases can be identified in the evolution of the EU law.

In a first step two directives—the "First Directive", n. 227/67, and the "Second Directive", no. 228/67—took care to introduce a general criterion for the definition and operation of the value added tax, which is uniform for all fiscal jurisdictions of the Member States. In a second step—through the "Sixth Directive", no. 388/77, 5/17/1977—it was further initiated the homogenization of the regulatory structure of the tax, with a uniform regulation of numerous procedural and substantial aspects of the VAT discipline.

After a careful phase of study and preparation about the regulatory assumptions, which ended with the preparation of the Cockfield plan, the discipline of VAT was further amended through three directives—n. 680/91 of 16.12.1991, n. 77/92, 10/19/1992, n. 111 of 12/14/1992—which established the replacement of the previous criterion related to the imposition of taxation in the country of destination with the principle of taxation at the country of source, the approximation of the rates and the tax bases, and finally the introduction of the compensation mechanism for the VAT paid in respect of the intra-Community trade. It is opportune to recall that the work of revising the VAT was accompanied by the enactment of three EU Regulations (mentioned in the previous paragraph) that have governed procedural aspects (related especially to the introduction of procedures for the administrative cooperation).

In addition to VAT even the field of excise duties has been deeply characterized by the EU rules; still in 1971 the EEC Commission had recognized the indispensability of a harmonization of excise duties in the interests of effective and concrete implementation of the common market, as it is a mechanism to impose taxes likely to affect significantly the degree of functioning of intra-Community trade. Such harmonization was not easily achievable for the resistance of the Member States to transfer portions of their sovereignty over a very significant form of taxation, as traditionally capable of producing a substantial revenue with a low level of resistance on the taxpayers. Only in recent times it has been realized a significant revision of the rules of excise and sales taxes, functional precisely to ensure harmonization at the EU level: so numerous excise duties and consumption taxes were repealed and amended, and the general architecture of these taxes has been conditioned to an overall reorganization of the discipline in order to standardize the methods of application of taxes and their rates according to the European model. In particular, a first directive—n. 12/92 2/25/1992—set the general rules applicable to the basic structure of the tax, while seven other directives—n. 79/92 and n. 80/92 of 10/19/1992 for tobacco, n. 81/92 and n. 82/92 of 10/19/1992 and no. 510/92 for mineral oils, n. 83/92 and 84/92 of 10/19/1992 for alcohol and alcoholic beverages—have provided specific rules on individual products which are usually subject to taxation by excise duties.

Still in the field of indirect taxation about the economic affairs it must be mentioned one of the first relevant EU acts on tax matters—namely the Directive. 335/69 of 17/07/1969, amended several times with other directives (No. 79/73 and n. 80/73 of 4/9/1973, no. 553/74 of 11/7/1974 and n. 303/85 of 06/19/1985)—which governs the taxation of capital raising, especially with reference to stamp duty on the issue, negotiation and entry into service of securities representing participation and debt securities, as well as the tax on contributions of capital to companies. The aim pursued at the EU level evidently consisted in defining a uniform level of taxation for acts involving the raising of capital in order to avoid discrimination or double taxation due to national laws.

Unlike the indirect taxation, the instrument of the Directives has been adopted very sporadically for the regulation of direct taxes. Indeed, in this regard only five cases can be considered:

- Directive n. 611/85 of 12/20/1985 relating to the taxation of capital and collective investment schemes;
- Directive n. 434/90 of 23.7.1990, concerning the regulation of mergers, divisions, transfers and equity trading in intra-Community nature;
- Directive n. 435/90 of 23.7.1990 concerning the regulation of relations between subsidiaries at EU level, with particular reference to the taxation of dividends (so-called Directive "mother-daughter");
- Directive n. 48/2003, of 3.6.2003. governing the tax treatment of capital income disbursed to non-resident EU citizens (so-called the Savings Directive);
- Directive n. 49/2003, of 3.6.2003, amended by the Directive. 76/2004 concerning the tax regime applicable to interest, royalties and royalty payments between associated companies of different Member States.

These regulatory measures have as their object the discipline of savings (directive n. 611/85, no. 48/2003 and no. 49/2003), as well as the regulation of specific situations of transnational relationships between companies belonging to the same group and in particular the distribution of dividends (directive no. 435/90), the payment of interest and royalties (directive no. 49/2003) and the realization of the extraordinary life of enterprise involving two or more entities resident in different Member States (Directive no. 434/90). Not only these provisions do not establish or define a tribute of European character, but not acting on the underlying structure of the existing taxes at the national level, they merely operate on profiles (although important) considered marginal with respect to the architecture of direct taxes. In substance it is a *special tax discipline of EU source* intended to be transposed into the national law, according to a typical mechanism of "surgical definition" of the national law by the EU law.

Evidently, it can be argued that the use of Directives in direct taxation takes on a completely marginal role, being confined to a sectorial and rather limited framework, with no significant influence on the structural aspects of the tax system background.

It should be noted, finally, that the instrument of the Directives has also been used in procedural matters and in particular:

- Directive n. 308/76, concerning the procedures for levying the tax claims of a State in other Member States;
- Directive n. 799/77 concerning the discipline of the exchange of information between administrations of Member States in the field of direct taxation;
- Directive n. 1070/79 which extended the procedures for the exchange of information in the field of VAT;
- Directive n. 1071/79 on the extension of the procedures for the collection of foreign tax credits;
- Directive n. 12/92 concerning the extension of the procedure for the exchange of information excise duties;
- Directive n. 44/2001 concerning the extension of tax credits allowed to the international debt recovery procedures.

3.2.4 The Use of the Instrument of the Multi-Lateral Agreement for the EU Discipline of Taxation

In addition to the typical mechanisms of the Regulation and the Directive the EU legal system provides an additional type of act to generate some regulatory effects that is represented by the EU convention.

This is an international convention, bilateral or multilateral, through which two or more Member States agree to the definition of aspects relating to the tax law. Like the other instruments of international law this EU source has the nature of a contractual law.

The EU convention differs, however, from the typical pattern of the International Convention for a set of procedural rules that apply to establish the roadmap for institutional enactment of the agreed regulations, taking it away from the sphere of the mere negotiation among the States and producing instead the involvement of the EU bodies.

In this case, it is expected that the typical procedure of diplomatic consultation between a plurality of States is started on the initiative of the EU bodies (and not by the individual States); moreover, the recognition of the European importance of the Convention is ensured by the ratification operated by the General Secretary of the Council.

Natural effect of the agreement is the possibility of a European interpretation by the Court of Justice, like all the legislations involving the EU, which is not permitted for the mere conventions.

The EU convention on tax matters was explicitly provided by the art. 293 of the Treaty of Maastricht (rule now deleted) as a tool for the regulation of direct taxes in order to avoid forms of double taxation, evidently with regard to the profiles of transnational economic relations. The Court of Justice has had occasion to point out that under art. 293 there was no direct effect, as this rule only assumed a programmatic nature, outlining the framework of initiatives that States will be able to take (case 11.7.1995, C-137/84, *Mutsch;* case 12.5.1998, C-336/96, *Gilly*).

This instrument has been used only once, in 1990, with the convention n. 90/436 of 07/23/1990 concerning the definition of a procedure for the amicable settlement or arbitration of disputes relating to transfer pricing between companies belonging to the same corporate group (known as the Convention on the transfer price). It was a regulatory instrument, which despite being readily implemented by some European countries, had failed to have a significant impact on the functioning of the concrete tax matters, since only a very few procedures were adopted by the Member States therein.

This rule set out by the art. 293 has been abandoned by the Treaty of Lisbon; it means clearly that the direct taxation may not be regulated by the instrument of the international convention, but it must be regulated by the procedures of the harmonization (therefore, not through the contractual agreements among the States, but rather on the common European basis, through the sources of EU law).

It also must be mentioned that a European convention was approved on 09/07/1967 in Naples on the mutual assistance between national authorities in order to implement the EU rules on customs. It is a multilateral act, of undoubted international nature, signed by the Member States of the European Communities in a primordial age, when there existed customs barriers and it was not established an unitary regulation of the customs duties. This convention has no basis in any of the rules of the Treaty, but simply expresses the will of the signatory States to lay down the general lines of administrative cooperation in order to prevent, to detect and to punish infringements of the customs laws.

3.2.5 The Adoption of the Soft Law Instruments to Regulate the Taxation Matters

It is definitely very frequent the recourse to acts by the EU Commission that express recommendations, resolutions, interpretative notes, communications, guide lines, invitations and suggestions to the legislative bodies of the individual Member States in order to agree to a common position regarding the regulation of the law. Such acts play a supervisory role, stimulating and address policy legislation as instrumental to the development of common models to be taken as a reference in national legal systems.

These acts are entitled as the European *soft law*, indicating the "light", essentially programmatic and non-binding capacity of the prescriptive formula adopted by the EU institutions.

It should also be noted that the acts of soft law, although not generally binding over the Member States, do not appear without legal effect. The recommendations addressed to the Member States contains an invitation to comply with a certain behaviour detected as a parameter of interpretation of EU rules and as a criterion for assessing the legality of action taken by the Member States (so-called "effect of legality"). The guidelines issued by the Commission in some areas of the law (for example, regarding the State aids) on the procedures and the methods of monitoring the activities of the Member States are also eligible to have legal effects on third parties and then may be appealed in front of the Court of Justice.

The soft law is adopted with some frequency in the tax area, as it is considered as an appropriate instrument to achieve at a gradual process of coordination and harmonization of national tax systems to the taxation models developed at European level. The use of a political and programmatic intermediate transition highlights once again the problem of the democratic legitimacy and the block of the EU institutions with respect to the decision to be taken for the regulation of tax (in line with what has been shown previously).

Even in this case it can be identified a basic distinction between indirect taxation and direct taxation.

The discipline of indirect taxation is taken into particular consideration for the soft law developed by the Commission. In fact, in the Neumark Report, approved in 1962, the process of tax harmonization of the European common market was divided into three stages, strongly denoted by the action in the field of indirect taxation: the first and fundamental step of integration concerned the tax reform of turnover taxes business, with the replacement of the cumulative multistage tax (so-called "cascading" tax), utilised in almost all the Member States, with the value-added tax, characterized by an operating mechanism which guarantees the neutrality of the economic production and marketing cycle; in the second stage it had to be abolished the consumption taxes, whose proceeds had a modest importance especially when compared with the obstruction and distortion to full competition of enterprises on European territory; and, finally, in the third and final phase, it had to be set up some mechanisms of administrative cooperation, especially with regard to the fraud and evasion relating to the intra-Community trade for the purposes of customs duties and value added tax. With regard to excise duty, the report merely stated that those charges have to be attached to the socio-economic characteristics of each country and therefore did not recommend the removal. It can be pointed out that the Neumark Report stated also some proposed revision of the discipline of direct taxes, which however took on a secondary position compared to the intervention on indirect taxation.

Subsequently, the issue of indirect taxation was analysed in an episodic and marginal way; so in the Werner Report in 1970, some recommendations were formulated on accelerating the process of harmonization of value added tax and excise duty through the approximation of the discipline (in partial contrast with the Neumark Report).

With regard to the direct taxation it can be recorded the existence of a large number of acts with programmatic content, typical expression of the EU soft law, which in essence are to set out general aims of the process of European integration. In this case, it clearly emerges the need to lead gradually to the elimination of fiscal disparities on the taxation of enterprises and corporations through a continuous approximation of national laws.

First of all, it must be mentioned the Neumark Report which discovered, as said before, next to the fundamental revision of indirect taxation also some interventions (although with a secondary axiological importance) in the field of direct taxation. In the first stage of the dynamic program defined in the Neumark Report, it was intended to set uniform criteria for the application of withholding tax on dividends and interest. In the second phase, however, the harmonization of corporation tax was identified as a crucial step in the process of fiscal integration of the common market: the main points of the program elaborated in the report are identified in the setting of a single rate at the EU level (to be determined by an approximation to the average tax rate of physical persons), and in the definition of appropriate regulatory mechanisms to prevent double taxation of intra-group dividends.

After the report Neumark, in 1967, it was developed the "program of tax harmonization" by the Commission, which, elevating the level of importance of direct taxation, fixed priority targets of economic integration such as a series of interventions related to the field of direct taxation, and in particular the elimination of international double taxation on dividends and interest, the homogenization of corporate restructuring and mergers, the harmonization of the tax base of the tax on business income with particular regard to depreciation.

In 1969, the Van der Temple Report contains a detailed study of different methods of taxation of corporate income and identifies the preferred criterion for the European integration in the "classic method", consisting in taxing either the company or the shareholder, because this method, although causing a phenomenon of economic double taxation, seems likely to ensure an adequate implementation of direct taxation, simple and free of distortions in the international relations (for example, the mechanism of the tax credit, which is excluded by the double taxation of company and shareholder, is not usually recognized in favour of non-resident). So it is developed the idea of "neutrality" at the European level—to be identified in the exclusion of interference with respect to the allocation of resources and investment (in line with the economic doctrine)—colliding with the "neutrality" at the internal level (to be intended as the elimination of taxation systems which could lead to double taxation).

Excluding the Werner Report, which was prepared in 1970 and is very briefly on the subject of direct taxation, in 1980 it is presented by the Commission a further act with a programmatic content very relevant to the Programme of approximating the legal arrangements for the taxation of companies: the Burke Report identifies as the primary goals of the process of European harmonization the definition of a common tax rate, the approximation of the criterion of taxation of partnerships to that one utilised for the corporation, the homogenization of the tax base, the solution of transactional relations (especially about the foreign income).

In 1990 it was presented by the Commission to the Council a detailed document for a fiscal study concerning the EU rules on companies ("*guidelines for corporate taxation*"), where it was stated for the first time the importance of the principle of subsidiarity in the field of taxation: with reference to the process of harmonization of direct taxes it was argued that the intervention of the European Union should be reserved only for those matters of tax law concerning transnational profiles that may not be adjusted by Member States in a manner consistent with the theoretical and liberalistic postulates of the European Union; accordingly, EU action should be restricted to a limited number of profiles of the tax law, and it was maintained at the national legislative the provisions to the regulation of all the other aspects having a typically internal relief. In this document six proposals were formulated concerning respectively the discipline of dividends between associated companies, the discipline of the extraordinary transactions, the international arbitration, the regulation of intra-EU flows of interest and royalties and, finally, the recognition of losses within the European area.

One crucial point of soft law in EU tax matters is surely identifiable with the presentation of the Ruding Report in 1992. In this document, the Commission faced in a comprehensive manner the problem of the taxation of companies and collective bodies in Europe, and defined not only the substantial fiscal discipline to be applied in each country, but also the mechanisms of taxation of shareholders, the tax benefits, the use of withholding tax. The report pointed out the existence of a very different situation in the various Member States, in terms either of the tax base or of the tax rates, which determined the phenomena of double taxation or tax arbitrage, introducing a model of general taxation structure which was not efficient and certainly not "neutral". Still remaining the recognition of the full sovereignty about taxation to the Member States, the Report Ruding formulated an articulated proposal whose core consisted of the adoption of a common rate for the taxation of companies (identified to the extent of 30%) and in a number of recommendations aimed to eliminate the double taxation of interest and royalties, to approximate the tax base and to reduce the tax burden on cross-border transactions.

3.2.6 In Particular, the Package "Monti" and the Importance of the Issue of Harmful Tax Competition

The advance of globalization of markets and the fiscal bleeding that ensued have increased the belief that tax competition between Member States not only alienates the EU integration, but also hampers the identification of a balance of taxation, creating situations of "fiscal crisis of the State". This has resulted in a greater awareness of the importance of coordination of tax policies of the countries of the European Union in order to avoid the introduction of regulatory standards whose main effect consisted in the erosion of the tax base.

Having this purpose, it has been issued a programmatic provision by the Commission in 1996, in a memorandum addressed to the Council, with the aim to contain the phenomena of harmful tax competition between States. This document has been expressly implemented by the ECOFIN Council, with a resolution of 9/1/1997 (so-called package "Monti" by the name of the Commissioner in charge).

At first, it established the approval of a "code of conduct", whose content is not legally binding and therefore expressing in the form of a political engagement, through which it is programmed: i) the blocking of new measures of direct taxation that, by supporting the localization of productive activities in a country, may produce competitive situations compared to other countries; ii) at a later time, the gradual dismantling of the existing tax rules which can generate competition between the States.

At second, in the memorandum it was formulated the proposal for a directive on interest and royalties between associated enterprises aimed to introduce the principle of taxation only in the country of residence of the recipient, in order to eliminate the complicate (and expensive) formalities required for the reimbursement of taxes.

Finally, it was defined as a proposal for a directive on the taxation of savings income of non-resident individuals, where it was prefigured an alternative system: i) the non-applicability of withholding tax and the obligation of communication and the exchange of information between the State in which the interest is paid and the State of residence of the recipient; ii) or alternatively, the application of withholding tax to the extent of 20% without prior exchange of information. The symbolic value of this solution seems to transcend the specific case: the traditional criterion of non-discrimination taxation of non-residents, which resulted in a kind of forced harmonization, was essentially abandoned in favour of a pragmatic solution that leaded to the reduction of competition tax through the coordination of the national systems, in compliance with the choices made by the individual States.

The feature of the package "Monti" is the choice of a regulatory solution which is no longer "surgical"—as it was expressed in the reports and documents previously formulated by the Commission on a programmatic issue, intended to interventions *à la carte*, limited to individual and specific topics of the direct taxation— but rather consists in the adoption of a global approach, aimed at addressing the issue of direct taxation in a general perspective in order to prevent some forms of harmful tax competition between individual States within the common market.

Therefore, this taxation plan is derived not only by the formulation of proposals for directives in order to important aspects of direct taxation and of the movement of capital, but also by the definition of a document of great axiological importance, which is the "code of conduct", intended to provide general guidelines for a coordinated action at EU level in order to reduce the distortions arising from the national tax laws.

3.2.7 The Translation of Soft Law in Binding Legislation by the EU Institutions

To assess the degree of effectiveness of EU soft law, it seems appropriate to observe a relevant impact that the papers mentioned above have exercised with respect to the formation of derivate EU law.

At first, it can be seen that the Neumark Report has exercised a profound influence on the European legislature, clearly inspiring the legislative solutions adopted for the VAT discipline. Indeed, as noted above, the Directives that have marked the gradual implementation of the process of harmonization of turnover taxes can be traced back to three phases roughly coincident with the three stages of the program outlined by the Neumark Report.

With regard to direct taxes, it can be observed that the relevant series of regulatory actions carried out in 1992 (the two directives on the extraordinary transactions and on the relations between the "mother-daughter" companies, as well as the mentioned Convention on the transfer price) drew its conceptual basis from the "Guidelines for the corporate taxation" as well as from the report Scrivener, which laid down the principle of the importance of tax treatment of companies with respect to the process of completing the internal market.

Rather limited, however, it appears the effect produced by other recommendations. Even the important information contained in the Report Ruding produced modest normative results, considering that there were not issued Directives, neither there were formulated proposals for Directives related to the findings of the Report; nor it can be found a successful program set out in other reports of the Commission, with a practical application in regulatory acts (or even for proposals aimed to legislative acts) of the European Union.

Emblematic, instead, was the fate of the "Monti" package, because the proposed Directives on the issues raised by the memorandum (particularly with regard to the taxation of interest and royalties) have resulted in the issuing of the final regulatory measures (and in particular of the aforementioned Directives n. 48/2003 and no. 49/2003). In regard to the Code of Conduct it may be noted a significant adhesion to the concrete program indicated in the memorandum of the Commission.

A first step was taken, on 3/9/1998, by the establishment of a Working Group (known as the Code of Conduct Group) called upon to undertake a constant monitoring on the rules adopted by the individual Member States. This group formed a voluntary organization among the States aimed to ensure a set of behaviours with the aim to produce a concrete effect to the instructions provided by the Code of Conduct.

Furthermore, in order to give more strength to the recommendations contained in the Code of Conduct, the Commission intended to bring its provisions to the procedure applied for the State aids. Therefore, it was allowed the application of the strict discipline established for the State aids, and in particular the obligation of the prior notification to the Commission concerning the new tax measures, as well as the penetrating powers of the Commission with regard to the control and supervision of the national legislation. In this way, the Commission attempted to circumvent the essentially political nature of the recommendations set out in the Code of Conduct, acting by means of interpretation in order to restore these requirements in a legally binding manner.

The impression is that the very enactment of the Code of Conduct represents a turning point in the process leading to the adoption of the European soft law: the attitude initially cautious of the EU bodies has imprinted with the issuance of the Code of Conduct a very significant acceleration to the scope of provisions contained in its recommendations, either from a methodological point of view (a setting of rules expressing a global approach rather than an atomistic programmatic intervention), or in terms of prescriptive regulation (proposing an interpretative reconstruction with the aim to increase the degree of the binding effect of the provisions). In this perspective, it seems possible to argue that the soft law instruments begin to become juridical mechanisms with a greater intensity compared to the programmatic function of the original legislation, thus assuming an increasingly important role in the process of fiscal integration within the European Union.

It should also be noted that the discipline of the Code of Conduct has been finally approved and converted into agreement legally binding on the Member States following the meeting of ECOFIN held on 6/3/2003.

3.2.8 A Final Assessment Regarding the Use of Sources of EU Derivate Law

The process of law-making bodies of the European Union has a constantly vibrating path, as characterized by the alternating phases of the law enactment.

In the first period, corresponding essentially to the second half of the sixties, the EU authorities have issued a large number of legal acts with regard to the indirect taxation, considered as a fundamental step in the process of economic integration of the common market. In particular, the implementation of value added tax and customs law, as well as indirect taxation of capital raising, have been set in its basic features with Directives and Regulations published between 1967 and 1969.

There has been, then, a long period of inactivity, interrupted occasionally by sporadic legal measures, which does not express a decisive importance with respect to the general configuration of the European taxation.

In the early nineties, there were really significant EU Regulations: following two Regulations in 1992 it was introduced the unique EU Customs Code; with three Directives of 1991 and 1992 it has been revised substantially the discipline of VAT, calling the move to the tax system prefigured as definitive (namely taxation in the country of origin); two basic Directives have been issued in 1992 in relation to the direct taxes; it was regulated in three Regulations, issued during the period 1991/1992, the stage of the proceedings and in particular the exchange of information and the administrative tax cooperation.

The most recent phase is marked instead by more meaningful instruments of soft law, and in particular by the definition of the Code of Conduct, which accentuated the effectiveness of soft law through the interpretative passage to the procedure of the State aids.

It is not difficult to bring these distinct phases of intensity of the EU legislation to as many crucial periods of the development of European integration. In the second half of the sixties it came into play the ability of the EU to give shape to the rules of economic freedom and trade under the Treaty, considered essential in order to start the functioning of the internal market; therefore, the adjustment of the tax on the affairs or on the business and the removal of customs barriers was considered, rightly, as an inescapable implementation of the European architecture. In the early nineties, it sharpened the common sensitivity to accelerate the process of economic integration of the Member States, which culminated with the signing of the Treaty of Maastricht in 1992; consistently, it was provided a significant impetus to the tax standardization, with a generalist approach and not limited only to indirect taxation, in the belief that the regulation of the phenomenon of taxation constitutes a fundamental means to implement the European development project. And finally, the most recent phase, essentially devoted to the harmonization of direct taxes, responds to the need to facilitate the introduction of the single currency for the common market, eliminating the phenomena of the harmful tax competition, which in a highly integrated economy may be distorting the competitive structure and, at least in the EU perspective, might alter the framework of fundamental freedoms.

It should also be noted that the legal sources of law used for the integration of EU tax law appear more clearly articulated than the framework of the principles expressed in the Treaty with regard to taxation, to the point of legitimizing the view that the derivate law surpass the primary law in the regulation of the phenomenon of taxation (also considering the need to protect the fundamental freedoms of the European Union).

However, it must be noted that the EU derivate law for taxation appears to be composed by a small number of sources: and indeed, in absolute terms, the sources of EU law that dealt with to adjust the taxation appear to be very few, especially when compared with the enormous production of the national tax legislation of the Member States.

The Role of the Jurisprudence of the Court of Justice Within the EU Taxation Law

4

Contents

4.1 The Role of the Court of Justice Within the System of the EU Taxation Law 79
4.1.1 The Judicial Power in the European Union 79
4.1.2 The Role of the European Court of Justice in the System of Sources of the EU Taxation Law 81
4.1.3 Considerations on the Contribution of the Advocates General to the Formation of the Decisions of the Court of Justice 82
4.2 The Main Guidelines Followed by the European Jurisprudence on Taxation 83
4.2.1 The Essentially Acknowledging Attitude of the Court of Justice About the VAT 83
4.2.2 The Casuistic Attitude of the Court of Justice on Excises or Duties, as Well as on the State Aids 84
4.2.3 The Creative Jurisprudence in Relation to the Direct Taxes 85
4.2.4 The Rule of Reason and the Balance of the European Interest with the National Interests 86
4.2.5 Some Synthetic Observations on the Role of Court of Justice Relating to the Regulation of the European Taxation System 87

4.1 The Role of the Court of Justice Within the System of the EU Taxation Law

4.1.1 The Judicial Power in the European Union

The Court of Justice of the European Union (also referred for convenience as the "ECJ") has the function of ensuring the uniform interpretation and application of EU law in all the Member States ("nomophylactic" function).

The ECJ is called (according to art. 267 TFEU) to give preliminary rulings concerning the interpretation of EU law and thus to carry out a hermeneutics reconstruction of the rules and the principles laid down in the Treaty and in the normative acts of derivate EU law. Indeed, even if the national courts are required to implement the EU rules into national law, because the law is directly applicable in the Member States (see what said earlier in the Chap. 2, Sect. 2.4), they can

P. Boria, *Taxation in European Union*, DOI 10.1007/978-3-319-53919-5_4

propose questions concerning the interpretation of EU law or the compatibility of provisions of national law with the European legal order.

In particular, the Court of Justice has been asked to rule on the *quaestio juris* (question of law) defining the meaning of the EU legislation relevant to the proceedings, while the national court is required to rule on the question of fact, thus arriving at a decision on the specific facts by applying the relevant standards (including the EU standards).

The content of the decision of the Court of Justice concerns not only the reconstruction of the EU rule (and thus the interpretation in the strict sense), but also often the compatibility of the internal rules with the parameter offered by the EU regulation. The historical fact tends to be considered in the judgment of the Court of Justice as the demarcation element of the *thema decidendum*, especially in order to establish the applicability of the EU law (and therefore the jurisdiction of the Court of the Justice).

The mechanism of the preliminary ruling—also referred to as "interpretive ruling of the European Union"—is presented as a faculty for various national courts and becomes an obligation only for the courts of last instance (for the decisions of which it is no longer possible to submit an appeal).

Through this judicial mechanism, the national courts are presented as a kind of "tool" of the process of European integration in order to promote the uniformity and the correct application of the EU law; thus avoiding that the courts of different Member States can form a jurisprudence conditioned by the local legal traditions, the preliminary ruling leads to a "judicial cooperation" between separate but coordinated legal orders, and seems destined to produce a centralized and European jurisprudence regarding the EU law, with respect to which the contributions of the national courts are valued as inputs and impulses from different legal systems that converge into a single regulated context.

The interpretative decisions given by the Court of Justice as a result of the preliminary ruling produce a binding effect for the national court which has required the intervention of the ECJ (and for the successive stages of the same trial). These decisions also are intended to expand their effects beyond the judgment to which they refer, as they relate to general issues; in this sense it can be argued that the interpretative judgments by ECJ may produce a binding effect on the national courts and the national public administrations.

As for the effectiveness of the temporal judgments of the Court of Justice, it applies the basic rule of the effectiveness *ex tunc* ("since then"), with recognition of the latitude of interpretation and validity of EU legislation from the original outset of the European regulation. Moreover, this criterion was often balanced with the requirements of legal certainty and of the protection of innocent third parties; so, particularly in economic and financial matters, the ECJ has recognized the effectiveness *ex nunc* ("since now") of the interpretative judgments where interfering with the conduct of third parties acting in good faith who had relied on the scope of the national legislation prior to the judgment of the ECJ.

4.1.2 The Role of the European Court of Justice in the System of Sources of the EU Taxation Law

The European Court of Justice has been specifying the size and the boundaries of EU law through a constant reading and "recognition" of the various legislative acts of the EU institutions.

In the literature, it has often been pointed out that the Court of Justice has made a significant contribution to the definition of the legal system of the European Union, with inputs of a creative nature and with the aim to compensate for the lack of reference standards into the system of EU legislation. The "creative" function was identified in particular in the autonomous creation of norms for the integration of EU law, primary and secondary, and in any case in the continuing search for general principles that could define the axiological horizon of the applicable European law.

In this perspective, it has been repeatedly observed that the jurisprudence of the ECJ has made a decisive contribution to the development of EU law, impacting also on the legislation of the European institutions through the indication of the general outlines emerging in the current regulations and the constant comparison with the fundamental purposes of the supranational integration.

Therefore, it seems obvious the assignment of a role of primary importance to the jurisprudence of the Court of Justice in the definition of the system of the sources of the various sectors of EU law (and of course also of the EU tax law).

With specific reference to the area of taxation, it should be noted that the ECJ has consistently been solicited over the years to intervene in its interpretation to settle doubtful matters, gaps and shortcomings of the EU law.

In particular, based on the examination of the case of a period of twenty-five years (and that is that included in the period 1978/2003) it has been identified some basic elements, which can be summarized as follows:

- total number of judgments in taxation matters: 329
- decisions on general principles: 77
- decisions on VAT: 136
- decisions on direct taxes: 16
- decisions on indirect taxes and duties: 100

The general quantitative data is very significant especially when compared with the number of legal acts of the EU institutions (as already mentioned in Chap. 3).

The judgments of the ECJ can then be grouped into four homogeneous groups, whose affinity index constitutes the object of the judicial decision. In this regard it is clear, since now, the really relevant position occupied by the judgments concerning the VAT (reaching about 42% of the total number of decisions of the ECJ in tax matters), understandable when compared with the increased importance of this form of taxation into the European legal system; also surprising is the large number of decisions on the general principles (about 23% of the total), namely the set of principles and rules which recognized the applicability of the EU tax regulation regardless of a specific legislative text reference; there are numerous cases concerning indirect taxes and duties (about 30% of the total); very few decisions appear related specifically to direct taxes.

It is also considered important to observe how the track chronology of tax case law indicates a vibrating and non-linear trend, so that it can be distinguished a grouping of decisions in some periods and an evident reducing of judgments in other periods. By examining the pattern of decisions it can be argued that in only three years 1982/84 there were 63 decisions in the face of a smaller number of decisions (60) over the next eleven years, as well as in the period 1996/2000 it can count up to 112 decisions amounting to about 34% of the total EU case-law that formed in twenty-five years taken as a reference.

However, beyond the considerations of statistics and classification, that provide reconstructive insights around the incidence and the role of the Court of Justice in tax matters, it is possible to point out some main areas of EU case law, so as to indicate the emerging general principles of the European regulatory law (and thus corresponding to a general and non-specific logic of the single tax) or to explain the position usually taken in the assignment of the discipline of a single tax (or a homogenous group of taxes).

4.1.3 Considerations on the Contribution of the Advocates General to the Formation of the Decisions of the Court of Justice

Very important in the process of formation of the EU case-law is the contribution made by the General Advocates, who through the submission of written conclusions provide a concise background of the present case, purified and adequately screened from possible deviations and compared to the legal arguments put forward.

Without a binding nature, the conclusions of the general advocates have an important influence on the decision of the Court of Justice because they contain a comparative analysis on the laws of the Member States and an accurate reconstruction of the previous case-law of ECJ that constitute most of the time the indispensable material to be used to produce the judgment of law.

Indeed, it is to be assumed that the overall contribution of advocacy, as an independent body with respect to the parties involved in the trial, aimed essentially at protecting the general interest of the European Union, is an important element of the formation of the judicial conviction and justifies keeping alive the connection between the specificity of the case and the plot of the value of the European law.

With regard to the tax matters it can be observed that the conclusions presented by the General Advocates have frequently been accepted in the judgments of the ECJ, as it can be inferred from the reasons given by the judges.

In particular, the contribution of General Advocates are attributable not only to the major reconstructive theories formulated by the case law concerning the regulation of VAT and other harmonized taxes, but especially to the "creative" thesis developed by the European Court of Justice with regard to the regulatory principles relating to direct taxes.

4.2 The Main Guidelines Followed by the European Jurisprudence on Taxation

4.2.1 The Essentially Acknowledging Attitude of the Court of Justice About the VAT

The greatest number of decisions of the ECJ certainly refers to the value added tax, given the typically European nature of this form of taxation.

However, it is significant that the Court of Justice in this area shows a trend characterized essentially by a mere reconnaissance of the existing rules, refusing to develop general principles to be utilized also for the discipline of other taxes. Particularly, the attitude of recognition is expressed through the detailed description of the rules laid down in EU measures of the secondary legislation (especially in the Directives concerning VAT) and through the clarification by way of interpretation of the semantic latitude taken by those rules.

It is true that the case law of ECJ has contributed significantly to single out the essential features of VAT on the basis of the rules set out in the various Directives: it was so recognized the legal nature of the tribute as a consumption tax; the qualifying elements of the VAT discipline have been identified in the general taxation of trading activities, in the proportionality of the rate, in the character of tax neutrality and in the multi-step procedure for the taxation of the several operations; the tax assumption has been determined with regard to the objective elements and to the subjective elements.

Moreover, the reconstruction of the guidelines of the tribute is often the theme of ECJ case-law also in the definition of the regulatory profiles for the application and the interpretation of the rules established by the Directives for the implementation of VAT (particularly regarding the deduction and the redraft, the chargeability of tax obligations, the procedural and instrumental obligations of the taxpayers etc.) as well as in the identification of the exceptions permitted by the internal discipline (exemptions or exclusions).

Sometimes, the attitude to the reconnaissance of the existing regulation operated by the Court of Justice with regard to the VAT is going to reduce in order to permit some reconstructions of the legal framework characterized by an evident "creative" spirit. Thus, in relation to the issue of the possible duplication of taxation on the same basis, the Court of Justice has defined the principle of prohibition of double taxation, not finding a specific normative reference (case 5.5.1982, C-15/81, *Schul*; case 25.2.1988, C-299/86, *Drexl*). Even with reference to the issue of the right to a refund of any overpayment, the ECJ has developed an approach that, despite the absence of explicit rules in the Directives, is to rebuild through an interpretation judgement the scope of individual rights and to limit the unreasonable compressions made by the internal discipline (case 6.7.1995, C-62/96, *BP Soupergaz vs. Greece;* case 2.12.1997, C-188/95, *Fantask*). It should also be mentioned the case of the abuse of law that was originally formulated specifically with reference to the discipline of VAT to contrast the negotiating artificial constructions made by taxpayers in order to gain an unfair tax savings (case 21.2.2006, C-255/02, *Halifax*).

However, such a "creative" attitude still occupies a marginal space in the case-law related to the VAT discipline, as the main issues brought to the attention of the Court of Justice find a solution through the work of reconstruction and the analytical case study of the EU rules in force.

4.2.2 The Casuistic Attitude of the Court of Justice on Excises or Duties, as Well as on the State Aids

About the subject of excise duties and customs duties the case law of the ECJ assumes a typically oriented position to the *case by case approach*, with the aim to resolve specific issues and cases by the interpretation and the application of the EU law. Indeed it is not easy to discover valuable theoretical guidelines in this regulatory area, since in the most part of situations the Court is required to order and to recompose quite detailed and minute cases.

A recurring theme is represented by identifying the concept of "taxes having equivalent effect" to the duties, with respect to which the case law seems to be consolidating the belief that the similarity of the products should be judged in relation to the classification of products in the same fiscal, customs or statistical category (case 04/04/1968, C-27/1967).

It should be noted, however, as the ECJ case law has repeatedly tried to identify the scope of the prohibition of "charges having equivalent effect" to the principle of non-discrimination relating to the indirect taxes. In this regard it was clarified the systematic difference of the two standards and the need to point out for each concrete case the reference to one or to another legal regime (case 1.3.1966, 48/65, *Luttick*; case 17.7.1997, C-90/94, *Haar Petroleum;* case 17.9.1997, C-130/96 *Fazenda publica*).

Sometime, in order to distinguish adequately between the cases related to the prohibition of "charges having equivalent effect" or to the principle of non-discrimination it was suggested to pay attention to the profile of the target of the taxation: in particular it has been held that, where the tax revenue is intended to support the product subject to taxation generating a benefit wholly compensated with the tribute to be paid, it can be identified a "charge having equivalent effect"; otherwise, in the case of a tribute restored only partially by the benefit received, it can be applied the principle of non- discrimination (case 11.3.1992, C-78/90 up to C-83/90, *Compagnie commerciale de l'Ouest*; case 27.10.1993, C-72/92, *Schartbtke*; case 17.9.1997, C-130/96 *Fazenda publica*).

A widespread casuistic attitude seems possible to be identified even in the case law of the ECJ regarding the area of the State aids.

This casuistic approach finds its conceptual foundation in the idea that the judgment on the applicability of the EU regulation must be formulated *a posteriori* (with a retrospective regard), concerning the material effects produced over the market fair competition and not the scopes and the political purposes pursued or declared by the national legislature. The provision of EU law, in fact, must be interpreted by the case law according to the purpose of preventing that the tax benefits granted by a Member State can affect some distorting effect on trade in the common market or may alter the regularity of the competitive game; the prohibition of the State aids is therefore not affected by the appreciation of the purposes of the national legislation, but rather it is defined in relation to the impact (and therefore to the global effects) that occurs on the system of competition (case 24.2.1987, C-310/85, *Deufil*).

It follows clearly the need to carry out, in the judgment of the Court of Justice, a careful analysis of the specific effects that are producing on the competitive structure of the common market in relation to the extent of the State aids established by the Member State.

4.2.3 The Creative Jurisprudence in Relation to the Direct Taxes

In contrast to what was seen for the VAT and indirect taxes, the Court of Justice has provided a decisively "creative" contribution to the reconstruction of the EU legislation applicable to the direct taxation.

At first, the ECJ has focused on the scope of the principle of tax non-discrimination in order to define precisely its scope: so, it is very significant that the first decision related to direct taxes expressly recognizes the prohibition of the direct discrimination against foreign citizens of a Member State by a national law (case 28.1.1986, C-270/83, *Avoir Fiscal*); later, it was clarified also the prohibition of the indirect discrimination, which is implemented by hidden or disguised forms of fiscal discrimination against the foreigner citizens of a Member State (case 8.5.1990, C-175/88 *Biehl*; case 13.7.1993, C-330/91 *Commerzbank*; case 27.6.1996, C-107/94, *Asscher*).

The effect of the discriminating national standard is judged by the Court of Justice not so much in terms of the actual outcome, but rather with regard to the mere potentiality of the damaging. Thus, it emerges a further characterization of the principle of non discrimination: this is intended as a simple risk of producing an alteration of the competitive structure of the common market and, therefore, as a potential limitation with respect to the equal treatment of economic operators, and not as an objective result to be determined on the basis of the material experience. Obviously this connotation of the principle of non-discrimination in terms of potentiality, carried out in the case law of ECJ, is to expand significantly the scope of the European action in relation to the wording of the rule contained in the regulatory EU law.

More recently, the Court of Justice seems to have shifted its focus from the pure discrimination to the restriction of a European freedom, independently by the analysis of the distorting effects produced by a discriminatory rule; therefore, the illegitimacy of the national rule can be judged as a restrictive regulation in relation to the effect of one of the four fundamental freedoms of the Treaty and not also with regard to the existence of a differentiation in the treatment between residents and non-residents. This jurisprudential trend (inaugurated with regard to freedom of establishment by the case 21.9.1999, C-307/97 *Saint Gobain*, and then resumed by the case 8.3.2001, C-397/98 and C- 410/98 *Metallgesellschaft* and the case 10.12.1998, C-127/96, C-229/96 and C-74/97 *Hoechst*) produces a significant widening of the judgment of compatibility of the national tax with the EU law.

It should however be noted that the reasoning of the Court of Justice, aimed at the verification of both the discrimination and the mere restriction, requires a judgment of comparability of the legal situations with respect to which exists a detrimental effect of the EU rules. Indeed, prior to establishing the unlawfulness of a national provision for the breach of the principle of tax non-discrimination or restriction of a European freedom, it must establish at first the similarity of the legal situations examined. So it was clearly stated, even in matters of taxation, "*that discrimination can only consist of the application of different rules to comparable situations or of the application of the same rule to different situations*" (case 14.2.1995, C-279/93, *Schumacker*).

It should also be noted that in the case law it is not easy to identify a recurring and unique pattern of comparison, being rather proposed evaluation formulas of legally relevant features that change because of the single and specific case. At this purpose, there can be identified two basic methods of the judgment on the comparison of the situations taken into consideration for the non-discrimination or for the mere restriction: sometimes it is taken a single and specific aspect of the legal relationship (so-called "limited comparison") or, otherwise, the comparison is established in relation to the overall economic and legal position of the subject (so-called "overall comparison").

4.2.4 The Rule of Reason and the Balance of the European Interest with the National Interests

The protection of EU principles expressed in the Treaty rules (which are precisely the prohibition of discrimination and the restriction of the fundamental freedoms) must always be balanced with the protection of the primary national interests.

The case law of ECJ has identified some public interests of the individual Member States that can lead to derogate from the EU regulations being regarded as causes of objective justification.

In particular, the Court of Justice has identified three reasons of overriding general interest of the individual Member States which are likely to confront dialectically—and therefore are possibly to lead to an exception—with the fundamental principles expressed by the Treaty in relation to taxation, namely:

- the coherence of the national tax system;
- the need to counteract fraud and tax avoidance;
- the effectiveness of controls and tax audits.

In this regard, it has been identified by the Court of Justice a test of judgment (so-called *rule of reason*), aimed at assessing the suitability of the national interests to justify an exception to the principles of non-discrimination and non-restriction of the fundamental freedoms of the Treaty. In essence, on the basis of an objective assessment (and not of the mere scopes pursued by the national legislature), the Court of Justice compares the risks and the potential disadvantages suffered by the domestic legal system with the benefits in terms of protection of the European freedoms according to an assessment of reasonableness.

This assessment of balance is an argument often decisive in the appreciation of the possible alternative solutions for the protection of the national interests to be pursued with a minor sacrifice of the interests represented by the European freedoms and to be carried out according to the typical pattern of judgment of proportionality.

It is to point out that the recognition of the national public interest worthy of protection and the test of comparison with the European freedoms is a clear moment of "creation" of the European law by the Court of Justice.

4.2.5 Some Synthetic Observations on the Role of Court of Justice Relating to the Regulation of the European Taxation System

In light of the analysis set out above some basic considerations may be drawn on the role played by the case law of the ECJ in the system of sources of European Union in the area of taxation.

In principle, it can be outlined a distinction between two groups of the decisions taken by the ECJ: the "creative" case law, mostly centered around the direct taxes; the "reproductive" jurisprudence, basically developed with the VAT and other indirect taxes.

The "creative" jurisprudence is characterized by the original contribution in the formulation of rules and principles with regard to the legal framework provided by the Treaty and by the derivate legislation, often compensating for the lack of reference standards and in any event by integrating the existing legislative order.

The "reproductive" jurisprudence, in contrast, takes a decidedly subordinate position to the legislative text, aimed to provide a merely interpretative reconstruction, mostly in an analytical key, about the rules laid down by the Treaty, the Regulations and the Directives.

It should be emphasized that the partition of the case law in the two groups indicates a significant consistency with the development of the EU legislation in the field of taxation: in fact, the "reproductive" jurisprudence is present in areas where there is a substantial amount of legislation, primary and derivate, providing a completed legal framework "decipherable" in the judicial action; on the contrary, with regard to the direct taxes, the "creative" jurisprudence connects to a regulatory framework which is almost empty, as a result of the lack of substantive laws (as seen in Chap. 3).

However, the importance of the role of the ECJ is basically referable to the contribution provided by the "creative" jurisprudence and in particular by the elaboration of general principles of taxation. Indeed, in a series of decisions concerning direct taxation, the Court of Justice has been able to devise rules and principles of general application aimed at ensuring the effective respect for the fundamental freedoms enshrined in the Treaty and to identify the limits and constraints related to the special interests of the nation-States that may object to a unconditional implementation of the aforementioned freedoms. The Court, thus, has been defining the fundamental dialectic of European tax law, identifying positive and negative elements of the developmental path of "tax liberalization" consistent with the aims of the European integration.

However, it should be noted that the ECJ case-law, and thus independently from belonging to one of the groups of the above mentioned decisions, declines and clarifies the principles of the "negative" taxation. The main subject of the decisions of the ECJ, in fact, regards the applications of the principle of non-discrimination and of non-restriction of the European freedoms and in particular cases where the exercise of the power of taxation by the individual States may hinder the regime of competition and affect, consequently, the functioning of the common market. Only in a very marginal number of decisions it is identifiable the profile of the harmonization of the tax laws of the Member States.

Also in this respect it is so evident a tendency of the EU bodies to reconstruct the phenomenon of taxation in an essentially "negative" dimension, as a possible distortion compared to a competitive structure of the common market and, therefore, as an obstacle to the process of trade and economic integration. It follows the inevitable tendency to develop rules and principles that restrict and deny, in fact, the power of taxation of the individual States rather than to seek for norms with a "positive" content about the architecture of the fiscal system.

Part II

The Principles

5 The Customs Union

Contents

5.1 The Abolition of the National Borders and the Customs Union as Founding Values of the European Common Market ... 91
5.1.1 The Abolition of the National Borders in the Relationships Among the States . 91
5.1.2 The Institution of the Customs Union ... 92
5.1.3 The European Customs Territory ... 92
5.2 The Customs Union ... 93
5.2.1 The Customs Union ... 93
5.2.2 The General Principles for the Functioning of the Customs Union ... 94
5.2.3 The Prohibition of Taxes with an Equivalent Effect ... 95

5.1 The Abolition of the National Borders and the Customs Union as Founding Values of the European Common Market

5.1.1 The Abolition of the National Borders in the Relationships Among the States

The first essential value related to tax matters in the European legal order may be identified in the abolition of the national borders in order to permit the freedom of circulation of goods and services in the common market.

Indeed, the primary purpose pursued by European Union consists certainly in the abandonment of the domestic borders among the Member States with the aim to set up a unitary European market without internal divisions to be substituted to the national markets (case 13.11.1964, C-90/63 and C-91/63, *Commission vs Luxembourg and Belgium*).

In this perspective, since the original Treaty the prohibition to use customs and duties, as for import as for export, in the commercial relationships among residents in the EU has been established as the main target of the European integration, being

P. Boria, *Taxation in European Union*, DOI 10.1007/978-3-319-53919-5_5

qualified as the first action for the execution of the general purposes (see the art. 3 lett. a TFEU).

The logical basis of this principle is identified in the link between the abolition of the national borders and the freedom of circulation of goods and services. Moreover, it is consolidated in the economic literature the conviction about the role of this principle in the process of European integration: the abandonment of the domestic borders and the institution of a free zone for the exchange of commodities are considered as the first legislative measure to be realized in order to achieve a real supranational common market.

5.1.2 The Institution of the Customs Union

In relation to the principle of the abolition of the national borders it may be linked the principle of the Customs Union (specifically mentioned in the art. 3 lett. a TFEU), whose institution is finalized to pursue an unitary customs policy at the European level with the aim to permit a homogenous treatment of the commercial relationships of the Member States with foreign States (extra EU). This is the further step after the abolition of the national borders, since it shows a higher level of integration of the Member States in the commercial area.

According to this principle, an exclusive competence is attributed to the European Union about the customs policy; the Member States are deprived of any competence in the customs matters and must comply to the discipline established by the European bodies.

The institution of the Customs Union determines the establishment of an unitary customs tariff to be applied to all the commodities coming from countries not belonging to the European Union; therefore, the positive discipline of the customs duties is defined in a unitary way through the European regulation.

This principle is to be considered as an unconditioned rule, directly applicable by the Member States and the European bodies. Every exception to this rule is to be interpreted in a restrictive sense and must be expressly established by the discipline (case 14.12.1962, C-2/62 and C-3/62, *Commission vs Belgium and Luxembourg*).

The institution of the Customs Union is considered as an essential factor of the functioning of the European Union because it assures the neutrality of the customs levy with respect to the circulation of the commodities in the European territories and, therefore, is connected to the fundamental freedoms of the common market (case 16.7.1992, C-163/90, *Leopold Legros*; case 14.9.1995, C-485/93 and C-486/93, *Maria Simitzi*).

5.1.3 The European Customs Territory

Currently the customs borders exist only at the limit of the European Union with the other countries not belonging to the EU (and however in harbors and airports) in order to permit the application of the customs duties for the commodities coming from the extra EU territories. After overriding the borders with the European Union, the commodities may circulate in the European territory without any obstacle or any taxation or levy (so, they are considered free from customs duties). Therefore, for the customs policy the borders must be identified with the borders of European Union.

It is recognized the existence of a customs unitary space at a European level, where are included the territories of the Member States (and obviously also the territories of the sub-State governments) and where all the principle of the European legal order are fully applicable.

The institution of a Customs Union could generate the problem of the conflict with the commercial relationships eventually established in international agreements. Particularly, the unitary customs tariff could counteract with the clause of "the most favored nation" established by the GATT agreements (and currently also by the WTO agreements), that imposes to apply any customs facilitation to all the countries belonging to the mentioned international agreements; it means that the abolition of the national borders and the unitary customs tariff should be applied to every country which has approved the GATT (or the WTO) agreements. This problem has been expressly solved with a rule that prohibits the application of "the most favored nation" clause in case of Customs Union.

5.2 The Customs Union

5.2.1 The Customs Union

According to the art. 28 TFEU it is established that the European Union sets up and includes a Customs Union which regards all the commercial exchanges among the Member States and determines the prohibition to apply restrictive measures with regard to circulation of commodities in the European territory.

This prohibition is to be considered as an unconditioned rule which does not suffer any exception for every tax; so, this rule fixes the general principle of the European legal order that the commodities may circulate without any obstacle or any tax in the European territory (case 16.3.1983, C-266/81, *Siot*).

The rule of art. 28 TFEU mentions some prohibited restrictive measures as well:

i. the customs duties for the import;
ii. the customs duties for the export;
iii. the taxes with an equivalent effect of the customs duties.

The prohibition of customs duties is justified because of the obstacles that these restrictive measures may produce, even though for a little relevance, with regard to the circulation of the commodities in the European territory (case, 16.7.1992, C-163/90, *Legros*). It is not relevant that the customs duties assume a protectionist function, being sufficient the mere existence of a levy with the feature of customs duty for the import or for the export or of a tax with an equivalent effect (case 1.7.1969, C-2/69, *Social Fonds Diamentarbeiders*).

In order to permit an homogeneous treatment of the commercial relationships with extra EU countries and, so, a full commercial integration in the common market it is established that the Customs Union produces the adoption of a customs common and unitary tariff for the regulation of the commercial exchanges among Member States and other extra EU States (art. 28 par. 1 TFEU).

The rules of the Customs Union are applicable for the circulation of the commodities with origin in EU countries and also for the exchanges of the commodities coming from extra EU countries which are considered in the regime of free circulation in the European territory (art. 28 par. 2 TFEU). At this purpose, are considered in the regime of free circulation the commodities coming from extra EU countries for which all the obligations, even formal, related to import have been complied and the taxes (including the customs duties) have been collected (without any recovery) (art. 29 TFEU).

5.2.2 The General Principles for the Functioning of the Customs Union

The functioning and the regulation of the Customs Union are regulated in the European legal order through some juridical principles recognized in the Treaty; they are general rules that presiedono the rules of the derivate legislation about the customs duties and the taxes over the circulation of commodities applicable to the commercial relationships with extra EU countries.

At first, according to the art. 30 TFEU it is prohibited the recourse to customs duties for import or for export in the commercial relationships among the Member States. This rule establishes that it is prohibited the recourse to every customs duties, including the fiscal levies, so as to solve any theoretical dispute about the juridical nature of the customs duties. This principle excludes the possibility for the Member States to set up a customs discipline at the national level, recognizing the exclusive competence of the European bodies.

At second, according to the art. 31 TFEU it is established that for the commercial relationships with extra EU countries are applied the customs duties regulated by the common customs tariff, determined by Regulation of the Council. On the basis of this common customs tariff the customs duties applicable in the Member States for the import or the export are homologated. This principle fixes a homogeneous criterion for the customs policy of the European Union and outlines the integration process required for the establishment of an effective common European market.

Moreover, with the aim to stimulate the cooperation in the customs policy it is expressly established the prohibition for quantitative restriction to the import (art. 34 TFEU) or to the export (art. 35 TFEU) or the establishment of taxes with an equivalent effect. There are not fiscal measures (therefore, to be distinguished from the real taxes) (case 4.4.1968, C-27/67, *Fzucht Gmbh*; case 20.3.1990, C-21/88, *Du Pont de Nemours*), which may include a compliance with a fiscal nature (as the issue of invoices, or other fiscal behaviors). Sometime, this quantitative restriction to the import or to the export may be admitted because of reasons of security, protection of health, protection of historical or artistic values, etc.; in any case this restriction admitted for public interest cannot become an instrument for the discrimination among European agents, nor a simulated restriction to the freedoms of circulation (art. 36 TFEU).

5.2.3 The Prohibition of Taxes with an Equivalent Effect

In the European legal order it is expressly established the prohibition of taxes over commodities passing through the national borders which may produce the same effect of the customs duties for import or for export. This kind of fiscal measures is called "taxes with an equivalent effect" to mean the suitability to impact over the commercial relationships among residents in the Member States and residents in other extra EU countries.

Evidently, this prohibition is connected instrumentally to the general prohibition of customs duties to be adopted by the Member States as a final rule of the Customs Union: indeed, even taxes different from the customs duties, but having the same capacity to impact over the circulation of commodities, may alter the free concurrence and generate an obstacle to the functioning of the common market (case 14.9.2995, C-485/93 and C-486/93, *Maria Simitzi*). The purpose of the prohibition of taxes of an equivalent effect is to avoid that the general prohibition of customs duties may be aggirato through fiscal measures with a different denomination or a different structure (compared to the customs duties) which are devoted to limit or to alter the free circulation of commodities.

The taxes with an equivalent effect are to be considered as monetary measures connected to the passage of the commodities through the national borders of the Member States and suitable to increase the price of the commodities. Particularly. The qualification of "taxes with an equivalent effect" is not related to the denomination or to the juridical structure of the monetary measure, being requested only that this measure is suitable to alter the rice of the imported or exported products compared to the domestic products (case 26.2.1975, C-63/74, *Cadsky*; case 25.1.1977, C-46/76, *Bauhuis*; case 9.3.1978, C-106/77, *Simmenthal*; case 31.5.1979, C-132/78, *Denkavit*; case 21.3.1991, C-209/89, *Commission vs Italy*). It does not assume relevance the existence of a discriminatory effect (case 16.7.1992, C-163/90, *Leopold Legros*), nor the destination of the fiscal flows (case 1.7.1969, C-24/68, *Commission vs Italy*).

The only admitted exception to the prohibition of taxes with an equivalent effect regards the institution of monetary measures to be qualified as the price of the services rendered by public bodies to the economic agent at the moment of the passage of the commodities through the national borders. In this case, the monetary measure is justified by the rendered service under a logic of commercial relationship (a sort of contract between the public body and the economic agent) and, therefore, excludes the qualification as a fiscal measure. To qualify these monetary measures as price of the service it is required (case 25.1.1977, C-46/76, *Bauhuis*; case 9.11.1983, C-158/82, *Commission vs Denmark*; case 31.1.1984, C-1/83, *IFG Intercontinentale*; case 29.7.1988, C-18/87, *Commission vs Germany*):

a. the coherence between the rendered service and the amount of the monetary measure;
b. the existence of a certain and specific benefit for the economic agent.

If the monetary measure is collected with respect to some control required by provisions of the European legal order, this measure cannot be qualified as a "tax with an equivalent effect", subject to the coherence of the amount of the measure itself with the cost of the control and subject to the existence of an obligation of the Member State about the control in the interest of the European Union (case 12.7.1977, C-89/76, *Commission vs United Kingdom*; case 2.5.1990, C-111/89, *Bakker Hillegom*). In this case, it is not necessary to verify the existence of a certain and specific benefit for the economic agent, because it is considered implicit in the European regulation of the control.

The European Freedoms and the Principle of Non-restriction for Tax Purposes 6

Contents

6.1 The Fundamental Role of the Freedoms of Movement Within the European Framework 97
6.1.1 The Freedoms of Movement as Founding Value of the European Legal System 97
6.1.2 The Principle of Non-restriction of the Freedoms of Movement for Tax Purposes 98
6.1.3 The Judgment Concerning the Non-restriction in the European Jurisprudence 99
6.2 The Free Movement of Goods 100
6.3 The Freedom of Movement of Services 102
6.4 The Free Movement of Capital 102
6.4.1 The Free Movement of Capital for Tax Purposes 102
6.4.2 The Exceptions to the Free Movement of Capital Expressly Provided by the Treaty 103
6.4.3 A Derogation from the Principle of the Free Movement of Capital: The Judicial Clarification of the Concept of "Lucrative Rights" Provided by Directive no. 69/35 105
6.5 The Free Movement of People 106
6.5.1 The Free Movement of Workers 106
6.5.2 The Freedom of Establishment 106

6.1 The Fundamental Role of the Freedoms of Movement Within the European Framework

6.1.1 The Freedoms of Movement as Founding Value of the European Legal System

It is well known that the underlying reasons of the accession to the supranational organization established by the European Union is to be found typically in the principle of the unity of the market and, consequently, in the assertion of freedom of movement.

Indeed, the freedom of movement in its traditional fourfold partition (free circulation of goods, persons, services and capital) applies to ensuring the effective

P. Boria, *Taxation in European Union*, DOI 10.1007/978-3-319-53919-5_6

pursuit of the basic goals of the EU integration according to an obvious instrumental relation with the principle of the unity of the European internal market.

These freedoms in fact express the need to promote a reduction of physical barriers and the legal restrictions imposed by the various nation-States and which mark the boundaries of the national sovereignty, in order to allow the implementation of a process of economic and trade unification at the level of the European Union.

It is not surprising, therefore, that the freedoms of movement are the subject of rules by the high symbolic content as part of the Treaty for years and point out the axiological primacy in the plot of the proper values of the EU law.

In particular there are some specific rule about the freedoms of movement:

- Art. 28 TFEU which states the free movement of goods;
- Art. 45 and art. 49 TFEU which recognize the freedom of movement of people;
- Art. 56 TFEU which establishes the free movement of services;
- Art. 63 TFEU which lays down the principle of the free movement of capital.

6.1.2 The Principle of Non-restriction of the Freedoms of Movement for Tax Purposes

The freedom of movement obviously has a specific relevance in tax matters, in order to exclude that nation-States can adopt protectionist or interventionist policy or otherwise obstruct or restrict the free movement of goods, persons, services or capital.

Indeed, on closer inspection it does not appear necessary to verify the existence of protectionist purposes in the national tax rule, since it is sufficient to recognize in the same rule an obstructive or distorting effect about the freedom of movement established by the Treaty.

In essence, it is forbidden to the Member States to adopt a fiscal discipline which has the effect of hindering the trade or the other economic mobility within the common market.

The prohibition of restriction for tax purposes is covered in reference to each of the fundamental freedoms of EU law—and therefore to the freedom of movement of goods, services, persons and capital—and possibly also with reference to specific profiles of a same freedom. Thus, for example, the restriction of a tax rule with respect to the freedom of movement of persons enacted by art. 49 TFEU can be established with regard to the principle of mobility of employees and with reference to the freedom of establishment of the enterprises.

It should be noted that a single national rule can collide with more freedoms of the EU law, because of the irreconcilability with a plurality of rules set out in the Treaty. Indeed, it is not uncommon to the experience of the EU case-law to find a national standard which contrasts jointly with the free movement of the persons and the free circulation of the services (case 10/03/2002, C-136/00, *Danner*; case 01/30/2007, C-150/04, *Commission vs. Denmark*) or with the free movement of capital and people (case 12/12/2006, C-374/04, *Test Claimants in Class IV of the Act Group Litigation*, case 05/24/2007, C-157/05, *Holböck*). Often the Court of Justice has ruled that the restrictive effects on the free movement of capital are to be considered as the inevitable consequence of an obstacle to the freedom of establishment of the enterprises and therefore both the freedoms must be included in the same judgment (case 09/12/2006, C-196/04, *Cadbury Schweppes*; case 10/03/2006, C-452/04 *Fidium Finanz*; case 05/15/2008, C-414/06, *Lidl*).

It is necessary to note that the protection of fundamental freedoms by the banning of restriction appears in many ways contiguous to the protection of the principle of non-discrimination, as the violation of freedom is mostly found in the presence of national measures which introduce a disadvantage towards residents of other Member States, and therefore produce a discriminatory effect. Moreover, the freedom of movement covers a broader spectrum of cases of the principle of non-discrimination—as mentioned earlier—as it applies to preclude national rules which restrict or obstruct intra-Community trade or economic mobility, even though they do not result in any discriminatory way. In this sense, it has been argued that non-discrimination is a *species* of the broader *genus* of freedom of movement.

It may be noted in this regard that in the case-law sometimes the protection of freedoms is the fundamental logical basis of the principle of non-discrimination and therefore deletes the axiological autonomy of the latter (so that the principle of non-discrimination may not be invoked separately by the restriction of the EU freedoms; case 28.1.1986, C-270/83, *Avoir Fiscal*); on other occasions, however, it has considered the independence of the two principles and thus the possible contextual and distinct proposal of the judgment about the principle of non-discrimination together with the principle of restriction of the EU freedoms (case 07/16/1998, C-264-96, *Imperial Chemical Industries—ICI*).

It should also be noted that the violation of the fundamental freedoms can be realized in the context of an international convention against double taxation through the simultaneous exercise of taxation by each Member State. In this case it is expressly formulated the theory of the "almost restriction" in order to indicate the uncertainty about the regulatory parameter to be taken by the judgment of restriction on fundamental freedoms, considering the inability to identify which of the two States should give up some tax power (case 05/12/1998, C-336/96, *Gilly*; case 09/14/1998, C-291/97, *Gschwing*; case 11/14/2006, C-513/2004 *Kerckhaert—Morres*).

6.1.3 The Judgment Concerning the Non-restriction in the European Jurisprudence

The principle of non-restriction has been formulated for the first time by the Court of Justice in the case *Dassonville* (case 01/28/1974, C-8/74) being expressly stated that "*all trading regulations enacted by Member States which are capable of hindering directly or indirectly, actually or potentially, intra-Community trade should be regarded as a measure having equivalent effect to the quantitative restrictions*".

So it is established that the judgment on the principle of non-restriction affects the legality of a national standard because of the obstructive and/or restrictive effects with respect to intra-Community trade. Therefore it must carry out a verification of the restrictive effects through an teleological assessment on the national rule.

In particular, the test of restriction is accomplished by the investigation of the disadvantage that the foreign person suffers in relation to the intra-Community trade as a result of the legislation of a Member State.

On the other hand, the restrictive measure can be justified in a matter of overriding national general interest according to the parameter of rationality. It is a complex evaluation that involves the balancing of the interests of the European Union with the national interests which will be examined in more detail later (see below, Chap. 7).

The judgment on the principle of non-restriction is therefore a typical binary structure as it is divided into two basic steps:

a. determination of a regulatory hurdle about the freedom of movement provided for by the Treaty;
b. assessment of a reasonable cause of justification that legitimizes the existence of a restrictive national measure.

The judgment of non-restriction has been frequently adopted by the Court of Justice also in tax matters, being expressed the conviction that the tax regulations of the Member States may not configure an obstacle to the freedoms of movement and however may not make less convenient the material use of the same freedoms.

The focus of the ECJ case-law is addressed in particular to some specific issues as the double taxation, the use of losses within the group, the anti-avoidance rules on *transfer pricing*, the *thin capitalization*, the *exit tax*. It is typically a series of issues concerning the direct taxes in which the rules of law are judged from the perspective of the principle of non-restriction, having to verify whether the national rule produces the deterrent effect with respect to the exercise of the freedom of circulation (mostly recurring in the freedom of collection and investment of capital and in the freedom of establishment).

6.2 The Free Movement of Goods

The free movement of goods is one of the primary targets of a supranational organization that takes the essential purpose of establishing a single market and a space free from frontiers and legal restrictions. Indeed, this principle is to characterize not only the European Union but also other forms of supranational organization (such as the WTO, NAFTA, etc.).

The principle of free movement of goods is fixed by the art. 28 TFEU, where it is forbidden the creation of the customs duties or of the charges with equivalent effect which can obstruct or limit the circulation of the goods (import and export) among the Member States; in the same rule it is established a Customs Tariff to be utilized as a common parameter for the trade relations (import and export) with foreigner extra-EU countries.

Therefore, the principle of free movement of goods is defined in the European legal order through tax limitations and constraints: the main limitation is determined by the reduction of the protectionist execution of the taxation power by the Member States. Therefore this principle is basically integrated by a series of specific tax regulations.

The free movement of goods is ensured mainly by the elimination of the customs barriers and the homogenization of the consumption taxes provided for in the various Member States. The first measure (elimination of the customs barriers) is devoted to avoid fiscal restrictions or taxes that prevent the free play of competition, submitting merchandise trade to protectionist or interventionist measures by the national laws. The second measure (homogenization of the consumption taxes) is functional to avoid the tax burden directly applied on the consumption of goods which may be a distorting factor for the free competition in the common market.

It should be noted that the policy of European Union about this principle has been executed since the origin through a very hard-hitting action of coordination of the national legislations which has been implemented by the following operations:

i) through the establishment of the Customs Union and the determination of a unified legal framework of the customs duties directly applicable in all the Member States;
ii) due to the harmonization of the regulations about the value added tax by several Directives;
iii) through the harmonization of the regulations about the excise duties, achieved through a series of EU Directives.

The principle embodied in art. 28 TFEU has thus found a detailed declination in the derivate EU law, whose target was to establish some European regulations devoted to conform the national fiscal discipline to the value of the free movement of goods.

It is significant, in this regard, that in the ECJ jurisprudence there are not almost cases for the judgment about the restriction of the free movement of goods. That means basically that the principle of the free movement of goods is not questioned in the tax jurisdictions of the Member States precisely because of the incisiveness and the accuracy of the guidelines contained in the EU regulations.

6.3 The Freedom of Movement of Services

The principle of free movement of services—that refers expressly to the industrial, commercial and professional activities—is contained in the art. 56 TFEU and is devoted to establish an essential freedom to the realization of a common market in the current economic context, considering the growing importance of services and industries in the configuration of economic and productive global system. Such freedom must therefore be fully protected by the European order with respect to the national regulations which may assume a restrictive or protectionist nature.

In the tax law, the free movement of services is basically ensured through a policy of harmonization of indirect taxes (especially with regard to the value added tax). At this purpose it may reiterate the comments made in the previous paragraph with reference to the freedom of movement of goods.

The increased importance of the freedom of movement of services in the area of taxation, however, concerns the discipline of direct taxes, where the national regulations can configure restrictive measures with respect to the principle. In particular, the restrictive effect was detected in two cases: the national tax rule may deter service providers from carrying out its activities in the Member State, or service recipients may be reluctant to seek or to receive the services by a national tax rule (case 01/30/2007, C-150/04, *Commission vs. Denmark*).

It should be noted that there is a significant case-law regarding the relevance of the principle of free movement of services in the regulation of direct taxes.

In relation to the matter of insurance benefits or supplementary pension, it has consolidated the conviction that constitutes an obstacle to the free movement of services the national tax legislation which has the effect of making the provision of services between legal entities of different Member States more costly or difficultly than the provision of services provided within the nation-State (case 04/28/1998, C-118/96 *Safir*; case 01/30/2007, C-150/04, *Commission vs. Denmark*).

Even in the field of treatment of interest paid to a bank (the mortgage loan being a case referred typically to the category of services) it was considered unlawful, because of the restriction of the principle enshrined in art. 56, the national provision which allows a tax advantage only if the loan was contracted with a lending institution authorized by the legislation of the Member State and not the loans received by resident banks or other credit institutions authorized in other Member States (case 11/14/1995, C-484/93 *Svensson—Gustavsson*).

6.4 The Free Movement of Capital

6.4.1 The Free Movement of Capital for Tax Purposes

Another freedom that plays a primary role in the EU legal system regards the movement of capital within the European common market according to the principle established in the art. 63 TFEU.

This freedom is evidently connected to the pursuit of the targets of economic and trade integration of the European Union since it allows the circulation of capital in the free space of the EU territories in order to allow the concrete development of productive initiatives and business.

The freedom of movement of capital is expressed through a variety of forms that can typically be traced to two categories of cases: the freedom to raise capital for the development of economic activities and enterprise (freedom regarded from the point of view of the "recipient"); the liberty to invest capital in order to achieve an economic return (freedom regarded from the point of view of the "investor").

The EU attention, however, seems to apply mainly to the first of the two mentioned cases, given the relevant relationship with the freedom of enterprise and, therefore, with the full implementation of the target of free competition in the common market.

In this regard it should be noted that the freedom of movement of capital often tend to overlap, or otherwise to combine with the freedom of establishment of companies; indeed, the raising of capital finds its natural expression in the constitution or in the development of enterprises, particularly with relation to the increase of the share capital or to the financial capacity of a company resident in a Member State other than that one of the investor (mostly the parent company) (case 11.11.1981, C-203/80, *Casati*; case 13.4.2000, C-251/98, *Baars*; case 3.10.2006, C-452/04 *Fidium Finanz*; case 13.3.2007, C-524/04 *Test claimants in the thin cap group litigation*; case 3.10.2013, causa C-282/12, *Itelcar)*.

National rules may not restrict the freedom of movement of capital by restrictive measures that are intended to put an obstacle to the free movement of capital. This prohibition applies obviously also, and perhaps above all, with the tax national laws that may not be configured to determine a disadvantage or at least a deterrent for non-residents with respect to the movement of capital.

So it was stated that national legislation involving a tax advantage limited to the capital gains arising from domestic investment constitutes a restriction with respect to the freedom of movement of capital under both of the forms mentioned above, since it discourages the citizens of that country to invest in other Member State and at the same time produces a restrictive effect with respect to investors resident in the other Member States to bring their own capital in the State (case 07/15/2004, C-315/2002, *Lenz*; case 01/19/2006, C-265-04 *Bouanich*).

6.4.2 The Exceptions to the Free Movement of Capital Expressly Provided by the Treaty

The freedom of movement is the only European freedom for which a restriction is permissible on the basis of a cause of justification recognized directly in a provision of the Treaty. For other EU freedoms, instead, the causes of justification are originated in the judgments formulated the Court of Justice.

A first exception to the freedom of movement of capital is provided in art. 65 TFEU, where it is established that the Member States may operate in the domestic legislation a distinction between taxpayers who are not in the same situation because of their residence or place of capital allocation (art. 65 let. a). Moreover the Member States may assume procedural regulation that can introduce some restrictions or limitations with regard to the free movement of capital (art. 65 let. b) in order to:

- take the necessary measures to prevent infringements of tax law and to permit the control of financial institutions;
- establish procedures for the declaration of capital movements in the tax return for the purposes of administrative or statistical information;
- assume regulations devoted to ensure the respect of public policy or public security.

In any case it is established that such regulations and procedures may not constitute a functional means to introduce forms of arbitrary discrimination or a disguised restriction with respect to the principle of free movement of capital and payments.

Therefore the Member State may introduce a legitimate distinction in the treatment of resident taxpayers with respect to non-resident taxpayers as long as it is justified by overriding reasons of general interest and does not constitute a means of arbitrary discrimination or a disguised restriction on the free movement of capital (case 06/06/2000, C-35/98 *Verkooijen*; case 01/19/2006, C-265-04 *Bouanich*).

A second form of derogation to the free movement of capital is expressly provided for by art. 64 TFEU where it is established that restrictions on the free movement of capital existing at the date of 12/31/1993 (and especially those concerning Bulgaria, Estonia or Hungary) are allowed—and thus fully eligible—in relation to third countries with regard to "direct investment", including investments in real estate, the establishment of enterprises or economic activities, the provision of financial services or the admission of securities to capital markets. This exception to the EU principle is also applied in tax matters, enabling national legislation to implement restrictions on relations with third countries provided that such regulations are pre-existing at the end of 12/31/1993 (case 05/24/2007, C-157/2005, *Holböck*).

It should be noted that the Treaty lacks a legal definition of "movement of capital" and the case law therefore has been referred to the elaboration formulated in the derivative legislation (in particular with Directive no. 88/361). Thus, according to the nomenclature annexed to that Directive, it is identified a set of circumstances that may be qualified as "direct investment" of capital; this category includes capital investment of any kind, made from physical persons or legal entities, intended to establish or maintain direct links between the investor and the business receiving the funds (case 12/12/2006, C-446/2004, *Test Claimants in FII Group Litigation*); however this list is illustrative, and not an exhaustive one (case 23.2.2006, C-513/2003, *van Hilten—van der Heijden*).

6.4.3 A Derogation from the Principle of the Free Movement of Capital: The Judicial Clarification of the Concept of "Lucrative Rights" Provided by Directive no. 69/35

The principle of free movement of capital is a partial exemption under the regulations of indirect taxes applicable to business contributions. In particular, according to the rule formulated by art. 10, let. c) of Directive 69/35, the taxation that affects the establishment or the registration of business in public registers is to be considered prohibited, including charges having equivalent effect, with the sole exception of the "lucrative rights" (within the meaning of art. 12, no. 1, let. e).

Indeed, the taxes referred to art. 10 let. c), although not affecting the capital contributions, are still collected on the basis of the formalities and requirements related to the legal form of enterprises and corporations, and therefore by reason of the structural tool prepared for the raising capital; so the maintenance of such charges and taxes might affect or obstruct the aims pursued by the Directive (case 31.3.1992, C-200/90, *Denkavit*).

The most significant point of the discipline laid down by Directive n. 69/35 concerns the application of the latitude of the exception established by the aforementioned art. 12, where it is stated that the prohibition of taxes does not affect the "lucrative rights". This concept is not, in fact, outlined in the EU Directive, nor adequately developed into the national legislation.

The legal scope of the category of "lucrative rights" was deepened by the Court of Justice which has identified a number of concrete indices relevant to determining the profitability of a "right" imposed authoritatively by law to some business because of the mere creation or entry in the public register. The Court held that the amounts charged for entry in the register of the companies must be calculated solely based on the cost of the formalities; these amounts may also cover the costs of minor services performed without charge. It was also pointed out that a Member State in order to calculate these amounts may consider all costs associated with the registration process, including the overheads attributable to them. It is also envisaged that a Member State is entitled to impose lump sum and to establish the amount for an indefinite period, subject to this amount it continues not to exceed the average cost of the public service.

Therefore, the focus of the case law concerning the "lucrative rights" is identified in the definition of the relationship between the amount of capital required by the public service and the actual cost of the same public service (according to the line conceptual indicated in the case 20.4.1993, C-71/91 and C-178/91, *Ponente Carni*).

It is also interesting to note that the issue of the juridical relations between the amount of the public charges and the cost of the public service is not a new issue for the case-law of the European Court of Justice.

In fact, already in a dispute concerning the interpretation of Directive no. 64/432, about the harmonization of the control on animal health, the Court of Justice observed (case C-46/1977) that controls and charges expressly permitted by the Directive may not be regarded as unilateral measures that impede trading or commercial activities, but, on the contrary, as operations designed to facilitate the free movement of goods, by neutralizing obstacles which may result in the freedom of trade. Therefore, monetary charges levied because of health checks and imposed by a provision of EU, having uniform character and being made before shipment in the exporting Member State, do not constitute charges having an equivalent effect to customs duties on exports, "*provided that their amount does not exceed the actual cost of the specific operations of the control*".

6.5 The Free Movement of People

6.5.1 The Free Movement of Workers

A fundamental freedom of the EU legal system regards the free movement of persons within the European area with the power to settle and take up residence in any territory of the European Union (art. 45 TFEU). This freedom constitutes a value typically attributable to one of the norms-symbol of the Treaty, namely the principle of non-discrimination on the basis of the nationality enshrined in the art. 18 TFEU.

As mentioned earlier, a first manifestation of this freedom concerns the mobility of workers (or, even, of the people looking for a job), being established the abolition of all restrictions based on nationality or residence of the employee in relation to employment, remuneration and other conditions of employment. In essence, it is granted the access and the execution of an employment in each Member State, without the necessity of a subjective requirement (regarding the nationality or the place of residence) of the employee.

This principle also applies to tax matter, since it is forbidden to assume a national regulation having a restrictive character about the aforementioned freedom of movement of workers. Thus, every tax rule that applies to introduce a taxation of the income coming from employment with a detrimental content with regard to the activities carried out by non-residents is to be considered unlawful and incompatible with EU law (case 12.12.2002, C-385/2000, *De Groot*).

It should be noted in this regard that the Court of Justice judged as a restriction of freedom of movement of workers the domestic discipline that does not permit the deduction of the "losses from negative rental" generated by citizens of a Member State with reference to the dwelling house owned in another Member State (case 02/21/2006, C-152/03, *Ritter*; case 07/18/2007, C-182/06, *Lakebrink*).

6.5.2 The Freedom of Establishment

A second manifestation of the principle of free movement of persons regards the right to establish a productive economic activity not related to an employment (and therefore a business or a professional activity) in each of the Member States (so called "primary" freedom of establishment). This freedom extends to the setting up of agencies, branches or subsidiaries by persons or legal entities resident in Member States (so-called "secondary freedom" of establishment). Indeed, in the ECJ case-law it is well recognized the right of each European citizen to establish more than one business center in the territories of EU countries (case 15.2.1996, C-53/95, *Inasti*).

This principle—enshrined by the art. 49 TFEU—is resolved in the illegitimacy of the rules of law which not only produce discrimination, direct or indirect, between residents and non-residents, but especially that produce the effect of preventing, obstructing or otherwise restrict the access to the market of a Member State through the establishment of the business. In essence, this principle permits to realize the conceptual passage from the protection of *market equality* to the protection of *market access*.

On the basis of the freedom of establishment the non-residents grant the right to access to the self-employed activities, including the power to proceed with the establishment of enterprises, under the same conditions defined by the national legislation for the residents.

This freedom is typically regarded in the perspective of the non-resident persons who exercise the economic activity; it is not considered instead the opposite hypothesis, namely the right of a resident person not to be hampered by national legislation if he decides to establish his economic activities in another Member State.

This principle is specifically considered by the ECJ jurisprudence in regard to tax matters, being prohibited tax regulations that take on a restrictive connotation compared to the freedom of establishment in the national territory by non-residents (case 09/27/1998, C-81/87, *Daily mail*; case 07/16/1998, C-264-96, *Imperial Chemical Industries—ICI*; case 04/13/2000, C-251/98, *Baars*; case 03/11/2004, C-9/2002, *De Lasteyrie du Saillant*). The Court of Justice has also observed that the freedom of establishment is a norm with a direct effect and it can be invoked by every European citizen in order to obtain the disapplication of the conflicting national regulation (case 13.12.2005, C-446/03, *Marks & Spencer)*.

So, the freedom of establishment is protected in the tax system, even if the choice to work in another Member State is carried out through a permanent establishment (case 07/16/1998, C-264-96, *Imperial Chemical Industries—ICI*). Particularly, the treatment of losses incurred by a permanent establishment may not be carried out by national law in a detrimental manner to the non-resident company as it would otherwise arise as a deterrent with regard to the freedom of establishment.

It should also be noted that the freedom of establishment requires the dual requirement of carrying on an economic activity and the existence of a minimum level of physical presence of the non-resident person who is established in the EU territory (case 04/23/2008, C-201/05). In particular, the execution of an economic activity implies an actual settlement in the hosting Member State and, conversely, excludes that the EU protection can be offered to the purely artificial settlement, that is made for the sole purpose of obtaining a tax savings; the minimum level of physical presence in the hosting Member State must be verifiable objectively in terms of premises, staff and equipment (case 09/12/2006, C-196/04, *Cadbury Schweppes*; case 04/23/2008, C-201/05).

For a company resident in a Member State the transfer of the place of the effective management or of the administrative body in the territory of another Member State does not fall within the area of the freedom of establishment, since it has to be considered as a mere organizational choice and not as the location of a stand-alone legal entity (and, thus, the residency is maintained in the same State of origin) (case 09/27/1998, C-81/87, *Daily Mail*).

The Principle of Tax Non-discrimination

7

Contents

7.1 The Principle of Tax Non-discrimination 110
  7.1.1 The Centrality of the Principle of Tax Non-discrimination Regarding the Trade Among the States in the EU Legal System 110
  7.1.2 The Types of the Principle of Non-discrimination 111
  7.1.3 The Judgment of Discrimination 112
7.2 The Importance of the Principle of Non-discrimination in Direct Taxes 113
  7.2.1 The Judicial Clarification of the Principle of Non-discrimination Regarding Direct Taxes 113
  7.2.2 The Comparability of the Situations for the Purpose of Application of the Principle of Non-discrimination 114
  7.2.3 The Evolution of the European Jurisprudence Towards the Overcoming of the Principle of Non-discrimination Through the Application of the Principle of Restriction 117
7.3 The Relevance of the Principle of Non-discrimination in the Regulation of Indirect Taxes 117
  7.3.1 The EU Regulations on the Principle of Non-discrimination for the Purpose of the Indirect Taxation 117
  7.3.2 The Prohibition of Discriminatory Internal Taxation on the Products of Other Member States 118
  7.3.3 The Distinction of the Non Discrimination Compared to the Prohibition of Taxes "with Equivalent Effect" to the Customs Duties 121
  7.3.4 The Implications of the Principle of Non-discrimination of Indirect Taxes and the Choice of the Country of Taxation 122

P. Boria, *Taxation in European Union*, DOI 10.1007/978-3-319-53919-5_7

7.1 The Principle of Tax Non-discrimination

7.1.1 The Centrality of the Principle of Tax Non-discrimination Regarding the Trade Among the States in the EU Legal System

A central role into the European Union in the field of taxation can be certainly attributed to the principle of non-discrimination.

It is a principle that finds its first formalization in the art. 110 TFEU (being enunciated previously in the art. 90 of the Treaty of Maastricht and in the art. 95 of the Treaty of Rome) where it is established the prohibition for the Member States to apply fiscal charges over the trade of domestic products of other Member States in excess of the fiscal charges applied to similar domestic products; moreover the EU provision forbids, in any case, to have recourse to an internal tax designed to protect domestic over foreign products.

Evidently this statutory provision expresses the need to assure a competitively neutral treatment to the commercial transactions carried out within the common market, excluding that Member States may take protectionist and interventionist positions which can encourage and protect the domestic production or, otherwise, can contribute to the elevation of tax barriers equivalent to customs duties and therefore are contrary to the target of free movement of capital, goods and services.

In this perspective, the rule laid down in art. 110 seems to refer mainly to the indirect taxes, having an immediate relevance on commercial transactions, rather than to the discipline of direct taxes, which instead may affect commercial traffic in a marginal and mediated manner (mostly through uncontrollable phenomena of transfer of tax over the price which are difficult to measure and to evaluate). Moreover, the general scope of the EU regulation about non-discrimination and still the nature of a fundamental principle into the fabric of European values make clear that this rule also applies to the area of direct taxes (such as it may be easily detectable by the case law of the Court of Justice).

The rule laid down by art. 110 acquires an essentially "negative" nature, since it only requires a foreclosure towards national regulations which permit favourable fiscal treatments or otherwise having a discriminatory essence, and not also defines a "positive" content to the tax treatment of the national systems. Indeed, it is not fixed any obligation to ensure equal taxation between domestic and foreign products, according to a "positive" criterion for a successful integration, but only it is forbidden to assume a less favourable tax treatment of foreign products, realized by the Member State (emerging the distinction of principle of non-discrimination with respect to the principle of equality).

The legal value to which it must be coordinated the above mentioned regulation, usually referred to as the "principle of tax non-discrimination", assumes a fundamental respect for the process of development of the European Union as it is sufficient to preclude the formation of tax barriers that might seriously question the primary aim of the free movement of the factors of production and the commercial products. At this purpose it is correctly observed that the principle is an instrumental rule to the pursuit of the four fundamental freedoms of EU law.

This value, as perspicuous since the denomination, is designed to contain the selfish excesses of the nation-States that are clearly in conflict with the process of the European integration, not even to indicate a path to facilitate the harmony of tax systems. In this sense, the principle of non-discrimination is configured as a "conservative" rule, direct to ensure the maintenance of a legal *status quo* (open borders in Europe) and not to pursue a gradual overcoming of the diversity in the national tax disciplines.

It appears the fundamental difference with respect to the principle of equality, especially in the "progressive" version (so-called "substantial" equality) commonly accepted in the Constitutions of the twentieth century: the principle of non-discrimination merely sets the elimination of distorting factors of access to the market and does not establish a rule of substantial equality of conditions and opportunities, which would act also for the individuals already existing on the market (as it would be in compliance with the principle of substantial equality).

Moreover, the principle of non-discrimination keeps some of the conceptual perspectives of the principle of equality, and in particular the need to verify the similarity of the legal situations taken as the basis of comparative judgment (appearing, in fact, entirely inapplicable the criterion of discrimination where such situations are substantially different from each other); so it might be the temptation to establish a sort of assimilation between the principle of non-discrimination and the principle of formal equality.

Indeed, within the European order the citizens are considered not as members of a changing society, connected by ties of solidarity and by the need to overcome the inequalities, but as *homines oeconomici* (economic agents) who operate as agents of the production system. So the equal treatment assumes an "horizontal" importance: the exercise of tax power is adjusted according to the principle of non-discrimination in order to avoid obstructive forms of freedom of movement, in order to ensure a levelling of the tax burden in each category of subjects, independently of social or equity assessments; the citizens, therefore, are equalized on the basis of the tax burdens in relation to the formal aspect of the production of a single event economically significant and not further discriminated with reference to the subjective position overall.

7.1.2 The Types of the Principle of Non-discrimination

In the jurisprudence of the Court of Justice it has been identified three types of discrimination incompatible with EU law, namely:

1. overt discrimination;
2. covert discrimination;
3. reversed discrimination.

The "overt discrimination" occurs when the national regulation achieves a discriminatory treatment on the basis of nationality or citizenship of the agent. In this case, for the legal entities the nationality is identified with regard to the registered office.

The "covert discrimination" is established where the national regulation introduces a discriminatory discipline in relation to the residence or to another factor of allocation, as an element which, while not representing the direct purpose of protection under EU law (namely the nationality or citizenship), resolves indirectly in a lesion of the same objective. This type of non-discrimination principle has been recognized in a dating judgment (case 02/12/1974, C-152/73, *Sotgiu*) where it was considered unacceptable any covert form of discrimination which leads to the same result of direct discrimination. In tax matters the qualifying element of indirect discrimination is identified in the residence (case 05/16/2000, C-87/99, *Zurstrassen*).

The "reversed discrimination" exists when the national regulation produces a discriminatory effect against the resident person, penalizing him with respect to the tax benefit or otherwise to a more favourable fiscal rule established for the not resident persons. In this case, the principle of non-discrimination is invoked by the citizen directly against his own country.

Usually the discrimination should find the constitutive source in a rule of domestic law; however, it can also be detected in a provision contained in international agreements to prevent double taxation. In tax matters such discriminatory effect was found in a conventional rule which was prejudicial to the application of a tax advantage to the permanent establishment of a non-resident company (case 09/21/1999, C-307/97, *Saint Gobain*).

7.1.3 The Judgment of Discrimination

The judgment about the principle of non-discrimination regards the legality of a national regulation with respect to the EU order because of the distorting and discriminatory effects that is likely to produce in the treatment of non-residents compared to subjects belonging to a Member State.

In particular, the discrimination test is done by checking if a similar situation is dealt with by the legislation of a Member State in a different way (and also if different situations are treated in the same way) with reference to the position of citizens or residents compared to the non- residents.

On the other hand, the discriminatory regulation can find an objective justification in a matter of overriding national interest according to the criterion of rationality. It is a complex issue that involves the balancing of the interests of the European Union with the national interests (which will be examined in more details later; see below, Chap. 8).

The evaluation of the principle of non-discrimination is therefore constituted by a typical ternary structure as it is divided into three basic stages:

1. assessment of the comparability of a situation involving a non-resident with the situation of a citizen or a resident;
2. verification of the existence of a rule with a discriminatory content, as appropriate to introduce a differential treatment of the two comparable situations;
3. existence of a reasonable cause of justification that legitimizes the adoption of the restrictive national regulation.

The judgment of discrimination has been repeatedly adopted by the Court of Justice in taxation matter, as a parameter for assessing the compatibility of national legislation with respect to the EU order. In particular, it will be examined in the following paragraphs the articulate orientation taken by the Court of Justice in the area of direct taxation.

7.2 The Importance of the Principle of Non-discrimination in Direct Taxes

7.2.1 The Judicial Clarification of the Principle of Non-discrimination Regarding Direct Taxes

The scope and the content of the principle of non-discrimination have been significantly developed in the case law of the Court of Justice.

The first decision of the ECJ regarding the importance of the principle of non-discrimination (and the first decision of its kind in the area of direct taxation) is the case *Avoir fiscal* of 1986, when a provision of the French law was found to be inconsistent with the Treaty, as it stated the attribution of a tax credit only to companies having their registered office in the French territory and not to the foreign companies that had a permanent establishment in the same territory; so it was stated that the dissimilar treatment in relation to a tax benefit (such as the grant of a tax credit) would have an unacceptable disadvantage to foreign companies and, therefore, violates the principle of freedom of establishment. That judgment expressly recognizes the prohibition of direct discrimination, that is the incompatibility with EU law of national provisions which determine preferential arrangements on the basis of the nationality of firms (or rather of the location of the registered office within the national territory).

Then with the case *Biehl* of 1990, the Court has examined the issue of indirect discrimination, through which the discriminatory effect upon the non residents is accomplished through a regulatory mechanism different from that directly precluded by EU law. In that case, the ECJ affirmed the illegality of a provision of national law which prevented the refund of amounts withheld during the year to a person employed in dependence of the single condition that the employee had left the territory of the State during the year same, since this condition may discriminate against nationals of other Member States in relation to the principle of equal payment treatment; and indeed the Court held the principle that "*the criterion that relates to the residence in the national territory any payback of the tax paid in excess, although it applies regardless of the nationality of the taxpayer concerned, may damage especially taxpayers who are nationals of other Member States, since these are often the last to leave the country or settle during the year*".

The latitude of the principle of non-discrimination, and in particular the prohibition of hidden or disguised discrimination, was further clarified by the ECJ in other decisions: in the judgment *Commerzbank* of 1993 it was expressly stated that the criterion related to the tax concession (in the case, the increase in the tax refund) applies to the tax domicile to discriminate against foreign companies because "*in most cases they are resident outside the territory of the State in question*"; in the decision *Asscher* of 1996 it was stated that the distinction in tax treatment depending on the criterion of residence (in this case the increase of the tax rate) "*is liable to operate mainly to the detriment of citizens of other Member States*".

Further characterization of the principle concerns the so-called "reversed" discrimination, which occurs when a national citizen of a Member State established in another Member State claims to be discriminated compared to other citizens because of tax rules. That finding was further deepened by doctrine rather than by the ECJ jurisprudence, which has addressed the issue sporadically. It may be cited the case *Werner* of 1993, which has advanced the question of illegality on the treatment of a German national resident in Belgium while working in Germany, who felt to be discriminated by a provision of the German tax reserved only for residents; in this situation the ECJ has not ruled on the merits for lack of connecting with EU law. In addition, in the aforementioned decision *Asscher* of 1993, it is expressly stated that it is not compatible with the Treaty the exclusion from tax benefits for nationals of a Member State "*where by reason of their behaviour, they are, with regard to their State of origin, in a situation similar to that of all other individuals who enjoy the rights and freedoms guaranteed by the Treaty*".

It should be pointed out that the prejudicial and discriminatory effect of the national regulation is judged by the Court of Justice not so much in terms of actual outcome, but rather in terms of mere potentiality. Thus, it emerges a significant characterization of the principle of discrimination: this is intended as a simple risk of producing an alteration of the competitive structure and, therefore, to determine a bias with respect to the equal treatment of economic operators, and not as an objective damage to verify (and to prove) materially. This connotation of the principle of non-discrimination in terms of the potential risk, carried out by the jurisprudence, is to expand significantly the scope of the European action in relation to the formal text of the rule contained in the Treaty.

7.2.2 The Comparability of the Situations for the Purpose of Application of the Principle of Non-discrimination

Consistent to the extension of the rule of reason, in all the decisions of the ECJ about the application of the principle of tax non-discrimination (even according to the tendency to turn the principle of non-discrimination in a sort of union with the restriction of an EU freedom) it is determinant the formulation of the comparability of the situations with respect to which the Member States occur a regulation with a discriminatory effect.

Indeed, according to one of the essential canons of the principle of equality (to which the principle of non-discrimination, as mentioned, is logically connected), to affirm the illegality of a discriminatory regulatory treatment (or of an unjustified restriction on an EU freedom) should first ascertain the similarity of the examined situations. As explicitly stated by the Court, "*a discrimination can arise only through the application of different rules to comparable situations or through the application of the same rule to different situations*" (case 14.2.1995, C-279/93, *Schumacker*).

It should also be noted that in the case law it is not easy to discover a consolidated or, even less, unique pattern of comparison, being rather proposed some evaluation formulas of the legally relevant traits that change because of the specific single case. Therefore it can be identified a typical casistic approach to the matter of the comparability of legal situations.

In the literature, the judgment on the comparison of the situations considered for the assessment of tax non-discrimination is usually performed through a dual approach, taking as the basis of comparison a single and specific aspect of the legal relationship (limited comparison) or the entire economic and legal position of the subject (overall comparison).

With regard to the first approach (limited comparison), it can be mentioned the cases *Avoir fiscal* and *Commerzbank*, in which the comparison was limited to the specific assessment of the taxation, regardless of an overall judgment on the entire position of the taxpayer.

With regard to the second method (overall comparison), a reference point is represented by the case *Schumacker* (case 14.2.1995, C-279/93), which constitutes a real *leading case*. In that decision, with reference to the taxation of persons resident in a Member State different than the State that emanates a regulatory provision concerning a differentiated tax system, the ECJ ruled that the legal position of a resident is not comparable *tout court* to the position of the non-resident, using some reasons for distinguishing the two situations: the non-resident receives part of their income in the country of production and usually the other part of the income in the State of residence; the overall ability to pay is easily assessable only in the State of residence, where it is possible to formulate a judgment about the general flow of income (while in the State of production it may form only a partial idea, limited to the portion of the income generated thereby). The difference between the two situations is, therefore, theoretically permissible to make a difference in the fiscal treatment of the income produced by the resident with respect to the non-resident and therefore to exclude the application of the principle of non-discrimination, given the lack of similarity for the considered situations.

In the same decision the ECJ, with the usual realism, pointed out that the differentiation of the two situations is least where the non-resident does not achieve a significant income in the State of residence, being found in an analogous situation of the resident. Indeed, in this case, the State of income is in the position to carry out the assessment about the overall ability to pay of the non-resident (since most of his income is produced there). Evidently, the Court has taken the view that the judgment on the comparability of situations is conditioned by the appreciation of the overall ability to pay of the non-resident; so the peculiarity of this decision is to have identified the determining factor for the judgment about the comparability not in the specific location of the individual taxpayer with respect to the Member State providing the tax regulation, but in the evaluation of the general situation of the taxpayer whose assessment can be formulated only taking into account the tax consequences arising from the combined regulations of two States.

The direction assumed by the case *Schumacker* was taken up with subsequent decisions: the ECJ reiterated that the judgment of comparison about the positions of residents and non-residents must cover the overall income (or, at least, the most part of the income) in the State of income so that it can occur an assimilation of the legal situations (case 11.8.1995, C-80/94 *Wielocks*; case 27.6.1996, C-107/94, *Asscher*); the same idea has been applied to legal entities, excluding the existence of an evident (or even a hidden) discrimination for the taxation of non-resident enterprises limited to the income earned in the country of production (case 15.5.1997, C-250/95, *Futura*).

In any case, the comparison must concern the regulations provided for by the same national legislation and does not extend to the international regulations; so it is excluded the possibility to compare a national regulation with the similar regulation of another State (even a Member State) (case 5.7.2005, C-376/03, *D*; case 6.12.2007, C-298/05, *Columbus container services*). Moreover, it is not relevant the fiscal treatment provided for by a State with regard to the taxation established in another State in order to find a cause of justification for the EU regulation (case 8.11.2007 C-379/05, *Amurta*; case 29.11.2011, C-371/10, *National Grid Indus*).

Therefore, in the ECJ jurisprudence which seems to be consolidating since the case *Schumacker*, the comparison between residents and non-residents is to be basically excluded, given the existence of significant elements of differentiation of the relevant legal situations; however, such general rule may be subject to significant deviations, and consequently it may admit the formulation of a judgment on non-discrimination, if it is detectable in point of fact an equivalence between residents and non-residents in relation to the overall ability to pay. It is possible to argue that such discrimination does not constitute simply a difference in the tax treatment between residents and non-residents, but rather a fiscal distinction which is not based on a reasonable assessment of the overall situation of residents and non-residents.

7.2.3 The Evolution of the European Jurisprudence Towards the Overcoming of the Principle of Non-discrimination Through the Application of the Principle of Restriction

The Court of Justice seems to have shifted the focus of the judgment from the discrimination to the restriction of a EU freedom, regardless to the analysis of the distorting effects produced by a discriminatory rule.

As a consequence, the assessment of the lawfulness of the national regulation is formulated not only in relation to the existence of a difference in the treatment between residents and non-residents, but especially with regard to the restrictive effect of one of the four fundamental freedoms provided for by the Treaty. It produces a significant enlargement of the judgment about the compatibility of national tax law with the European order.

Indeed, the Court of Justice, while evaluating national regulations with a potentially discriminatory content, has focused the judgment on the restrictive scope of the national tax provisions relating to the freedom of establishment (case 10.12.1998, C-229/96 *Hoechst*; case 21.9.1999, C-307/97 *Saint Gobain*; case 8.3.2001, C-397/98 *Metallgesellschaft*); moreover, the ECJ has considered restrictive of the freedom of movement of capital a rule that allows a tax exemption for dividends paid by a company resident in the national State (case 6.6.2000, C-35/98 *Verkooijen*).

The reasoning of the Court of Justice, addressed to the verification of both the discrimination and the mere restriction, is always to be balanced with any other interest worthy of protection that may justify a derogation from the implementation of the EU freedom. This introduces the theme of the extension of the rule of reasonableness (to be understood as balancing for the conflicting interests) to all cases related to the principle of non-discrimination, imposing a type of analysis casuistic (and not deductive) in order to the application of the same principle.

7.3 The Relevance of the Principle of Non-discrimination in the Regulation of Indirect Taxes

7.3.1 The EU Regulations on the Principle of Non-discrimination for the Purpose of the Indirect Taxation

The Treaty about the functioning of European Union contains several provisions which specifically regulate the exercise of the power of taxation with regard to the area of the indirect taxation.

The provision of art. 110 TFUE (already contained in the art. 90 of the Treaty of Maastricht and in the art. 95 of the Treaty of Rome), taking up a similar content by a rule formulated in another international context (with reference to art. III, no. 2 of the GATT Treaty) prohibits Member States from applying charges to domestic products of other Member States in excess of the charges applied to similar domestic products, and moreover to establish an internal tax designed to protect domestic over foreign products.

The provision of art. 111 TFEU (already established in the art. 91 of the Treaty of Maastricht and in the art. 96 of the Treaty of Rome) precludes the use of internal tax rebates in excess of the taxes actually levied for goods exported to the EU, so as to avoid forms of tax shelter designed to promote exports to other Member States.

And finally the art. 112 TFEU (already established in the art. 92 of the Treaty of Maastricht and in the art. 98 of the Treaty of Rome) states that the discipline of taxes different from the indirect taxes can permit some remissions and repayments for the export or may introduce compensation fees (applicable to imports from the Member States), subject to the approval of the EU bodies (and in particular of the Council by a qualified majority on a proposal coming from the Commission) and to an application covering a limited period of time.

These regulations show a common ideological background, which is to be identified in the pursuit of a neutral treatment of the commercial transactions conducted within the common market, so as to prevent the national States from taking tax positions which produce a favour for domestic products or otherwise conflicting effects on the free movement of goods and services.

These rules express a logic of protection about the economic freedom and the value of market competition, appearing clearly designed to contrast national tax policies which have a discriminatory content with respect to products or services of other European countries. In other words, the aim pursued by the mentioned regulations typically consists in the definition of a condition of tax neutrality with respect to the trade and the movement of goods and services in the EU market.

Similarly to what was seen for the direct tax, the provisions of articles 110, 111 and 112 are related to the "principle of tax non-discrimination", aimed at eliminating the formation of tax barriers that would preclude or limit the achievement of the primary purposes of free movement of products on the EU market. Indeed, the principle of tax non-discrimination has found a preferential field of application with regard to the area of indirect taxation, given the immediate relief in terms of obstacles to freedom of movement that the toll on business or on consumption is capable of producing.

Evidently, it can recur in this regard all the general considerations already formulated with regard to direct taxation about the scope and the legal significance of the principle of tax non-discrimination.

7.3.2 The Prohibition of Discriminatory Internal Taxation on the Products of Other Member States

The rule enunciated in the art. 110 TFEU provides, as mentioned, the prohibition of a discriminatory internal taxation which is compared to the products coming from other Member States, with the obvious aim of ensuring the free movement of goods and services by any State of the European Union under neutral conditions in the common market.

It is a rule of great systematic relevance which has repeatedly been qualified by the Court as a fundamental element of the European order with regard to its primary purpose of the proper functioning of the common market (case 7.12.1995, C-45/94, *Ayuntamiento de Ceuta;* case 17.6.1998, C-68/96 *Grundig Italia vs. Ministry of Finance*).

The prohibition laid down by art. 110 is capable of producing immediate effects in the legal relations between the Member States and the residents thereof, not being subject to any condition nor subject to the adoption of any normative measure either by the EU institutions or the Member States (case 1.3.1966, C-48/65 *Lutticke*; case 17.2.1976, C-45/75 *Rewe*; case 22.3.1977, C-74/76 *Iannelli e Volpi*; case 27.5.1981, C-142/80 and C-143/80 *Essevi e Salengo*); in other words it is a rule having a direct effect that can be invoked by a Member State or by an individual resident in the territory of the European Union.

This prohibition is presented as a consistent rule to the principle of abolition of customs barriers enshrined in art. 23 and 25 TFEU. Indeed, if the national States are allowed to implement tax charges that fall only on products coming from other Member States (and not even on domestic products), it would inevitably repeat the same discriminatory effect that is intended to exclude by the abolition of the customs duties. How effectively it has been suggested by the Court of Justice (case 14.12.1962, C-2/62 and C-3/62, *Commission vs. Belgium and Luxemburg, Pan pepato*), the norm of art. 110 applies to prevent "loopholes" of fiscal nature which may be hidden behind a protectionist tax policy.

Moreover, even for such a rule it can be proposed the exemption made by the national interest tax and other national policy objectives, provided that the compression of the principle of non-discrimination is reasonable and not arbitrary (case 14.1.1981, C-140/79 *Chemical farmaceutici*). Also in this connection it may propose the same considerations made above with reference to the direct taxation.

As to the content of the provisions contained in the above mentioned rules of the Treaty, it should be noted that they preclude the levy of any tax to the State institutions, to the local authorities, and also to any other public bodies with powers of taxation and regardless of the tax revenue beneficiary (which could, in limit, also be different from the State or local authorities, as may occur, for example, with purpose taxes). Neither it is relevant the quantitative dimension of the taxation, falling in the latitude of the application of the ban also minor tributes as long as likely to hinder the free movement of goods and services (case 16.2.1977, C-20/76 *Schottle*; case 3.7.1985, C-277/85, *Commission vs. Italy, Marsala*). The prohibition contained in the art. 110 extends also to the products of countries not belonging to the European Union if these products find in the situation of "free practice" (case 7.5.1987, C-193/85 *Co-frutta;* case 17.7.1997, C-90/94 *Haar petroleum*; case 17.6.1998, C-68/96 *Grundig Italia*).

In the category of the products covered by the prohibition of discriminatory internal taxation there are primarily the "similar" products, namely the products which, irrespectively of the nominalist category or of the Customs statistics, in the perception of consumers show similar characteristics and meet the same functions and requirements with regard to the origin, the manufacturing process, the taste etc.

(case judgments *Rewe* of 1976, *Hansen* of 1978 and *Walker* of 1986). In addition, on the basis of the provision of the second paragraph of art. 110, into the same category of products protected by the tax protectionist effect are to be included also the "competing" imported products, which express a competitive position (even if only potential or indirect) with the domestic products; in particular the ECJ has identified the existence of a competition between two products, when they—although showing some significant differences of a qualitative nature—are presented to the consumer as the terms of a possible alternative of the actual and concrete consumption (alcoholic wine and beer in the case 25.4.1985, C-207/83 *Commission vs. United Kingdom*; or rhum and brandy in the case 18.2.1986, C-35/84 *Commission vs. Italy*).

The case-law formulated by ECJ about the tax discrimination through the indirect taxes is considerably large. At first, it has been established that any discriminatory effect introduced by the national regulations must be considered prohibited according to the rule of art. 110, regardless to the formal element involved in the discrimination; the discriminatory effect has been recognized by reference to the rules on the tax base or the tax rate, to the rules pertaining to tax relief or even to the procedural rules which impose additional burdens for the imported products. So it was considered illegal a criterion of assessment, while differentiated for domestic products and for imported goods, which generates detrimental effects for the imported products (case 2.4.1998, C-296/95 *Outokompu oy*, where it has identified the illegality of a system of taxation of the same product which established several tributes over the national products and a unique tribute on the imported products, producing a higher burden over these ones); the Court of Justice has also syndicated the validity of a consumption tax whose base was calculated net of expenses for transportation and marketing with regard to the domestic products and gross of the same expenses for the imported products (case 17.6.1998, C-68/96, *Grundig Italy vs. Ministry of Finance*); the ECJ has also judged unlawful a mechanism for deferred payment of taxes which was admitted only for the national companies, as distorting the financial position of the firms resident in other Member States, which imported the same products in the territory of the State (regulation therefore discriminatory in terms of competition) (case 17.6.1981, C-113/80, *Commission vs. Ireland*).

The Court of Justice has focused on the concrete and substantial identification of the tax discrimination in order to verify the actual discriminatory effect over imported products, without any regard to the formal structure of the regulation (and therefore beyond the purely textual provision of the national legislation); particularly the ECJ has given attention to the effective and real incidence of the taxation on domestic products and imported products, comparatively considered, and therefore to the concrete existence of some form of tax discrimination: thus, such discrimination was found in the presence of a special tax on cars that exceed a certain power determined in order to include only imported vehicles (case 9.5.1985, C-112/84 *Humblot*); or where a diversity of application of the tax due by the carrier according to the national or international shipment involves the substantial exemption for the national product (case 16.2.1977, C-20/76 *Schottle*); or even when the tax, although not apparently affecting the import, regards typically the use of an imported product for a specific aim (case 3.3.1988, C-252/86 *Bergandi*). Moreover, a very high tax burden on certain products, that is going to hit in point of fact only imported products (as it is completely missing in the productive capacity of the national production of those products) may not be discussed in terms of legality by the Court of Justice as devoid of an actual discriminatory impact (case 11.12.1990, C-47/88, *Commission vs. Denmark*, where it is explicitly stated that the provision of the Treaty "does not allow to censure the excessiveness of the level of taxation which the Member States could establish for certain products in the absence of any discriminatory or protective effect").

However, it is significant that according to the Court of Justice, in the presence of uncertain situations, namely when it is not entirely clear whether the national rule produces a discriminatory effect over the imported products, it is up to the State the burden of proof about the legitimacy of the national rule (case 19.2.1991, C-374/89 *Commission vs. Belgium*; case 16.12.1992, C-210/91, *Commission vs. Greece*). This is not a rule of judgment based on a relative presumption of illegality of the conduct of the national legislature (which would probably be unacceptable in terms of legal logic), but rather it is a mechanism for the involvement of the Member State in the analysis of the economic and legal effects of the tribute, justifiable considering the inadequacy of the tools available to the Court of Justice.

7.3.3 The Distinction of the Non Discrimination Compared to the Prohibition of Taxes "with Equivalent Effect" to the Customs Duties

The rule of the art. 110 is to be distinguished with respect to the scope of other rules of the Treaty which show some affinity or at least a functional contiguity of content.

In particular, the distinction must be demarcated with respect to the provision that provides for the prohibition of recourse in national legislation to taxes "with equivalent effect" to the customs duties in accordance with art. 28 and art. 30 TFEU. It is a rule which, like the principle of tax non-discrimination relating to indirect taxes, aims to eliminate disguised restrictions on the movement of goods and services in the common market and therefore, ultimately, is devoted at fostering the neutrality of taxation of trade between companies belonging to EU Member States.

The legal scope of the two standards is substantially different. The prohibition of taxes "with equivalent effect" refers typically to charges applicable only to the imported products and therefore should be referred to the regulations of customs duties; and so it determines the absolute illegality of the conflicting national legislation. On the contrary, the regulation of art. 110, correlating with the principle of fiscal non-discrimination, concerns an internal tax (or a taxation system, possibly articulated on a plurality of internal taxes) which, while causing a difference in the tax treatment between domestic production and imports, affects a generality of products and therefore involves both domestic products and imported products with a substantial indifference with regard to the origin of the goods; it produces a "relative" illegality, which is to take effect only when (and to the extent that) the national tax norm is applied in order to achieve a discrimination between domestic products and imported products (coming from other Member States).

Therefore, the national regulations conflicting with the prohibition of taxes "with equivalent effect" are to be considered completely and definitively illegitimate and should be immediately abolished; on the other side, the rules that conflict with the provision of art. 110 can maintain the legal validity if they are interpreted and applied so as to avoid the tax discrimination with respect to the products of companies imported from other Member States (cases 11.3.1992, C-78/90 to C-83/90 *Compagnie commerciale de l'Ouest*; case *Charalampos Dounias*).

The difference between the two regulations justifies the theory according to which it is forbidden the contextual and cumulative application of both regulations, since a unique factual context would be ascribed to two fundamentally distinct legal regimes (case 1.3.1966, C-48/65 *Lütticke*; case 17.7.1997, C-90/94 *Haar petroleum;* case 17.9.1997, C-130/96 *Fazenda Publica*).

Sometime, in order to distinguish adequately between the cases related to the principle of non-discrimination and the prohibition of taxes "with equivalent effect" it has been suggested to pay attention to the profile of the functionality of the tribute; so if the revenue generated from the tax is used to finance public activities in support of the product subject to taxation (or otherwise related to its production)—as it typically happens with the "purpose taxes"—it assumes relevance the extent of the received benefit, especially where this benefit is fully offset by the tribute paid in the presence of a tax with equivalent effect (while in the case of a charge only partially restored by the benefit received it falls within the scope of the principle of non-discrimination tax) (mentioned cases *Compagnie commerciale de l'Ouest and Fazenda Publica*).

7.3.4 The Implications of the Principle of Non-discrimination of Indirect Taxes and the Choice of the Country of Taxation

A final issue concerns the possible implications of accepting the principle of non-discrimination in respect to indirect taxes with regard to the identification of the country where the imposition of goods or services is carried out.

In particular, the prohibition of tax discrimination between domestic and imported products leads implicitly to accept the same normative criterion with respect to the profile of the territoriality of the tax benefit, showing clearly that the possible differentiation of treatment can determine a discriminatory regulation. Indeed, if foreign products are taxed in the country of origin while the imported products are taxed in the country of destination (or vice versa), it would be generated a differentiation of tax criteria difficult to justify in terms of systematic logic; that differentiation is capable to produce an effect of harmful concurrence to foreign products and therefore is to be considered inconsistent with the EU legal order as colliding with the principle of non-discrimination.

It should be noted that already in the disciplines of the GATT Treaty it is provided for the acceptance of the principle of taxation in the country of destination. It is a fiscal policy that neutralizes the effects of different tax systems with respect to international trade, ensuring that the diversity of the economic measurement of tax affects only the final price (and therefore the final consumers) and not also the remuneration of the product (remaining indifferent to the competition among the companies).

This principle of taxation in the country of destination seems to have been accepted as a primary criterion in the EU framework. Indeed, the use of the opposite principle of taxation in the country of origin could produce distortions in the competition among the firms, as any differences in taxation (particularly in the tax rates) in the legislation of the country of origin would be maintained also in the exporting countries and thus lead to a consumer price of imported products differently than domestic products.

The acceptance of the principle of taxation in the country of origin would allow more easily the abolition of customs barriers, preventing any form of control of imports for fiscal reasons (also according to the so-called *Cockfield report*). On the other hand, until it is very advanced the process of harmonization of indirect taxation and it remains a sensitive difference in the taxation between the Member States, the acceptance of the principle of taxation in the country of origin—as said—could lead to distortions in the competition on the market and therefore collide with the fundamental principle of non-discrimination.

In this perspective, it may be outlined a sort of connection between the principle of non-discrimination and the principle of harmonization: the choice of the territoriality for taxation, which is seen to represent an implication of the principle of non-discrimination, constitutes a typical manifestation of the policy of tax harmonization as it involves general evaluations in order to define the relations between the tax legal systems of the various Member States.

8 The Tax Interest of the National States and the Balance with the European Values

Contents

8.1 The Relevance of the Fiscal Interest of the National States in the European Order . . . 126
8.1.1 The Principle of the Efficiency and Preservation of the National Taxation Systems as Value of the EU Legal System . . . 126
8.1.2 The Dialectic Confrontation Between the Principle of the Efficiency of the National Public Finance and the EU Freedoms . . . 127
8.2 The Identification of the National Interests Qualified as Objective Causes of Justification with Respect to EU Values in the Jurisprudence of the Court of Justice 128
8.2.1 The Creative Jurisprudence Regarding the Causes of Justification with Respect to the Application of EU Freedoms. The So-Called "Rule of Reason" . . . 128
8.2.2 The Emergence of the Overriding Reasons of General Interest as Cause of Justification with Respect to the Principles of Non-discrimination and Non-restriction: The Tax Coherence of the Internal Taxation Systems . . . 129
8.2.3 The Jurisprudential Openings to the Principle of Territoriality . . . 130
8.2.4 The Jurisprudential Appreciation of the Risk of International Tax Evasion or Tax Avoidance . . . 131
8.2.5 The Protection of the Effectiveness of Tax Controls and Audits . . . 132
8.3 The Balancing of the Court of Justice Between the EU Interest and the National Interest 133
8.3.1 The Use of the Principle of Reasonableness in the EU Jurisprudence as a Balancing Formula with Respect to the Principle of Tax Non-discrimination . . . 133
8.3.2 The Recourse to the Principle of Proportionality as a Mechanism for the Mediation of the Possible Axiological Conflicts . . . 134
8.3.3 Some Considerations About the Balancing of the National Tax Interest and the Individual Rights in the Jurisprudence of the European Court of Human Rights . . . 135

P. Boria, *Taxation in European Union*, DOI 10.1007/978-3-319-53919-5_8

8.1 The Relevance of the Fiscal Interest of the National States in the European Order

8.1.1 The Principle of the Efficiency and Preservation of the National Taxation Systems as Value of the EU Legal System

Among the values outlined in the EU legal system it is specifically relevant the general interest in the proper application of the taxation systems of the national States, which qualifies as a specific interest of the European Union to be considered with precedence over the single interest of the nation-State and the peculiar interests of groups or categories of economic operators.

This principle finds an explicit statement in the art. 119 par. 3 TFEU, where it is established that the economic purposes of European Union, especially the monetary policy, require, among other essential requirements, "healthy public finances"; moreover, it also seems easily deduced by the rules set out in art. 121 TFEU, according to which the Member States should regard their economic policies as a "matter of common interest", and in the art. 126 TFEU, where it is stated that States must avoid an excessive public debt based on predetermined parameters (and particularly in relation to the ratio of public debt to gross domestic product).

Natural corollary of this principle is that the European Union must ensure, at the European level, the establishment of some appropriate regulatory mechanisms to allow individual Member States to research an efficient public finance, even (and perhaps mainly) in terms of the proper functioning of the tax system.

In this regard, it may point out two different lines of regulatory intervention teleologically related to the principle of efficiency and preservation of the national taxation systems.

At first, the European Union must ensure the concrete pursuit of the taxation of the nation-State as a determining factor for the achievement of the flow of tax revenues needed for the optimization of the public budget; in particular this involves the recognition of the legitimacy of national standards established to cover the tax obligation through the limitation of the phenomena of tax evasion and tax avoidance, even when in conflict with other rules of European inspiration.

At second, there is a need to develop the full reciprocal assistance of the tax administrations of the Member States, mainly through the information exchange and the cooperative mechanisms, in order to guarantee a constant monitoring and, consequently, a greater degree of efficiency in the supervision and control of the conduct of taxpayers. Evidently, this responds to the idea that the cooperation between Member States in terms of administrative efficiency may permit to ensure concretely the national tax obligations, increasing the level of deterrence with respect to the evasive or elusive conducts and, in any event, the functionality of the tax systems.

It should be noted that it is not explicitly mentioned in the Treaty the principle of the "danger of tax evasion" as a possible limit to the general defense of the fundamental freedoms. The only exception in this regard is provided by the rule on freedom of movement of capital (namely art. 65, first paragraph TFEU) in which it is determined that the Member States have the option of applying the national tax provisions which distinguish among taxpayers according to the place of residence or allocation of invested capital and have the right to take all necessary measures to prevent violations of the tax legislation.

8.1.2 The Dialectic Confrontation Between the Principle of the Efficiency of the National Public Finance and the EU Freedoms

The principle of the efficiency of the national public finance plays a prominent and often conflicting dialectical role, as compared to other EU values which are functionally correlated with economic freedoms forming the basis of the common market. In fact, the preservation of a "strong" nucleus of sovereignty about taxation in each Member State shows a real contrast with the needs of market opening, likely to lead to tensions in the axiological declination of the EU legislation.

On the regulatory side it may be noted that the axiological comparison between the opposing values is particularly noted in the relevance of the principles of tax non-discrimination and of restriction of EU freedoms.

Indeed, the value of consistency and integrity of the national tax systems may well collide with the demands of the tax non-discrimination and of the abatement of fiscal frontiers, if it determines obligations for non-resident taxpayers (including those resident in other Member Community) identified as "fiscally dangerous"; therefore in this context it must be verified time after time, through a balancing of values, the priority of the principle of the integrity of national public finances or, otherwise, the primacy of the EU freedoms (as a consequence of the elimination of the factors of fiscal discrimination).

However, the conceptual basis of the principle is to be found in the same underlying logic of EU law: the protection of the national public finances should never be understood in a conservative sense, as a nation-State yearning to resist to the process of European integration, but rather as the necessary protection of the fundamental mechanisms of the common market (namely the protection of the national economic systems as necessary part of the economic European order). To prevent or, at least, to contain the "fiscal crisis" of the nation-State will increase the degree of efficiency and soundness of the common market, according to a consolidated logic in a globalized economy, in which the national economic systems develop constantly and progressively through close interdependencies.

8.2 The Identification of the National Interests Qualified as Objective Causes of Justification with Respect to EU Values in the Jurisprudence of the Court of Justice

8.2.1 The Creative Jurisprudence Regarding the Causes of Justification with Respect to the Application of EU Freedoms. The So-Called "Rule of Reason"

The Court of Justice has repeatedly been called upon to rule on the eligibility of national laws to escape from the fundamental principles of EU law.

The various forms of balancing of conflicting values (EU interest and national interest) have been defined with particular regard to the protection of the principles of non-discrimination and non-restriction of fundamental freedoms.

Despite it is not easy to remark a line of constant and unequivocal judicial behaviour, varying with regard to the different intensities of the EU rule (namely depending on the reference of the prohibition to the area of restriction or to the area of non-discrimination), it may be noted as the reasoning of the Court starts from the selection of public interest worthy of appreciation by the EU legal order and from the assessment of the suitability of the national restrictive or discriminatory rule to pursue the same public interests.

Therefore, the Court of Justice has proceeded according to a typically "creative" logic to identify the national public interests which, although not explicitly mentioned in the Treaty, can be regarded as implicitly appreciated by European Union as "overriding reasons of general interest" that may justify derogations from the rules of EU law. It was also pointed out that these "reasons of general interest" should be appreciate as causes of objective justification and not mere intentions of the national legislature (to be considered as subjective reasons).

In particular, the Court of Justice has identified three reasons of overriding general interest of the individual Member States which are likely to confront dialectically—and are possibly to justify an exception—with the fundamental principles expressed by the Treaty in relation to taxation, and namely:

- the coherence of the national taxation system;
- the need to curb tax evasion and tax avoidance;
- the effectiveness of controls and tax audits.

It has been so formulated by the Court of Justice a test of judgment (so-called *rule of reason*), aimed at assessing the suitability of the national interests to justify an exception to the principles of non-discrimination and non-restriction of the fundamental freedoms of the Treaty. In essence, on the basis of an objective assessment (and not of mere intentions or purposes pursued by the national legislature), the Court produces a judgment of balance by a comparison between the risks and potential disadvantages suffered by the internal taxation law with the benefits obtainable in terms of protection of the EU freedoms according to an assessment of reasonableness and proportionality.

Moreover, it should be noted that the Court of Justice has ruled out the acceptance of a compensation between the tax disadvantages which affect the discriminated taxpayer and the other benefits or tax advantages which the same taxpayer may enjoy in other respects, still under national tax law (case 13.7.1993, C-330/91 *Commerzbank*; case 27.6.1996, C-107/94, *Asscher;* case 21.9.1999, C-307/97, *Saint Gobain*). Indeed, in this case, it would appear a sort of financial compensation that may not be appreciated as a reason for admitting the exclusion from the application of the EU rules, since this reason cannot be considered as an "overriding reasons of national interest"; otherwise, this reason could be considered as an index of the difference of the situations to be evaluated when comparing the cases.

8.2.2 The Emergence of the Overriding Reasons of General Interest as Cause of Justification with Respect to the Principles of Non-discrimination and Non-restriction: The Tax Coherence of the Internal Taxation Systems

The first overriding reason of the general interest which has been repeatedly recognized as a cause of justification such as to justify a derogation from the protection of the principles of non-discrimination or restriction is identified by the ECJ case-law in the coherence of the tax system.

Thus, the Court of Justice, ruling on a case of taxation on insurance, held that it is permissible and not objectionable the discrimination between resident enterprises and non-resident enterprises with regard to the application of a tax benefit (deduction of insurance premiums), precisely because of the need to ensure "coherence of the taxation system" (case 01/28/1992, C-204/90, *Bachmann*). Particularly, it was argued that the coherence of the tax, which is a matter for each Member State, is a decisive factor for the balance of the national public finances, as it allows to ensure compliance with the tax structure, and consequently to avoid artificial and uncontrollable leakage of tax revenue. Therefore, it is undoubtedly an "overriding reason of national interest" which deserves to be considered as a suitable value of the European Union to be evaluated in a judgment of balancing with respect to the principle of non-discrimination.

However, the ECJ, before admitting the exception to the principle of non-discrimination, evaluates the existence of alternative ways which can be adopted by the nation-State to ensure compliance with the coherence of the tax system. It may be inferred that the value of the cohesion of the tax system must be examined with reference to the specific nature of the concrete case, and it is not likely to be primarily applied in the abstract to the principle of non-discrimination. It almost seems that the ECJ, while recognizing the full worthiness of such national value in the EU legal system, intended to establish a sort of axiological ranking, giving it a secondary (or recessive) character with respect to the principle of non-discrimination.

The Court has deepened the issue of the fiscal coherence in a subsequent decision, especially to define better (and to restrict substantially) the scope of that justification. So, it was pointed out that the coherence of the tax system must show a structural and systematic character, to be considered with reference to a whole complex of taxation and not only to a single and limited case (case 08/11/1995, C-80/94, *Wielocks*).

Since the judgment *Wielocks* the ECJ has repeatedly rejected the argument of the fiscal coherence as an "overriding reason of general interest", requiring a direct and immediate link between the renunciation of the imposition and the subsequent taxation; it was so pointed out that the relationship between the deduction of the costs and the taxation of the income must cover the same objective and subjective scope, referring essentially to the same tax and to the same taxpayer (case 14.2.1995, C-279/93 *Schumacker*; case 14.11.1995, C-484/93 *Svensson*; case 16.7.1998, C-264/96, *Imperial Chemical Industries—ICI;* case 28.10.1999, C-55/98 *Vestergaard*; case 13.4.2000, C-251/98 *Baars;* case 6.6.2000, C-35/98, *Verkooijen*).

In essence it can be seen that the cause of justification due to the criterion of coherence of the national tax system does not seem to be currently an effective argument to safeguard the validity of the conflicting national provision with the EU legislation in front of the Court of Justice.

It should also be noted that the "fiscal coherence" has been identified as a value that works on two different levels of legal sources. On the one hand, the coherence has been identified as a specific requirement of the law, that is to be evaluated exclusively for the aims and functions defined by the national law (see the mentioned case *Bachmann*). On the other hand, it has been attributed a relief to the conventions against double taxation between the Member States, in which the criterion of judgment is made by the respect of the reciprocity of the rules applicable to the contracting States (and not consistent with the objectives and purposes of national law) (see the mentioned case *Wielocks*). Therefore it has been argued that the Court recognizes two dimensions of fiscal coherence, to be appreciated differently according to the regulatory framework, national or international.

8.2.3 The Jurisprudential Openings to the Principle of Territoriality

A variation of the criterion of fiscal coherence has been identified by the Court of Justice in the protection of the principle of territoriality functional to ensure the taxation in a Member State of the income produced in the territory of that Member State by a non-resident.

Particularly it was stated that "*the protection of the allocation of the taxation powers between the Member States may also require for the economic activities of companies established in one of those States only the application of the tax rules of the latter, both for profit and for losses*" (case 12/13/2005, C-446/2003 *Marks & Spencer*; case 07/18/2007, C-231/2005 *OY AA*; case 05/15/2008, C-414/2006 *Lidl*).

It thereby acknowledges that the purpose of the national regulation that brings the taxation to the country in which it is established the economic activity responds to "an objective of general interest" and as such it can determine a derogation from the principles enshrined in the Treaty and from other EU regulations (case 25.2.2010, C-337/08, *X Holding*; case 29.11.2011, C-371/10, *National Grid Indus*).

In essence, the case law attaches particular importance to the exercise of the power to tax by the Member States intended to ensure compliance with the principle of territoriality.

On the other hand, the Court of Justice has explicitly led the protection of the principle of territoriality to the area of the coherence of the taxation system, stating "*that it will be no longer guaranteed a coherent taxation if the transfer abroad would make impossible to tax on the income occurred during the residence in the State of origin*" (case 7.9.2006, C-470/2004 *N Van Dijk;* case 29.11.2011, C-371/10, *National Grid Indus*).

Therefore it must be excluded that the protection of the principle of territoriality constitutes a independent and distinct cause of justification from the coherence of the national tax system).

8.2.4 The Jurisprudential Appreciation of the Risk of International Tax Evasion or Tax Avoidance

A further profile of the national tax interest emerging in the ECJ case law as a cause of justification with respect to the derogation of the provisions of EU law, in particular as the limit of the principles of non-discrimination and non-restriction, concerns the appreciation of the risk of international tax evasion (or tax avoidance).

It should first be noted that the Court of Justice does not seem to give relief, at least in principle, to the danger of tax evasion or otherwise to the risk of revenue losses due to tax arbitrage of taxpayers as possible causes of justification with respect to the violations of fundamental EU freedoms (case 16.7.1998, causa C-264/96, *Imperial Chemical Industries*; case 09/21/1999, C-307/97 *Saint Gobain*; case 06/06/2000, C-35/98 *Verkooijen*; case 8.3.2001, C-397/98 and C-410/98, *Metallgesellshaft*; case 09/12/2006, C-196/2004 *Cadbury Schweppes*).

Indeed, the cause of justification was found by the Court of Justice in the need to prevent the tax avoidance as a topic that is to weaken the effectiveness of the tax systems of the nation-States.

In particular, most of the issues brought in front of the ECJ deals with cases of allocation of fiscal losses or tax benefits in favour of the parent company within a group of companies with offices in different Member States, in order to allow the shifting of the taxable profits from the production site to the place with lower taxes (case 12/13/2005, C-446/2003 *Marks & Spencer*; case 07/18/2007, C-231/2005 *OY AA*).

In this regard it should be noted that the Court of Justice denied that the contrast to the tax avoidance, to be intended as a special operation devoted to gain an unworthy fiscal advantage compared to the general purposes of the national taxation system, could be allowed in order to permit derogations from the EU regulations.

Indeed it is frequent the statement in the ECJ case-law that the mere use of tax advantages by taxpayers, due to the choice of certain assets in transactions, does not constitute an abusive situation, unless it does not result in the application of artificial schemes aimed at obtaining the exclusive or the main purpose of tax benefits (case 03/09/1999, C-212/97 *Centros*; case 09/30/2003, C-167/2001 *Inspire Art*; case 09/12/2006, C-196/2004 *Cadbury Schweppes*).

In other occasions the Court of Justice has excluded the eligibility of a cause of justification for the contrast of the tax avoidance on the basis of the non-recognition of a rigorous evidence about the risk of tax evasion (case 07/17/1997, C-28/95 *Leur-Bloem*) or because of the lack of proportionality of the measures of internal contrast of the tax avoidance (case 05/15/1997, C-250/95 *Futura Participation SA*; case 07/16/1998, C-264/96, *Imperial Chemical Industries—ICI*).

In essence, the EU legal system recognizes the abstract need for the protection of the national taxation system with respect to the behaviours of taxpayers related to the tax avoidance or tax evasion, but at the same time it identifies a number of limitations and restrictions on the use of this principle as a cause of justification compared to the fundamental freedoms of European law. Evidently, the ECJ warns the risk of an indiscriminate use of such reason of national interest as a possible latch to open the EU legal order in favour of protectionist and selfish purposes of the Member States, and therefore comes with circumspection to the protection from the risk of tax evasion or tax avoidance.

8.2.5 The Protection of the Effectiveness of Tax Controls and Audits

Another overriding reason of general interest—conceptually very close to the second mentioned above—has been identified by the Court of Justice in ensuring the effectiveness of the controls and the tax audits.

At first, with reference to the indirect taxation, the Court of Justice has recognized the relevance of the reasons of "safeguard of the effectiveness of fiscal supervision" as a cause of justification with respect to the EU framework (in particular case 20.2.1979, C-120/78 *Cassis de Dijon*).

Subsequently, this belief has also been reaffirmed in the area of the direct taxation, especially where the rules of national law were intended to prevent an arbitrary determination of the tax base in the tax return (case 01/28/1992, C-204/90, *Bachmann*; case 05/15/1997, C-250/95 *Futura Participation SA*; case 8.7.1999, C-254/97 *Baxter*; case 28.10.1999, C-55/98 *Vestergaard*).

In the mentioned cases the Court of Justice has recognized the legitimacy of the national legislation which introduced some control measures and monitoring requirements intended to limit a possible tax evasion, as long as it was avoided the discrimination between residents and non-residents and in any case was respected the principle of proportionality. However, just the assessment of the degree of proportionality often led the ECJ to qualify as unlawful the domestic law.

Particularly, with reference to tax accounting it has been observed that the regulation of a special accounting system for a permanent establishment, compatible with the rules of the State in which the permanent establishment itself is located, is a rule disproportionate to the purpose of ensuring effective fiscal controls, that would force the foreign company to adopt an organizational level too costly (consisting of both the accounting records required for the permanent establishment and for the ordinary activity of enterprise), such as to conflict with the needs of non-discrimination with respect to the resident companies (for which there is the only ordinary accounts) (mentioned case *Futura*).

Even the setting of absolute and even relative assumptions, where suitable to produce a discriminatory or restrictive effect about the EU fundamental freedoms, were judged inherently disproportionate (mentioned cases *Baxter* and *Vestergaard*).

It should also be noted that, while being recognized the general right of the Member States to proceed with the adjustment of the tax obligations according to the specific requirements of the national law and especially with the purposes of simplicity, rationality and effectiveness of the tax levy, the ECJ has repeatedly held that the mere need of the public administration can never justify the derogation from the basic principles of EU law (case 26.1.1999, C-18/95 *Terhoeve*; case 16.5.2000, C-87/99 *Zurstrassen*).

8.3 The Balancing of the Court of Justice Between the EU Interest and the National Interest

8.3.1 The Use of the Principle of Reasonableness in the EU Jurisprudence as a Balancing Formula with Respect to the Principle of Tax Non-discrimination

The declination of the principles of non-discrimination and non-restriction by the Court of Justice makes clear the recourse to mechanisms of conciliation and balance between the conflicting interests: in particular, the verification of the comparability of regulatory situations, in order to identify the scope of the principle of non-discrimination, requires an assessment of the taxation of residents and non-residents; above all, the definition of the derogation function of the national tax interest, in its various forms, inevitably leads to the search for the balancing with the principle of non-discrimination.

It emerges also in the ECJ jurisprudence (in line with what is typically done in the constitutional jurisprudence of the nation-States) a dialectical tension between the values of equivalent axiological level belonging to the same legal order.

Moreover, in a complex regulatory system, in which the fundamental values of European integration are constantly subjected to the verification of functionality about the basic needs of subsistence and self-regulation of the Member States, it is inevitable that there are axiological contrasts. The EU integration aspirations clash with the selfish positions of the nation-States; the enhancement of freedom of European law collides with the protectionist intent of national markets and domestic enterprises; especially the opening towards a fully competitive structure may well conflict with the need to preserve the efficiency of the national public finance system.

Thus the fundamental values of the European system may not be taken in their uniqueness, unrelated in comparison with the values formulated in the Constitutions of the individual States—while also relevant from an European perspective—as if these values, taken in the purity of the original regulatory concept, do not allow the coexistence with other values. On the contrary, the pursuit of a mediation legislation and the balancing of conflicting values indicate the acceptance of "open" solutions, which may be calibrated differently also because of the peculiarities of historical contingency and politics.

For the definition of the axiological antinomies produced by the implementation of the principle of tax non-discrimination, the Court of Justice shows a preference for combined solutions centred around criteria of composition and mediation rules articulated according to the preferred model of the principle of reasonableness.

In this regard it may be noted how in the ECJ jurisprudence it is entirely infrequent the recourse to the usual logic diagrams of the principle of equality, that is to say the "ternary" method of the judgment of inequality (known as founded on the verification of the *tertium comparationis*); otherwise, it is preferred to make use of the "binary" method, typical of the control of reason, through which the Court verifies the conformity of the national standard syndicated with the ratio of the European regulations. Thus, from time to time, the control of reasonableness regards the functional connections or the compatibility of the legal aims with respect to the system of EU values. The topic of the disparity degrades from the level of an assumption of the logical reasoning to the level of rhetorical argument (such an element having a purely argumentative valence).

It produces, however, a markedly "realist" attitude of the Court, which identifies the regulatory solution in relation to the specific elements of the case and to the peculiar features of the national tax regulation which is assumed to be incompatible with EU law.

As a further corollary, the argumentative strategies employed by the ECJ to support the balancing of conflicting interests are not easily traced back to be classified according to constants and stabilized models of judgment. This seems to induce a fractional and somewhat distracting reconstruction of the ECJ jurisprudence on the point, to the detriment of a legal framework characterized by the juridical certainty.

8.3.2 The Recourse to the Principle of Proportionality as a Mechanism for the Mediation of the Possible Axiological Conflicts

After the verification of the existence of an axiological conflict between the European regulation and the national regulation, inspired and justifiable because of an "overriding reasons of general interest", the Court is called upon to assess the degree of compression of the EU rule according to the parameter expressed by the judgment of proportionality.

Basically the Court of Justice is required to use a criterion for evaluating the suitability of the substantial scope assigned by the national legislature to the tax regulation under an objective and systematic perspective.

In particular, the judgment of proportionality operated by the Court follows a twofold policy: at first, it seeks to verify the suitability of the national norms to the pursued purpose of the legal system; at second, the control is aimed at verifying the necessity of the national provisions and therefore at the evaluation of other alternative regulations that may produce a minor sacrifice of the EU values.

It is precisely on this line of reasoning that is increasingly operating the balance between the national values and the EU values in the judicial appreciation.

Sometimes the tax provisions adopted in the law of a Member State are considered to be non-proportional, and therefore excessively invasive of the EU values, as they can be replaced with other measures involving a minor sacrifice of European law (case 7.9.2006, C-470/2004 *N Van Dijk*).

On other occasions the Court of Justice has adopted intermediate solutions, recognizing the lawfulness of national provisions derogating from the European principles and, at the same time, the respect of a particular principle of law as a condition of eligibility for the cause of justification (case 12/13/2005, C-446/2003 *Marks & Spencer*; case 05/15/2008, C-414/2006 *Lidl*).

Finally, in some decisions the Court has recognized that the tax provisions adopted by a Member State do not produce some regulations overly invasive than the EU values, because they seem appropriate and proportionate to the pursued legal aim (case 07/18/2007, C-231/2005 *OY AA*; case 07/12/2005, C-403/2003, *Egon Schempp*; case 02/28/2008, C-293/2006 *Deutsche Shell*).

It must observe, however, that the judgment of proportionality constitutes inevitably an evanescent parameter for the teleological measuring of the national provisions, since the application of this judgment is entrusted to a probabilistic quantitative evaluations and to the analysis of the prognostic character on purposes of the law, which reflect the significant risk of a large degree of subjective appreciation and, consequently, of indeterminacy.

8.3.3 Some Considerations About the Balancing of the National Tax Interest and the Individual Rights in the Jurisprudence of the European Court of Human Rights

Some interesting considerations regarding the balance between the conflicting values of the tax interest and the protection of individual rights can be drawn from the case law of the European Court of Human Rights (ECHR), where some profiles of the axiological relationship are defined in order to lead to a reconstruction of the plot of articulated values applicable internationally.

Indeed, in the European Convention for the Protection of Human Rights it has established a guarantee of protection of personal assets with respect to the discriminatory and unreasonable power to tax, which can infringe the essential liberty to the enjoyment of its wealth (see art. 1 of the First additional Protocol).

At first, the Court has punctuated the suitability of the tax interest of the nation-State to prevail over the rules protecting the wealth of the individual, positioning as a preeminent axiological rule, provided that it complies with certain guarantees of formal order, and in particular with the application of the law (case *Sro Spacek vs Czech Republic*). Indeed, the Court expressly stated that the right of nation-State to impose regulations which seem necessary to secure the payment of taxes is subtracted typically to the scope of the principle on the protection of the individual wealth (cases *Gasus Dossier and Fordertechnik Gmbh*).

Moreover, this rigorous position is partially mitigated by the consideration that the taxation must still be implemented through the non-discriminatory rules: while recognizing the primacy of the national tax interest, the Court stated that the tax rules must comply with two conditions: i) the existence of a "legitimate aim" and ii) a reasonable relationship of proportionality between the tax provisions and the normative *ratio* (cases *Darby* and *Van Raalte*). Particularly, considering the legitimate aim, the Court has syndicated the taxation rules adopted by a State, as directed to facilitate the mere perception of taxes and not to intervene substantially on the structure of the tax system; therefore the Court drew a balance of values in a recessive manner considering purely the interest of the public administration (and not the interest of the "State-community") compared to the primary values of the axiological plot as defined in the Convention for the Protection of Human Rights.

In contrast, the prevalence of the interest of the "State-community" with regard to the values of the defensive sphere of individual ownership is confirmed by the jurisprudence that recognizes the legitimacy of retroactive tax rules, as designed to avoid, or at least to contain, the tax avoidance: in the balance between the protection of the individual values and the basic needs of the national community the Court attaches a prominent character to the latter because of the fundamental importance of the reasons for economic solidarity among the members of a community (cases *Koln, National & Provincial, Leeds and Yorkshire building permanent vs. United Kingdom*).

Unlike what was seen in the EU legal system, the international agreement discipline, due to the European Convention for the Protection of Human Rights, seems to confirm the dynamics of the relationship between individual values and collective values present in national Constitutions: the tax interest is expressly recognized as an autonomous axiological macrostructure, suitable for interrelating with instances of the defensive sphere of the individual wealth; in respect of the judicial balancing it emerges the primacy of the tax interest of the State-community, and instead, the recessive and secondary grade of the interest of the fiscal public administration; in any case the balance of the conflicting values is attributed to an area of discretionary assessment of the national legislature, though not exuberant than the limits of the principles of reasonableness and proportionality.

The Tax Harmonization

9

Contents

9.1 Tax Harmonization in the European Legal System 137
  9.1.1 The Notion of Tax Harmonization 137
  9.1.2 The Implementation of Regulatory Instruments in the European Harmonization 139
9.2 The EU Harmonization of Indirect Taxes 139
  9.2.1 The General Rules of the Harmonization of the Indirect Taxes 139
  9.2.2 The Harmonization of VAT 140
  9.2.3 The Harmonization of Excise Duties 142
  9.2.4 The Harmonization of Customs Duties 144
9.3 The Harmonization of Direct Taxes 145
  9.3.1 The General Rules of the Harmonization of Direct Taxes 145
  9.3.2 The Policy of the Harmonization of Direct Taxes Followed by the European Union 146
9.4 The Regulatory Framework of the Principle of Tax Harmonization Within the EU ... 148
  9.4.1 The Determination of Taxation Models as a Qualifying Result of the Process of Tax Harmonization 148
  9.4.2 The Recessive Nature of the Principle of Harmonization in the EU Legal System 149

9.1 Tax Harmonization in the European Legal System

9.1.1 The Notion of Tax Harmonization

A primary principle of EU taxation system is represented by the harmonization of taxes which is explicitly stated in the art. 113 TFEU (formerly art. 93 of the Treaty of Maastricht and art. 99 of the Treaty of Rome). In this rule it is defined the aim of the harmonization of the laws of the Member States in function to the turnover tax, the consumption tax and other indirect taxation to the extent that harmonization is necessary to ensure the establishment and functioning of the common market.

This rule is clearly intended to achieve a homogenous regulatory framework in the European Union which tends to harmonize the tax systems of the various

P. Boria, *Taxation in European Union*, DOI 10.1007/978-3-319-53919-5_9

Member States, reducing the specific aspects of each national system to some details or, at least, to marginal elements which do not affect the structure and the function of the taxes, so as to identify a methodological criterion for the European integration.

The tax harmonization is a process by which some States by mutual agreement or the EU institutions define the legal framework of a certain taxation through the adaptation of the essential structure of the tribute "according to a single model" (in line with the classic definition given by the doctrine).

Evidently the notion of tax harmonization is to be found in the following topics:

- the definition of an unitary taxation model
- the reduction of the diversity of each national law with respect to the unitary model.

The legal model imposed at an European level does not imply a real unification of the national tax laws, but requires the adoption of a legislative point of reference around which to implement the convergence of the domestic law of the various Member States.

The reduction of the diversity in the discipline regulations of the Member States is the logical counterpart of the adoption of a unitary tax, as it is to express the degree of compliance of national legislation with respect to the legal basis chosen as European parameter.

The tax harmonization can be achieved with reference to the qualifying structure of a tribute or to the individual segments of the discipline by the legal systems of taxation.

Just with regard to this distinction has been proposed repeatedly in the literature the distinction between "harmonization" and "approximation" of tax systems (also on the basis of textual indications given in the rules of the Treaty), assuming that the two legal institutions are aimed at pursuing a different goal: the harmonization would be finalised to reach the uniformity of national laws through the elimination of specific diverging provisions; the approximation would pursue a homogenous regulatory European framework through the revising of national tax legislations with respect to the structure of taxes.

In any case, it seems that this distinction cannot be indicative of an axiological difference between the two institutions, so as to draw a clear line of distinction between them, appearing on the contrary more correct to assume that both the harmonization and the approximation constitute (possibly) different modalities to achieve the same goal of the convergence of the national tax systems towards a single model defined at a European level.

9.1.2 The Implementation of Regulatory Instruments in the European Harmonization

The tax harmonization of the national taxes, while finding an explicit reference in the Treaty (mentioned in art. 113), is typically performed through normative acts attributable to the EU law, and therefore, by means of Regulations, Directives and acts of the soft law.

It should be noted in this regard that the act preferentially adopted for the harmonization of the national taxes is certainly represented by the Directive, such an act designed to establish the general principles and the basic structure of the tax and, at the same time, to leave the national law allowed to define the specific rules of the detailed implementation.

The rulemaking procedure to be adopted for fiscal harmonization (particularly in the area of indirect taxation) is specifically regulated in the Treaty; expressly it is provided for the use of the method of the prior consultation of the Parliament, which is mandatory but not binding on the Council. Evidently, in the belief of the European legislature, the tax harmonization is a very important phase of the integration process that calls into question some main characters of national sovereignty and therefore may not be entrusted solely to the judgment of an executive and intergovernmental branch, impregnated by assessments often connoted by only economic opportunities, but it has to go through the parliamentary debate, even if only on a consultative basis, which undoubtedly has the capability to operate the balancing of the involved legal values.

Moreover, it should be noted that under a procedural standpoint the scope of the principle of harmonization, as envisaged by the EU Treaty, appears unsatisfactory overall, because it does not include the adoption of the principle of qualified majority being on the contrary required the unanimity in the decision of the Council. The Commission, in the White Paper on completing the internal market, found that the harmonization of indirect taxes, which is considered essential for the completion of the process of European economic and trade integration, must be accelerated properly under the procedural point of view, since the principle of unanimity constitutes an often insurmountable obstacle for the effective implementation of the same principle.

9.2 The EU Harmonization of Indirect Taxes

9.2.1 The General Rules of the Harmonization of the Indirect Taxes

The principle of tax harmonization, as mentioned earlier, is explicitly established in the art. 113 TFEU with specific regard to the area of indirect taxation (and thus, in particular, relating to value added tax, excise duties and import duties).

The harmonization of indirect taxes is qualified as a primary value of the European unification process, since it is likely to have a decisive influence on the functioning of the internal market (in this sense it can be assumed the prescription of art. 26 TFEU).

It is clear, in fact, how a disparity of taxes on commercial transactions and affairs between the different Member States should be to affect a regulatory framework where the economic sensitivity is most acute and, therefore, could easily lead to harmful tax competition, capable to generate competitive mechanisms driven so as to accentuate the centrifugal tendencies within the European community.

Consequently the attention of European legal order has been focused primarily on the area of indirect taxation, with specific reference to turnover taxes, excise duties and excise duties, given the suitability of these forms of taxation to change the price of a good or service to the consumer, thus altering the competitive neutrality of the market.

The harmonization of the various taxes has been made in different periods of time and in a heterogeneous manner, making essentially impossible to formulate a unitary reasoning on the process of harmonization of indirect taxation. Otherwise, it seems preferable to conduct a fractional analysis about the tax harmonization, broken down by the different sectors of taxation, on the basis of the principles laid down in the EU legal system.

9.2.2 The Harmonization of VAT

One of the primary aims of the program for the realization of the common market, as laid down in the Treaty of Rome establishing the European Economic Community, was definitely identified in the harmonization of the tax laws of the Member States with regard to taxation on the amount of business. Evidently, the reduction of fiscal imbalances on the price of goods and services that were circulating within the European common market was regarded as one of the main factors for the freedom of competition between economic operators in the European Union.

A common model of tax on turnover was determined by reference to the *Taxe sur valeur adjoteè* (TVA) applied in France and was elevated to the benchmark for a unified regulatory indirect taxation on consumptions in each Member State (Directive of 04/11/1967 n. 67/227).

In particular, it was established the principle that each Member State should apply "*to the goods and services a general tax on consumption exactly proportional to their price, whatever the number of transactions take place in the production and in the distribution process before the stage of taxation*" (art. 1 par. 1 of Directive no. 67/227).

The process of EU harmonization of VAT was then continued through a series of subsequent regulatory actions by the governing bodies of the European Union and can be ideally divided into three periods:

a) the first period since the establishment of the Economic Community up to 1992;

b) the second period that begins with the abolition of fiscal frontiers and coincides with the transitional arrangements for the taxation of trade between the Member States;
c) the third period in which the definitive system of intra Community trade entered into force.

During the first period, a decisive contribution to the harmonization of the laws of value added in the Member States has been done through the enactment of the Sixth Directive of 05/17/1977, which provides a detailed guidance on the formation of a uniform tax base. Subsequently other Directives have been formulated that have clarified the scope of the tax (among which it may be mentioned the Eighth Directive of 12/06/1979 no. 79/1072/EEC and the Thirteenth Directive of 11/17/1986 no. 86/560/EEC).

The second period of harmonization is characterized by the abolition of fiscal frontiers, as a stage of completion of the European Common Market, and involves for VAT purposes the intervention on the rates and on the tax base in order to establish uniform rules in the Member States and to facilitate the intra Community trade (Directive n. 92/77/EEC and then Directive. 95/7/EC). It is further confirmed the validity of the so-called "VAT transitory regime", which provides for a taxation in the State of destination of economic transactions and trade, as this discipline was considered easier to run than the so-called definitive scheme (which instead provides for a taxation in the State of origin).

In this period some secondary (or non-structural) profiles of the value added tax discipline are also regulated. Some EU acts have been enacted in order to regulate the special disciplines applicable to certain economic sector (Directive n. 94/5/EC which governs the application of the tax for used goods and antiques; Directive of 05/07/2002 no. 2002/38 on the subject of e-commerce and electronic services rendered by remote). On a procedural level some EU regulations were finalised in order to regulate innovative forms of fulfilment of the instrumental obligations (Directive of 12/20/2001 n. 2001/115 concerning the simplification of the emission, transmission and storage of invoices). Furthermore, in order to foster fiscal supervision and cooperation between administrations of different Member States it was adopted the Regulation 01/27/1992 n. 218/92 which provided for the establishment of a common system for the exchange of information by electronic means in relation to intra Community transactions.

It is also noted that the EU legislature has felt the need to reorganize the whole matter by adopting the Directive of 11/28/2006 no. 2006/112/EC (in force since 01/01/2007), which assumes great importance as it replaces some 33 previous Directives, becoming today the reference text on value added tax in the European framework.

The last phase of regulatory changes in VAT will progress since the adoption of the definitive system through the criterion for the taxation of intra Community trade in the State of origin. At this purpose, it seems inevitable to undertake an overall rethinking of the mechanisms of implementation of the tax, with particular regard to the discipline of transactions between residents of different Member States, being difficult to operate specifically on the texts of existing legislation.

And in fact, one of the aspects of greatest sensitivity of the VAT regulation concerns the trade between persons resident in different Member States, since it poses the problem of identifying the place where to tax the transaction. As already observed, at the present stage in which the definitive system for the application of VAT in the country of origin has not yet entered into force on, it must apply the criterion of taxation in the State of destination. Therefore, until it will not be reached a sufficient degree of alignment of national legislation to the definitive system, the intra Community trade is governed according to that transition period in which the taxation is referred to the country where it is verified the final consumption.

The main aims of the VAT harmonization have been substantially pursued as the national regulations show a strong convergence at least for the structural elements of the value added tax. There are still differences related to tax rates and other elements of the discipline of the tribute that create diversity of application in the various States, but still do not seem to compromise the unitary model of reference.

In particular, the main characteristic of value added tax—which is detectable in each Member State—certainly could arise in the performance of tax neutrality with respect to the various stages of production or distribution, since the taxation was intended to be charged only to the final consumer and regardless of the number of transactions and of the circulation of the goods or services in the relations between economic agents (namely between entrepreneurs or professionals).

In this respect it may be noted a full compliance of the VAT harmonization with respect to the general principles of EU law. Indeed, the neutrality of VAT is one of the most significant applications of the principle of fiscal neutrality as a fundamental value for the establishment of a common market: the taxation, as a factor likely to produce distortion with respect to the natural ability to function of the market, is considered as an interference regarding the organization of the optimal competition between economic agents and thus an element to be attenuated and limited by law.

9.2.3 The Harmonization of Excise Duties

The excise duties are taxes on the production or manufacture or consumption of the products in the territory of a Member State. Therefore, like the value added tax, these taxes are able to affect significantly the circulation of goods and services in the European market and, thus, appear as factors that might alter the free unfolding of the competitive mechanism. It seems natural that such taxes have been the subject of a number of EU measures aimed at achieving a process of harmonization of the different national rules.

The aim pursued by the EU evidently consists in finding a tax structure common to all Member States so as to achieve a tax coordination in the European area, in order to avoid forms of harmful competition between countries (through the application of different rates on the same types of products) and, furthermore, to cope with the impossibility of customs controls for trade within the European market, while safeguarding the national fiscal sovereignty.

The current general rules about the excise duties have been established in the Directive of 02/25/1992 n. 92/12/EEC which defined the general framework of the discipline of excise duties in order to standardize the rates and methods of application, and at the same time to decree the repeal of the excise and consumption patterns existing in national legislations and incompatible with the EU discipline.

It should also be noted that the harmonization involves a limited number of excise duties, namely:

- the excise tax on mineral oils and related products (Directive n. 92/81/EEC and n. 92/82/EEC);
- the excise tax on alcohol and alcoholic beverages (Directive n. 92/83/EEC and n. 92/84/EEC);
- the excise tax on tobacco products (Directive n. 95/59/EEC, n. 92/79/EEC, n. 92/80/EEC, modified by the Directive n. 2010/12/EU);
- the consumption tax on electricity (Directive n. 2003/96/CEE);
- the excise tax on natural gas (Directive n. 2003/96/CEE).

The harmonization concerns in particular some general features of the tribute discipline: the identification of the tax assumption, the taxpayers, the methods of applying the tax, the rules for the movement of the goods subject to the excise duties, the checks audits and investigations.

However, it remains a significant difference in the laws in force in the various nation-States with regard to the determination of the tax base, the fixing of rates and the identification of alternative schemes. In essence in the face of a single model, which acts as a regulatory parameter of the structure of the taxation, is accorded a wide discretion to the States for the definition of the concrete and specific level of taxation. Consequently, it is still possible to produce some tax asymmetries in the treatment of the transactions subject to the excise duties that can generate some distortions to the EU objective of free competition.

It must be observed that there are many existing excise duties in the Member States which have not been subjected to any process of harmonization and which are currently covered in a totally dissimilar and unique way in each national legislation.

At this purpose, the Directive n. 92/12/EEC allows the Member States to introduce other forms of indirect taxation to the same goods subject to excise tax. It is then admitted the possibility of establishing non-harmonized taxes, which respond only to the fiscal or extra-fiscal needs of the national order (unless they give rise to formalities connected with the custom procedures of the goods at borders).

Thus, the process of harmonization of excise duties, despite having made significant advances, is far from reaching at the final stage, having to be considered as a relevant cause of distortion of competition within the common market and even as a generator of protectionist practices by the Member States.

9.2.4 The Harmonization of Customs Duties

The matter of customs duties has been subject to a process of harmonization within the EU system that has produced a regulatory framework basically stabilized in the national legislation of the Member States.

Indeed the removal of customs borders to allow the free movement of goods and services within the European area constitutes a fundamental rule for the establishment of the common market, which finds also an explicit recognition in the Treaty (where the banning of customs duties or charges having an equivalent effect on goods entering and leaving the State is listed as the first among the key actions of the European Union which should preferably be pursued for the attainment of the European integration).

The harmonization of customs duties has been achieved with a series of regulatory measures and in particular:

European Customs Code, established by EEC Regulation of 10/12/1992 n. 2913, which defines the assumption, the taxpayers, the methods of determining the customs debt (quantity, quality and classification, price and value of the goods) and the specific customs regimes;

Implementing Provisions of the European Customs Code, arranged with the EEC Regulation n. 2.7.1993. 2454 (consisting of 915 articles and 113 attachments, lists and forms);

Common Customs Tariff, set out in Regulation EEC of 07/23/1987 n. 2658.

The unitary discipline provided by the European Union states that customs duties are imposed on goods coming from outside the EU and intended for consumption in the territory of the European Union (which constitutes the customs territory). Taxes are paid, levied and assessed by the customs offices of the Member States, but they are destined to flow into the EU budget as a typical source of income belonging to the latter.

The determination of the tax liability is realized through a single customs tariff that applies to all goods coming from countries outside the European Union; this is a policy that realizes the "customs union", which constitutes a further step than the abatement of the customs borders, capable to indicate a higher level of integration of the Member States in the trade relations with Extra EU countries.

By virtue of the process of harmonization, the customs barriers currently exist only at the borders with countries outside the European Union (and in any case in ports and airports) in order to allow the application of customs duties on goods coming from outside the European territories. Once crossed the borders with the European Union, the goods can move within the European market without any additional tax burden (and thus they are "cleared").

9.3 The Harmonization of Direct Taxes

9.3.1 The General Rules of the Harmonization of Direct Taxes

The harmonization of direct taxes is not subject to specific regulation in the European Treaties. The process of harmonization of the tax on income, involving relevant aspects of the fiscal sovereignty of the Member States, is not regulated expressly by the European norms.

Indeed, the loss of a decision-making authority on relevant portions of the taxable national basis in favour of arrangements defined by the EU and the consequent weakening compared to the choices of economic policy, is an event that is considered not readily absorbed by the Governments of the Member States. So, the harmonization of direct taxes represents one of the most consistent issues of the process of European integration of national tax systems.

At this purpose, it is significant that in the Treaty of Lisbon it is abandoned the rule, previously stated by the art. 293 of the Treaty of Maastricht (former art. 220 of the Treaty of Rome) that required negotiations between the Member States aimed at ensuring the abolition of double taxation within the European Union. It substantially means that it must be excluded the recourse to dense network of bilateral (or multilateral) agreements between the various Member States in order to solve the problem of the taxation of income generated in the international transactions within the European Union. The general aim of the harmonization of direct taxes and the specific aim to avoid double taxation within the European market is a task to be charged to EU bodies and institutions.

It is applicable to the harmonization of direct taxes, the general rule laid down by the art. 115 TFEU (former art. 94 Treaty of Maastricht and art. 100 Treaty of Rome), by virtue of which the Council, with an unanimous decision and with the previous consultation with the Parliament and the Economic and Social Committee, can establish some Directives for the approximation of the national legislations to the extent to develop the process of integration of the common market.

This rule has been interpreted as the axiological foundation of the use of recommendations and of soft law mechanisms addressed to Member States by EU bodies concerning the progressive approximation of the national provisions relating to the taxation of income (and especially to the taxation of business and savings). This *soft law* produces, evidently, a level of approximation of national legislation with a lower grade than the harmonization of indirect taxes (for which it was formulated the figurative definition of "elastic convergence").

It should also be noted that the need to start the harmonization of tax legislations, especially with regard to direct taxation, must be coordinated with the fundamental principle of subsidiarity; therefore the tax harmonization is to be regulated by European bodies with regard to transactions or operations carried out in the European territories which may actually affect the functioning of the common market; otherwise there is an exclusive competence of the individual Member States for the regulation of the taxation at an essentially domestic level.

The harmonization constitutes a mechanism to search for a uniform model only for the taxes common to the Member States, with the consequent inapplicability to special or atypical taxes of each State (if not solved in measures having an effect equivalent to the common tax). Similarly, because of the general protection of the European market, it was excluded the applicability of the principle to local taxes, which are territorially confined to a restricted community and thus appear overall to be unsuitable to affect the general freedom of movement protected by the EU law.

9.3.2 The Policy of the Harmonization of Direct Taxes Followed by the European Union

Since the Sixties many study groups organized by the EU institutions have examined the direct taxation as a possible subject of a program of tax harmonization.

In the Neumark Report of 1962, despite being excluded an opportunity to unify the structure of the tax systems of the Member States, it was called for the harmonization of direct taxation mainly in order to avoid possible forms of double taxation. In particular, it was proposed the hypothesis of a harmonized tax on companies and it was prefigured the approximation of the laws in relation to the taxation of the income of natural persons.

Later in the Memorandum on the harmonization of direct taxes in 1965 and 1966 with the Report Segre it was underlined the need to arrive at an approximation of the structure of direct taxation in the Member States in order to eliminate the differences in the treatment between residents and non-residents and to exclude forms of double taxation so as to achieve a real European capital market.

In 1970, with the Werner Plan, the harmonization of direct taxes was seen as a necessary step for the effective realization of economic and monetary union; thus were formulated a number of purposes related to the approximation of systems of direct taxation in the various national laws, which appeared fully consistent with the logic of a federal finance.

The intentions expressed in the various study groups did not produce concrete results and indeed were repeatedly disregarded in the EU regulations. So for a long time the subject of harmonization of direct taxes was largely set aside by the EU development policies.

At the end of the eighties the theme is taken up in the debate on the establishment of a monetary union: so with the Delors Report in 1989 the approximation (or at least the coordination) of direct tax systems of the Member States is regarded as a crucial step in the process of European integration.

So in 1990 the first two directives are issued on the subject of direct taxation (namely the Directive n. 90/434 concerning the operations of corporate organization and Directive n. 90/435 relating to the treatment of dividends between parent and subsidiary companies) and it was approved a multilateral Convention between the Member States (Convention n. 90/436 on the arbitration procedure for the elimination of double taxation).

Just a short time later, in 1992 the Ruding Committee, appointed by the Commission to identify the major distortions of tax with respect to the functioning of the common market, identifies the minimal aims of a program of the harmonization of direct taxes in the establishment of an uniform tax base, in the prediction of a range of tax rates to be applied on the profits of the enterprise and in the transparency of the incentives of a fiscal nature granted for investments made by businesses throughout the country.

The EU institutions also show considerable reservations about the implementation of the harmonization agenda outlined by the Ruding Committee, judging inopportune an interference about the political needs of individual States and considering the degree of maturity of European integration.

So the new regulatory initiatives in the field of direct taxation took at long time (13 years) after the Directives mentioned above. In 2003 there were issued two Directives concerning the fiscal discipline of the intra Community capital investment (namely the Directive n. 2003/48 on the taxation of interest paid to non-resident individuals and Directive n. 2003/49 concerning the taxation of interest and royalties paid between companies belonging to the same group and resident in different Member States).

Currently there is not any implementation of the proposals for Directives made at the time about other profiles of the harmonization of direct taxation (for example in terms of withholding taxes on dividends, coordination between corporate taxation and taxation of dividends, approximation of the tax rates and of the tax base, determination of business income, treatment of the fiscal losses, taxation of labour income earned by workers circulating in the European Union).

On a closer inspection it can be seen that the direct tax harmonization measures taken by the EU institutions typically involve the area of income flows generated in a cross-border dimension, covering a number of Member States (or at least between two of them). Legislative acts concerning the approximation of the direct taxation of income flows which remain within the single territory of a Member State, have not had a positive outcome (and thus remained at the stage of mere proposals formulas without becoming mandatory regulations).

It may therefore draw the conclusion that the harmonization of direct taxes currently employs a marginal degree, as typically intended to regulate certain income profiles of intra-Community nature and thus appearing to be unfit to regulate important aspects of the overall structure of direct taxation in the national laws. Clearly, the resistance of the nation-States to transfer the fiscal sovereignty on direct taxation in favour of the European Union represents a determinant brake towards the implementation of the policies of the European tax harmonization.

9.4 The Regulatory Framework of the Principle of Tax Harmonization Within the EU

9.4.1 The Determination of Taxation Models as a Qualifying Result of the Process of Tax Harmonization

The qualifying features of tax harmonization are to be found in the definition of an unitary model of taxation and in the reducing diversity of each national legislation with respect to the unitary model.

Therefore the principle of harmonization produces a configuration of the tax disciplines of the Member States that would be compatible with respect to the unitary and integrated taxation models defined at an European level.

It can be argued that the specific and qualifying effect of the process for tax harmonization achieved at an European level is the determination of a common tax model that operates as a benchmark for the taxation of economic activities in the European territory.

The model of taxation may assume different contents:

- it can be identified in the regulation of the integral prototype of a European tribute, whose essential legal structure is defined directly by the EU sources and becomes binding for the Member States;
- or it may consist in the determination of principles and general rules of the tax regulation, which are intended to outline the legal framework governing the national tribute.

The first type of tax model is essentially traceable to the more complex and advanced forms of tax harmonization, which cover the entire discipline of a tribute and are in any case aimed at defining the key elements of the tax structure (assumption, taxpayers, taxable base, tax rate). This model is typically found in the area of indirect taxation (as noted in the previous paragraphs): therefore, often in the literature the value added tax, the customs duties, and (sometimes) the excise duties are qualified as European tributes, with the aim to indicate that the definition of the tax is basically made through a legislation attributable to the EU institutions.

The second category of tax model can be ascribed to forms of sectorial harmonization, which are limited to segments of the discipline of a tribute and not aimed at defining the basic structure of the tax or fundamental aspects of the structure of taxation. This model of taxation can be observed especially in the area of direct taxation, where the European harmonization covers limited aspects of the fiscal discipline.

9.4.2 The Recessive Nature of the Principle of Harmonization in the EU Legal System

In the perspective mentioned above, the principle of harmonization is presented as a guiding principle with a "positive" content that is intended to establish a rule of gradual integration of the national tax systems and not a mere delimitation and foreclosure. Indeed the establishment of a common and unified model of taxation and the reduction of differences between the national laws are to be considered as factors of aggregation and homologation of the national legal systems with respect to the power of taxation.

In particular, the principle of harmonization provides for substantial indications in relation to the development of the national tax systems: the need to promote a co-ordination of the fiscal policies of the nation-States in order to overcome particularism and selfishness that have traditionally denoted the evolution of the legal systems of the States does not only respond to the aim of achieving faster the European integration, but it also seems to correlate with the purpose of encouraging the establishment of programs for the taxation of mobile factors of production more in line with the outlook marked by the globalization.

It can so be argued that the principle of harmonization arises in a logic of countertrend with respect to the principle of non-discrimination and to other general principles of EU law relevant to tax matters which are oriented (as observed in the previous chapters) to neutralize the potentially distortionary scope of the national taxation. In other words, the principle of harmonization expresses a "positive taxation", namely where the tax power exercised by the Member States shall be directed to unitary models and to purposes generally agreed and compatible with European aims, unlike the principle of non-discrimination and other general values that indicate instead a "negative taxation".

However, even the tax harmonization shows the common ideological background of the other general principles applicable to tax matters, detectable in the acceptance of the values of freedom and economic development of the common market acknowledged as the primary interest of the European Union. This is consistent with the clear propensity taken by the EU to identify safeguards and guarantees for a competitive structure of the market in the belief that trade and economic integration constitutes the main engine of a political and social integration.

Moreover it appears very significant on a symbolic level that the principle of harmonization plays a very recessive role, in comparison with the principle of non-discrimination and with other general values of EU law, showing itself as a value of less binding form and sometimes with a mere programmatic purpose.

First of all, this value may not be implemented directly by the legal interpretation, as it requires the necessary mediation of a legal act of derivate legislation. Unlike the other European principle (tax non-discrimination, prohibition of restrictions on EU freedoms, opening of customs barriers, prohibition of State aid) the tax harmonization may not be directly applied by the Member States and by the EU institutions, nor may find a direct application in the case law. It necessarily requires the definition of a model imposed in a legislative instrument

(Directive or Regulation) that expresses the options accepted in the specific discipline of a harmonized tax.

Therefore, the value of harmonization does not necessarily apply as the other values laid down in the Treaty, but it requires the formation of a political consensus in the EU institutions relevant to the enactment of the legislation rules. This means that, for the practical implementation of this value, it is required the principle of unanimity in order to ensure the acknowledgment of the fiscal sovereignty of each Member State.

It should also be noted that the tax harmonization has not a general character, as it can be traced primarily to a narrow legal context, identified with the area of indirect taxation; in fact it does not apply (having only a marginal relevance) to the most important sector of direct taxation.

In this perspective, the recessive tendency of the principle of tax harmonization and the primacy of the principle of non-discrimination (and other principles) are to confirm at the European level the existence of a "negative taxation", which is lacking of a positive connotation of the tax power, consistent with the ideological postulates assumed in the economical constitution of the European Union.

The State Aids

10

Contents

10.1 The General Framework Regarding the State Aids 151
10.1.1 The Prohibition of the State Aids as a Measure to Promote the Free Competition in the Common Market 151
10.1.2 Procedural Nature and Degree of Competence of the EU Guidelines on the State Aids 152
10.1.3 The Character of the State Aids Prohibited Under the EU Law 153
10.1.4 The Procedure for the Judgment on the EU Compatibility of the State Aids 154
10.1.5 A Progressive Perspective Regarding the Exceptions to the Prohibition of the State Aids 155
10.1.6 The Preventive Regulation for the Exceptions to the Prohibition of State Aids 158
10.1.7 The Eligibility of de minimis Aids 158
10.2 The Tax Relief as a Possible State Aid 159
10.2.1 The Qualification of Tax Relief as a State Aid 159
10.2.2 The Eligibility of Tax Incentives at a Regional or Local Level 160
10.2.3 The Urban Free Zones 162
10.3 The Recovery of the State Aids 162

10.1 The General Framework Regarding the State Aids

10.1.1 The Prohibition of the State Aids as a Measure to Promote the Free Competition in the Common Market

One of the issues with respect to which is more important the problem of resolving conflicts between national law and EU law is the provision of financial differentiated treatments arranged and facilitated by a Member State in favour of certain categories of domestic enterprises or economic activities.

The establishment of a common market presupposes the establishment and the operation of a unified economic space in which the exchange of products and services, and in general the commercial transactions can take place under the same conditions as those applying in the domestic market. Therefore it is necessary

P. Boria, *Taxation in European Union*, DOI 10.1007/978-3-319-53919-5_10

not only that barriers and obstacles to the free movement of goods and services are removed, but also that the competition between enterprises resident in the European territory is not distorted by the financial measures taken by the Member State that produce an economic benefit confined to a narrow audience of national subjects.

Therefore, it must reconcile the two requirements to avoid that the national legislation more favourable may collide with the EU freedoms on which the common European market is founded and to allow, at the same time, that Member States maintain their margins of autonomy in decision-making regard to the choices about economic policy and internal tax. The point of balance between the conflicting interests (EU aims and national demands) can be essentially identified through the distinction between permitted measures and prohibited measures.

In this context the provision of the art. 107 TFEU (formerly art. 87 Treaty of Maastricht and art. 92 Treaty of Rome) prohibits the granting of the State aids which, by favouring certain economic activities or certain products, may affect trade so as to distort (or threaten to distort) the system of free competition; the admitted benefit, however, must necessarily be selective, since it is suitable to benefit certain firms (or sectors of economic activities) and not even the majority of the firms (in which case there would not be a State aid, but rather a controllable measure of support to national enterprises, to be detected with respect the principle of non-discrimination).

The aim pursued by the rules of the State aids is thus clearly related to the promotion and the protection of an open European economic space, in which it is definitively removed the possibility of a centrifugal and self-referential economic policy, direct to pursue some selfish goals of the nation-States, in favour of the development of the European integration through the removal of a power of financial facilitation potentially distorting the free competition.

10.1.2 Procedural Nature and Degree of Competence of the EU Guidelines on the State Aids

The discipline laid down in the art. 107 establishes that, through a complex procedure, the Commission is required to initiate a "formal investigation", in principle with a preventive nature, about the compatibility with the EU law of the financial measures taken to support the national enterprises and decided by the Member State in order to issue (or at the opposite to deny) the relevant authorization regarding the national financial measure recognized as a State aid.

Therefore it is not established the principle of the absolute and automatic inadmissibility of the State aid, but rather it is defined the jurisdiction of the EU body with regard to the assessment of compatibility of the most favourable national rules with the principles and rules of the EU law.

It is a rule that applies to establish an area of competence in favour of the EU institutions (and especially the competence of the Commission).

In fact, the extent of benefit provided for by the internal discipline of a Member State until it was expressly approved by the Commission is to be considered devoid of a direct and immediate legal effect. The act of the national legislation comes formally into force, but substantially remains suspended until the decision of the Commission approving the norm by judging the compatibility with the EU law. The approval of the Commission arises as a legal condition of the effectiveness of the national law providing for a measure of domestic advantage.

In this perspective it can be argued that the discipline of the State aids, although it contains some descriptive elements of the prohibited measures, does not assume a substantial connotation, but is to be qualified as a discipline essentially with a procedural nature.

10.1.3 The Character of the State Aids Prohibited Under the EU Law

The State aids consist in the attribution of a financial benefit to the recipient by a provision of a Member State, such as to affect trade within the common market and to distort the free competition between the European firms.

The qualifying features of the State aids are to be regarded as constituting a plurality of elements:

- the public nature of the entity which materially pays the financial measure;
- the financial nature of the resource to be given to the domestic recipient;
- the allocation of selective financial resources;
- the potential distortive effect on the free competition among the European firms.

For the classification of a financial measure as a State aid, it is required at first that the subject called upon to provide the financial resources is a public entity; in this category it can be included the territorial or non-territorial entities, public administrations or governmental bodies, or even a private entity acting under a power delegated by the State or other public body.

The resource used for business (or other economic agents) must have a financial content, to be clearly identified in an increase of financial liquidity for the recipient and not even in a mere utility economically significant. Especially it is to be considered in the area of the State aids either the positive financial measure (consisting in financial contributions) as well as the "negative" financial measures, which resulted in a reduction of the costs that would ordinarily sustain the beneficiary. Consequently the taxation benefits can be ascribed to the category of the State aids, because they may be assimilated peacefully to the reductions of the burdens and charges imposed over the business (or over the economic agents).

A decisive character for the recognition of the State aids is to be found in the selective destination of the financial measures taken in support of the business (or of the economic agents). The selectivity of the financial measures is the guiding principle in the verification of the compatibility of the State aids with the EU law, imposing the need to check case by case the existence of the selective destination.

Finally, it is consolidated the belief in the EU bodies that is necessary to evaluate the actual effectiveness of the financial measure determined by the Member State in terms of potential obstruction with respect to the freedom of competition in the common market. In particular, it must be verified the potential effect that may occur with regard to the transactions on the market for the economic agents who are not beneficiaries of the measure of support, also in order to establish the existence of possible specific disadvantages that could limit the presence on the market or, in any case, penalize the business action.

If the elements described above are found as a result of a positive judgment made by the Commission, the facilitative extent decided by the Member State qualifies as a State aid and therefore it is to be considered inadmissible under the EU law as a prohibited measure.

It must be distinguished with respect to this last figure the "illegal" aid, in which the judgment of compatibility has not yet been made by the Commission, but the support measure decided by the Member State has not been notified to the Commission; in this case, the aid is to be considered illegitimate for failure to observe the procedure required by the art. 108 TFEU.

It should also be noted that no new State aid can be found compatible with the EU law until the beneficiary of a previous unlawful State aid has failed to return it (case 15.5.1997, C-355/95, *Deggendorf*). This is clearly a rule of fiscal caution intended to protect the EU interest with respect to the recurrence of violations to the rules on State aids in favour of the same beneficiary.

10.1.4 The Procedure for the Judgment on the EU Compatibility of the State Aids

As mentioned above, the discipline of State aid has as its primary goal the establishment of a procedure for the assessment of the financial measures taken to support domestic enterprises (or other economic agents) adopted by the Member States.

The competence to decide on this matter is expressly conferred on the Commission (art. 108 TFEU) and is regulated by some specific rules of implementation (Regulation of 03/22/1999 n. 659).

Member States are required to notify the Commission "in good time" the draft legislation devoted to grant or to modify some financial measures in favour of domestic enterprises (or other economic agents) that are potentially qualified as State aids. Member States are also obliged not to give effect to the support measures before the Commission expressed about the admissibility of the same measure with the EU law (art. 108 par. III).

Therefore, by the EU law, there are two specific obligations for Member States that wish to proceed with the establishment of financial measures in their national territory:

- a positive obligation, consisting in the communication of the proposed aid to the Commission;

- a negative obligation, having the contents of a *non facere* (not to do), defined in terms of a prohibition to implement the same support measures.

In this regard it should be noted that often the Member States include in the national law which introduces a support measure a referral clause about the effectiveness of the financial arrangement pending the authorization of the Commission (standstill clause). This is clearly a rule of precaution dictated by the need to avoid the complex procedures of the recovery of the State aids in the event of a negative decision on the compatibility of the national measure with the EU law.

The Commission shall conduct an examination about the financial measure determined by the Member State, judging the compliance of individual items to the model of the State aid. Particularly, the investigation focuses on two aspects of the facilitative selectivity of the measure and of the potential distortion of the free competition. The verification is typically accomplished with a casuistic approach, through an examination of the effects of the aid on the relevant market according to an assessment of a prognostic kind conducted in the same way of the normal parameters of the economic evaluation.

The investigation concludes with a decision of the Commission on the admissibility of the financial measure designed by the Member State. The decision may be positive (and therefore admitting the eligibility of the national aid), or negative, as it establishes the incompatibility of the State aid with the EU law. The decision may also predict a "conditioned eligibility", subject to some appropriate actions to be taken by the Member State in order to make compatible the financial measure with the EU law.

The Member State is bound by the decision taken by the Commission on the State aids, subject to a recourse to the Court of Justice to challenge the content of the decision. In the event of failure to comply with the decision of the Commission, the State is liable to the infringement of the proceedings.

The Commission has also the power to declare in advance for some economic sectors the compatibility with the European law and therefore the inapplicability of the procedure mentioned in art. 108 (in accordance with Regulation n. 994/98). In application of these Regulation some categories of "horizontal" State aids, for which it is possible to formulate a previous judgment about the admissibility, can be exempted from the prior notification to the Commission.

In this regard it should be noted that the Commission has adopted a code of some best practices in the field of the State aids, for which it is established a simplified procedure for the approval of the support measures adopted by the Member States (Communication of 04/29/2009).

10.1.5 A Progressive Perspective Regarding the Exceptions to the Prohibition of the State Aids

The interest of the European Union begins to take on a "social" connotation with regard to the guidelines on the State aids. Some indicators of this approach may be found typically in the State aids considered to be compatible with the EU law, which promote settlement mechanisms of social conflicts or otherwise are aimed at encouraging acts of solidarity towards "weak" categories.

Particularly, some kinds of State aids are expressly considered eligible by the Member States, as always compatible with the European framework:

- the social aids granted in favour of individual consumers, subject to the exclusion of any discrimination with regard to the origin of the products (art. 107 par. II, let. a);
- the aids devoted to recover the damages generated by natural disasters or extraordinary events (art. 107 par. II, let. b);
- some aids recognised in favour of some territories of Germany, as a consequence of the national unification (art. 107 par. II, let. c).

In these cases, it is excluded a discretionary evaluation by the EU bodies about the compatibility of the State aids with EU law; however, the Member States must notify to the Commission the national provision in order to permit the acknowledgment of the case with the EU law.

For other kinds of State aids the Commission may formulate a discretionary judgment about the eligibility of the facilitation under the EU law; especially in this category are considered the following cases:

- aids to promote the economic development of areas where the standard of living is abnormally low or where there is a high level of unemployment (art. 107 par. III, let. a);
- aids devoted to promote an important European project or to remedy a situation of serious distress or disturbance in the economy of a Member State (art. 107 par. III, let. b);
- aids aimed at facilitating the growth and development of certain regions or certain economic activities as long as the distortion of competition is not contrary to the EU interest (art. 107 par. III, let. c);
- the aids for the promotion of the cultural initiatives and the protection of the artistic and cultural assets (art. 107, par. III, let. d);
- the other categories of aids decided by the Council on the basis of a proposal coming from the Commission (as the aids for promoting the employment or the development of small and medium enterprises) (art. 107 par. III, let. e); it must be noted that, for this last case, it has been issued the Regulation n. 994/1998 which has entitled the Commission to verify the compatibility with the European discipline about the national State aid regarding the promotion of small and medium enterprises, the research, the protection of the environment, the development of the employment.

With regard to these cases, it is attributed a wide discretionary power to the Commission for the balancing of the interest promoted by the State aids (and so the social or political aims pursued by the Member State) with the European freedoms and principles (case 15.5.1997, C-278/95, *Siemens*; case 19.9.2000, C-156/98, *Germany vs. Commission*; case 17.5.2001, C-310/99, *Italy vs. Commission).* Therefore, the Commission is required to operate a global evaluation of the State aids, considering the functionality, the proportionality and the consistency of the national provision in the general European framework, in order to judge the eligibility of the same provision as a derogation to the ordinary prohibition of State aids which can distort the free competition on the common market (case 21.3.1991, C-303/88 *Italy vs Commission*; case 9.1.2003, C-157/00, *Greece vs. Commission).*

From the mentioned catalogue of State aids deemed eligible by the EU law some significant indications emerge.

At first, it may be identified a traceable interest (as a collective interest of the European Union) to promote the economic and social development of the Member States. In this respect the choices of economic policy, although theoretically conflicting with the rules of the competitive game, are to be compatible with the EU law as belonging to the same "social" purpose of collective development. The State aids relating to the social and ideological purposes are considered eligible with the European legal framework, although they produce a definite impact on the competitive neutrality of the market, since it is well appreciated the promotional value of the benefit to the general community and the solidarity intent involved in such facilitation measures.

In particular, it is assigned a specific relief to the "European interest" as a term of reference for the assessment of compatibility of certain categories of State aids, appearing clear the axiological dimension of the European community with respect to the "social" purposes.

Secondly, in the list of the allowed aids there are some cases which recall the general social needs, not only due to macro-economic purposes, nor to instances of the development of certain territories. This can be read as a recognition of the need to promote (or, at least, to admit) tax rules that favour a promotional character of the social evolution according to a plan to raise the situations of under-protection.

Although the social policy has not been the central component of the European integration process, it seems possible to some extent to establish a connection of this profile of the European Union with the principle of substantial equality in the EU legal framework; in fact, it can be acknowledged, as a reference for the assessment of collective interests, an evolutionary process directed to the removal of economic and social obstacles that reduce on a factual level the freedom and the equality of European citizens, so as to hinder the development and the self-realization of the person. The goals that make up the teleological and axiological horizon of the EU legislative action may not be reduced to the mere protection of the values of freedom and of economic efficiency (even though they are taking a prominent relief), but shall be combined with the promotion of the progressive social values in order to support an overall growth of the European Union such as to promote the personal elevation of the individual citizens.

10.1.6 The Preventive Regulation for the Exceptions to the Prohibition of State Aids

According to the art. 109 TFEU it is recognised the possibility to regulate preventively the State aids admitted by the EU legal order, defining the category of measures which are exempted from the procedure of authorization.

At this purpose it has been issued the Regulation n. 994/1998 that establishes the power of the Commission to adopt specific regulations for the execution of the discipline of the State aids, with the aim to identify the categories of measures which do not need to be authorised by the Commission.

Then, several Regulations have been issued time by time by the Commission in order to admit specific categories of State aids with a preventive decision. Especially, the Regulation n. 800/2008 (also called "general regulation of the exemption for categories") defined the general criteria for the preventive determination of the compatibility of the national measure in favour of the enterprises with the European discipline of the State aids and, therefore, the exemption from the compulsory procedures to be followed in front of the Commission.

Particularly, it is expressly established the application of some general principles of the European legal order for the evaluation of the specific categories of State aids:

- according to the principle of the benefit, it must considered the benefits obtained by the European Union for the process of the European integration and related to the State aids to be introduced; this benefits are to be compared with the distortion of the common market coming from the State aids; if the comparison produces an advantage for the European union superior than the distortion, the national measures can be considered allowed;
- on the basis of the principle of transparency, the impact of the State aids over the common market must be evaluated through a clear and verifiable analysis, also applying some mathematic parameters (so called "ESL") in order to verify the grade of intensity of the national measure.

Periodically, the Commission elaborates some general reports, applying the mentioned principles and through a cooperation with the Member States, with the aim to specify the regional areas which need some contributions (or other measures of support) and the categories of State aids allowed. In these reports (so called "regional papers") the Commission usually identifies the kind of disadvantage of the regional areas compared to the national or European average.

10.1.7 The Eligibility of de minimis Aids

The Commission considered that the State aids of a minimum content do not fall under the regulations provided by the art. 107 TFEU—and therefore are not subject to the prior notification—on the assumption that these measures are not likely to have a significant impact on the international trade and may not lead to distortions of the competition among the economic agents in the common market. Those measures of small size are usually referred to as *de minimis* aids regulations (from the Latin sentence: "*de minimis non curat lex*").

In particular, the benefit measures are mostly targeted at the small and medium-sized enterprises whose dimensions are fixed by law. Into the category of *de minimis* aids are considered the measures that do not involve an advantage over € 200,000 over three financial years for the individual beneficiary (according to the Regulation of 12/28/2006 no. 1998). This limit, however, has recently been raised up to € 500,000 by the Commission (with the communication of 11/26/2008 no. 800), as part of the European economic recovery plan as a result of the global financial crisis (so-called *European economic recovery plan*).

Where the total amount of the State aids exceeds the above mentioned limit, the full extent of the benefit will be submitted to the European guidelines on the State aid (and therefore it may not be included in the exemption even the part of the aid that fits within the limit).

10.2 The Tax Relief as a Possible State Aid

10.2.1 The Qualification of Tax Relief as a State Aid

The national provisions which introduce a tax relief in favour of domestic enterprises (or in favour of the products generated in the national territory) can surely be included in the conceptual area of the State aids as measures potentially devoted to distort the free competition in the same way of the expenditures (and indeed in the literature the two facilitation measures are considered equivalent). In this sense, it is often expressed by the Court of Justice that the category of the State aids includes not only subsidies and public services with a positive content, but also the public measures that result in a reductions of the burdens on business (case 03/15/1994, C-387/92 *Banco Exterior*, where the problem has been examined for the first time; case 05/08/2003, C-328/99, *Italy and SIM 2 multimedia*; case 09/14/2004, C-276/02, *Spain vs. Commission*).

In fact, the tax benefits, resulting in a favourable treatment to the beneficiaries, are likely to reduce the cost of production and thus are detrimental to the competition on the common market.

Otherwise, the "purpose taxes" or the special contributions do not seem to fall within the scope of the regulation on the State aids, since any assessment of compatibility with the EU law does not apply to the structure of the tribute, but rather to the destination of the fiscal flows (and so to the expenditure made as a result of the tax revenues).

The restriction of the European regulation on the State aids with regard to the adoption of tax facilitations looks like a typical application of the principle of non-discrimination (and therefore it recalls the scheme of the "negative" taxation), as it introduces a limit to the power of taxation of the nation-States.

Naturally, the national provisions to be included in the discipline of the State aids must be qualified as tax benefits and thus they have to produce a tax advantage which derogates from the ordinary fiscal regulation, regardless to the favourable elements of the norm (so the advantage may regard the assumption, the taxpayer, the tax rate or the tax base). Therefore the national provision must present a "promotional" nature, devoted to promote some constitutional values with a prevalence over the tax interest of the national State (such as the protection of the family, health, work, savings, etc.). Consequently, the tax rules which appear as a consistent implementation of the ordinary structure of a tribute or which are a deductive application of the general principles of the national tax system may not be qualified as tax reliefs as they miss the promotional nature; so these rules are not covered by the discipline on the State aids (Communication of the Commission C-384/98).

Obviously, the tax benefits, according to the general rule formulated by the art. 107, must present a selective nature, regarding limited categories of beneficiaries or specific sectors of productivity and not also referring to the general economic agents.

It should be further noted that the selectivity of the tax benefits is to be considered, according to the prevalent doctrinal opinion, not with regard to the mere event that the benefit can actually regard only a few individuals, but rather with regard to the pursuit of singular and specific aims of economic policy, not related to the logic of development of the general productive system as a whole.

On the contrary, the national measures intended for the generality of economic agents and productions are to be considered eligible under the EU law. In fact, although the general tax facilitations may determine some advantages for the domestic enterprises or the national production, for the purposes of the regulations on the competition such facilitation falls within the area of the sovereignty of the Member States and is not objectable by the European law (except for the processes of harmonization to be achieved on the basis of the EU legislation).

10.2.2 The Eligibility of Tax Incentives at a Regional or Local Level

One of the most topical issues of the discipline on the State aid is the suitability of tax benefits determined by the sub-state legislation, given the need to prevent forms of decentralization of the tax power which may circumvent the ban on the State aids.

This issue has been repeatedly examined by the Court of Justice which defined the guidelines of the applicable European regulation.

First of all, it is not excluded that the provision of a tax relief restricted to a certain regional or local territory automatically integrates the requirement of selectivity (which, as mentioned above, is one of the features of the provisions to be qualified as State aid) (case 09/19/2000 C-156/98, *Commission vs. Germany*). Instead, it is required that the Region (or the sub-state territorial entity) has a statute (of fact and law) to be considered sufficiently autonomous in relation to the central government of a Member State in order to play "a key role in the definition of the political and economic environment in which the business operates" (case 09/06/2006, C-88/03 *Azores*).

In particular, the Court of Justice has identified three different types of legal relations between the national tax system and the local tax system (case 09/06/2006, C-88/03 *Azores*, to be evidently considered a leading case):

- the State unilaterally decides the tax to be applied in a limited territory and the Region suffers such a decision;
- all the Regions (and all the local authorities placed on the same level) have the power to determine the tax advantage as a competence conferred directly by national law (symmetrical federalism);
- only some Regions have the power to set the tax relief in their territory pursuant to a regulatory autonomy attributed by the national law (asymmetrical federalism).

In the first case, the Court identifies a clear manifestation of the territorial selectivity, appropriate to generate a situation of State aid, considering to be able to verify only the existence of the reasons of social and political solidarity that justify some derogations from the general EU prohibition.

In the second case, the existence of a territorial selectivity is excluded as the rules about the tax benefits can be taken by each local authority, thus assuming a general nature and not limited geographically. Clearly, the facilitation must be available to all enterprises and to all sectors of the economy and not be subject to a further selection of an objective or material nature (because otherwise there would be a form of material and non-territorial selection).

In the third case, finally, the adoption of a tax relief can be considered legitimate if the fiscal advantages are limited to the territory of the Region of decision and, above all, it is verified the existence of an adequate regulatory autonomy. In this latter regard, some parameters are identified, whose compliance is decisive for the verification of the existence of a sub-state decision-making capacity of the regional institution:

- *institutional autonomy*, identified on the basis of the existence of a political and administrative statute which confers distinct and autonomous decision-making powers compared to the central Government
- *decision-making autonomy*, by virtue of which the final decision is taken by the regional entity without direct intervention of the central government (being admitted, however, processes of consultation in which the final decision is left in any case to the regional entity);
- *economic and financial autonomy*, which is to recognize in the ability of the regional authority to assume a regulatory determination regarding the extent of the tax benefit that is established without financial compensation and/or financial assistance from the central government (through grants or direct subsidies to compensate for the lost revenue resulting from the tax facilitation).

These elements are functional to verify that the Region plays a "key role" in the definition of a political and economic context in which the economic agents operate and not be constrained by decisions taken at the level of the general economic policy of the Member State. Indeed, the real test of the local financial autonomy (namely the third parameter above mentioned) is crucial for the verification of the eligibility of the tax facilitation, since it clearly expresses the amenability of the effects of the tax advantages to the territory and to the economic capacity of the regional institution which issued the facilitation norm. It should be noted in this regard that in the ECJ jurisprudence it has been identified a large series of financial relationships that can occur between national tax system and local tax system in order to verify if there is a State coverage of the tax advantages decided at the local level (case 09/11/2008, C-428/06 and C-434/06, *Basque Country*; Tribunal of First Instance, 12/18/2008, TE-211/04 and TE-215/04, *Gibraltar*).

10.2.3 The Urban Free Zones

The European regulation on the State aids also applies to the provision of tax measures which are devoted to introduce some benefits for disadvantaged geographical areas, mostly attributable to urban centres with reduced economical and industrial capacity (so-called "urban free zones").

The Commission approved and authorized these favourable provisions (with specific reference to urban free zones initially envisaged by France) as falling within the exception subject to the aids of social economic and political solidarity (as provided by art. 107 par. III, let. c). Moreover, these measures are to be considered proportionate as they were limited to a restricted number of the national population and therefore not likely to be an element of distortion of general competition and trade.

The conclusions reached by the Commission have been collected in a separate document ("*State aid and regeneration of deprived urban areas*" of 2007) in order to give a general nature to the information contained therein.

10.3 The Recovery of the State Aids

The recovery of the State aids unlawfully granted by the Member States is substantiated through a series of administrative measures intended to recover the benefits unduly received by the economic agents and hence to restore the financial balance foreshadowed by the EU law.

There are no specific EU rules governing the procedures for the recovery of the unlawful State aid, being left to the laws of each Member State to identify the steps necessary to perform the recovery action.

Moreover, there is a general application of the principles of equivalence and effectiveness of the recovery (communication of the Commission C-272 of 2007). In particular, it is expected that the procedures of national law applicable to the recovery of incompatible State aids are to be implemented without delay and must not be less favourable than those governing similar domestic rules nor make excessively difficult the recovery of the illegitimate tax facilitation measures. In essence, according to the EU law the discipline of the recovery of the State aids must ensure an immediate and effective rebalancing of the financial situation unlawfully determined by the facilitation provision granted by the Member State.

Therefore it seems to be excluded the configurability of specific provisions of the internal law of the Member States dedicated to the recovery of the unlawful State aids, precisely by reason of the application of the principles of equivalence and effectiveness.

On a theoretical level, a matter of considerable complexity is represented by the legal classification of the act of recovery. At first, it is argued that such an act acquires the same nature as the measure of advantage granted by the Member State, having to qualify the administrative power (and the relative procedure) in the same perspective of the rule of facilitation; therefore, in the case of the tax relief, the recovery act should take the fiscal nature. On the other hand, it is argued that the administrative activities carried out for the recovery of State aid are to be considered as a merely satisfying activity which reflects the execution of a legally binding normative instrument of the EU institutions, qualified by reference to the due and non-discretionary administrative acts; in this respect, the recovery act lacks its authoritative character and becomes simply and executive activity of the European law; so it is excluded that the act of recovery can be classified as a fiscal activity (or a fiscal procedure).

In the literature it seems to be consolidating the belief that the recovery act has a fiscal nature, also in consideration of the administrative competence entrusted to the tax authorities and the jurisdiction often accorded to the tax or administrative courts.

For the recovery of the tax benefits qualified as State aids is often required the issuance of a notice of assessment in respect of the beneficiary containing the invitation to a refund of the tax benefit as a result of the unlawful State aid.

It should be noted that if the internal legislation has produced the legitimate entrust in the beneficiary in order to the eligibility of facilitation domestic measure, the recovery order may not be executed (art. 14 of Regulation no. 659/1999). The evaluation of the circumstances that led to the legitimate expectations of the beneficiary should be carried out by the national court applying the usual parameters of the ordinary diligence of economic operators (case C-280/95, *Commission vs. Italy*).

The Harmful Tax Competition 11

Contents

11.1 The Harmful Tax Competition as an Emerging Value of the EU Legal System 165
11.1.1 The Notion of "Harmful Tax Competition" 165
11.1.2 The "Harmful Tax Competition" as a Paradigm of the Limitation of National Taxation 166
11.2 The Fight Against Harmful Tax Competition Within the EU Legal System 168
11.2.1 The "Monti Package" and the Introduction of the Code of Conduct 168
11.2.2 The Content of the Code of Conduct 169
11.2.3 The Effects of the Code of Conduct. The Assimilation to the State Aids ... 170

11.1 The Harmful Tax Competition as an Emerging Value of the EU Legal System

11.1.1 The Notion of "Harmful Tax Competition"

The topic of "harmful tax competition" has been for many years one of the main arguments used by international organizations (and therefore not only by the EU) to assess the compliance of decisions taken by the individual States in relation to the tax advantages with respect to the development purposes and even to the peaceful coexistence of the States in the international context.

The recruitment of national measures involving tax benefits in favour of those economic agents that are allocated in the State is in fact able to distort materially the ordinary rules of business competition, producing discrepancies and distortions with regard to the normal operation of the market. Therefore, the international organizations that promote the value of free competition in the market have gradually developed a strategy to contrast with the rules and the practices adopted by some Member States for promotional purposes of its territory.

In this perspective, the definition of the tax policies with emphasis on territorial facilitation, aimed in particular at promoting the localization of economic activities

P. Boria, *Taxation in European Union*, DOI 10.1007/978-3-319-53919-5_11

or capital investment in the country, were judged as an expression of choices which are "harmful" to the processes of globalization and international integration and, therefore, as an element to counteract or at least to restrict. Thus, some forms of integration of fiscal policies of individual States are promoted by international organizations in order to reduce the fiscal competition between the States.

Consistent with that approach in the EU law it has gradually been shaping the belief that tax competition exerted between the various Member States is to be judged as a negative factor, potentially suitable to alter the operation of the common market and then to distort the effectiveness of the principle of free competition.

Although it is not formulated a specific definition of "harmful tax competition" in the EU law, it has been progressively identified an area regarding the behaviours of the States (and in particular the regulatory regimes adopted into national law) which may be judged incompatible with the general principles expressed in the Treaty and in any case inadequate to permit the process of European integration.

The "harmful tax competition" is so identified with the adoption of fiscal policies by a Member State which determines, at least potentially, a subversive tax order compared to the majority of the other States, as it introduces elements of fiscal facilitation or, however, some tax benefits that induce the economic agents to be located in the territory of the same State, including the allocation of resources and factors of production, at the expense of the State of residence (and therefore with a disregard to the "natural" development of business).

Typical expression of the fight against the harmful tax competition in the EU law can be found in the adoption of the "Code of Conduct" (following the ECOFIN decision of 1997, as part of the "*Monti package*") intended to achieve the block of new favourable fiscal measures and, above all, to promote the gradual dismantling of the existing tax regulations, devoted to encourage the location of economic activities in a given country, which are capable of producing competitive situations compared to other countries. The rules established by the Code of Conduct have been able to render concrete and effective the value of harmful tax competition within the European legal system.

11.1.2 The "Harmful Tax Competition" as a Paradigm of the Limitation of National Taxation

At a first glance, the fight against the "harmful tax competition" seems to look like a mechanism of protection of national taxation with respect to the tax policy of foreign States, avoiding or at least mitigating those forms of interference with respect to the behaviours of economic agents which are resident in the national territory. In this perspective the discipline to contrast the "harmful tax competition" may be ascribed to the category of acts realised in defence of the fiscal sovereignty of the individual State.

On a closer inspection, indeed, the conceptual background of the harmful tax competition expresses a completely different logic than the protection of national fiscal sovereignty.

It is well known that the use of tax relief operates as a mechanism for promoting economic and social assets to be pursued in line with the fundamental aims laid down generally in the national Constitutions. Particularly, the adoption of tax incentives represents a means, often inescapable, to ensure the economic recovery of depressed areas or to facilitate the rise to a level of a minimum acceptability for some business underdeveloped categories.

In this perspective, the tax relief, which is used to determine the reduction or even the cancellation of the ordinary tribute, where it introduces a discrimination with respect to the generality of the associates, who are in an objectively better starting situation, pursues the achievement of the substantial equality of the members of the civil society according to a primary goal of the Constitution. The provision of promotional tax rules is so understood as a fundamental option for the fiscal sovereignty of each State, through which are effectively and substantially realised the core values of the protection of human dignity and individual development. The tax benefits contribute, therefore, to mark the pace of the sovereign State towards a path of equality and justice in the direction of the economic development and social support.

The compression of national fiscal policies pursued by the international organizations (and among them also by the European Union) is proposed actually to ensure the full equality of the Member States and to protect the competitiveness of business in the international market by excluding that the tax factor can be distortionary compared to the allocation of resources.

Evidently the idea of the harmful tax competition between the Member States lies in the conviction that there exists a *standard* tax, that is a consistent level of tax burden on the international market, in which the main national tax legislation will be lining up—at least as a trend line—resulting in a treatment which is broadly equivalent for the corporate and business taxation over the economic agents. Sensitive deviations from the *standard*, and in particular the facilitations of the tax burdens, are regarded as a clear interference with respect to the allocation decisions of economic agents and thus are essentially classified as acts of "international tax competition", aimed to attract capital and enterprises in the national territory distracting them from the territory of residence.

The perspective through which the rules related to the harmful tax competition are framed must be identified around the market values: the normative acts of the State which introduce some mechanisms to facilitate the ordinary taxation are not considered as an expression of concern to fiscal sovereignty, nor as a search for a balance between the different constitutional values or as an instrument for the development of the substantial equality, but rather as obstructive acts which distort the international market, almost as a gesture of defiance for the other countries that comply with the standard tax policy.

This transfiguration of a legislative act in a competitive behaviour is evident in Europe, where the emerging trend is to counter not only and not so much the actual "tax havens", which proclaimed the absence of any withdrawal tax and therefore can actually produce serious distortions to the international allocation decisions, but also the single and specific regulations of tax relief adopted by each Member State as likely to determine a sectorial interference compared to the ordinary taxation applied in other States.

Therefore, the "harmful tax competition" aligns conceptually the "negative" taxation of the EU legal order, connecting to the same liberal axiological system. It expresses, on the one hand, the desire to contain and to limit the national fiscal sovereignty and to eliminate the expansionary potential, at least compared to a promotional use of taxation as an instrument of development and restoration of the substantial equality; on the other hand, it denotes the opening towards the "market" as a reference point of the fiscal choices, clearly showing the collapse of the fiscal sovereignty to the logic of full competition of enterprises and economic agents in the common market.

11.2 The Fight Against Harmful Tax Competition Within the EU Legal System

11.2.1 The "Monti Package" and the Introduction of the Code of Conduct

As mentioned before, a key role with respect to the fight against the harmful tax competition is covered by the package of programmatic provisions issued by the Commission on 10/01/1997 and endorsed by the ECOFIN Council in the form expressed in its Resolution of 12/01/1997 (so-called "*Monti package*"); in this document a key element is expected to be the enactment of a "Code of conduct", whose content is not legally binding, having the characteristics of a political commitment, which lays down rules designed to contain the phenomena of harmful tax competition between the Member States.

Harmful tax competition is presented as a growing source of conflicts between the Member States because of the ability to influence the choices of economic and tax policy taken at the national level, which must be countered through a strong coordination at the EU level.

Unlike the OECD report on harmful tax competition, the European Code of conduct is not directed so much to counter the relocation of financial assets or business which could lead to costs to the firm (and therefore to modify the determination of the tax base in the territory where ordinarily operates the company), but rather to slow down the logic of an artificial location of the business in countries with a more convenient tax regime. The Code of conduct is typically in contrast with the fiscal practices that may result in substantial benefits so as to change the allocation choices of the firm in an area different from the usual one (or where it is expressed the main economic activity).

It is to point out that harmful tax competition is identified as a major cause of the shift of tax burden from capital to labour by the Member States. In fact, the provision of preferential tax regimes is able to attract especially the inputs with greater mobility (such as capital and enterprises), but not also the labour that is configured as a factor strongly rooted to the native territory and poorly mobile.

Therefore, the mobility of capital and business triggers a vicious circle: to counteract the shift towards preferential tax regimes, the States lessen the tax burden on these factors, and conversely are forced to increase the tax burden on the factor of the labour in order to maintain stable the tax revenues. In this view, the contrast to the harmful tax competition is considered as a functional element not only to the pursuit of free competition within the common market, but also as an element of social healing, directed to redressing the balance in the level of taxation on labour and capital and ultimately to promote the growth of employment in Europe.

Given the nature of a political commitment, ineffective to condition the legal system (given the absence of specific obligations and especially of sanctions in the event of default), the Code of conduct was originally implemented for a prolonged period by embodiments spontaneously adopted by the main Member States.

Subsequently, following the agreements reached during the ECOFIN meeting on 06/03/2003, the Code of conduct has found an explicit recognition in the EU law with the final agreement on the forms of harmful tax competition determined through some company regimes deemed "harmful", particularly with regard to the profile of the taxation of business income (except to establish a temporary extension for some of these schemes). In this document have been identified five categories of potentially harmful measures: the intra-group services, the financial services, the offshore companies, some sector-specific schemes, the tax incentives of a regional nature.

11.2.2 The Content of the Code of Conduct

The Code of conduct is applied at first with reference to the business taxation that significantly affects (or influences) the choice of location of the economic agents in the European territory. Secondly, the Code of Conduct also applies to special tax regimes reserved to the employment which may be conditioning on the location of the business activities.

The tax provisions considered by the Code of conduct are those contained in the national legal acts (laws and regulations), as well as those resulting from administrative practices held in the Member States.

The Code of conduct provides basically two distinct categories of prescriptive directions.

At first, it is programmed to block new provisions of direct taxation which, by encouraging the location of production activities in a national territory, produce competitive situations compared to other countries (so-called *standstill clause*). In essence this rule determines a sort of freezing on some existing tax reliefs in the Member States, preventing that they can grow in quantity and quality.

At second, it is foreshadowed the gradual dismantling of the fiscal provisions established in the Member States which produce the effects of the harmful tax competition (so-called *rollback clause*). This is a more effective measure, as instrumental in achieving a fair competitive fiscal structure through the elimination of preferential tax regimes that can produce distortions of the natural allocation of the business in Europe.

The guiding principle of the contrast to the harmful tax competition is identified in the express recognition of a parameter for the identification of the incompatible cases: the national tax provisions are considered potentially harmful, when they lead to an effective level of taxation in the privileged territory which is smaller than the taxation generally applied in the other countries.

The facilitation effect can be achieved through the tax rate or through the tax base or even through other elements of the structure of the tribute.

In order to proceed with the assessment of tax favourable regimes some indices of harmful tax competition are determined in the Code of conduct:

- tax relief that is intended only to non-residents or only to transactions with non-residents;
- tax relief that is isolated from the national economy and do not affect the overall tax base of the State;
- tax relief that is attributed regardless to any genuine and material business activity carried out in the national territory;
- rules for determining the operating result of the business (profit or loss) which sensibly differ from those provided usually at international level (with particular reference to the models developed by the OECD);
- tax provisions that lack transparency and disclosure, including cases where the tax benefits are granted by the administrative authorities.

It is also established that the control of the fiscal provisions is to be carried out not only by the Commission but also by the Member States, which may request information directly to the State which applies tax benefits deemed potentially liable to be qualified as harmful tax competition. This is a generalised form of control about the fiscal competition in Europe, that may emphasize the compliance with the instructions contained in the Code of conduct.

To ensure a constant monitoring of the implementation of the commitments undertaken with the Code of conduct has been set up a "monitoring group" which is open to all Member States, whose main task is to examine the tax favourable provisions adopted by the Member States and to verify the potentially distorting effects that can be produced on the common market.

11.2.3 The Effects of the Code of Conduct. The Assimilation to the State Aids

The Code of conduct is essentially a political document, which is expressly qualified as a non-legally binding commitment. Therefore it is an act that can be classified typically in the category of the European *soft law*.

It has been repeatedly observed that the fiscal provisions capable to produce harmful tax competition show an undoubted affinity with respect to the State aids, given the amenability of both cases to the category of tax benefits. This affinity seems to constitute the logical assumption for the application of the rules on State aids envisaged by the Treaty also to the tax provisions regulated by the Code of conduct.

Indeed, in the Code of conduct it is expressly recognized that some of the tax provisions potentially amenable as an expression of harmful tax competition fall within the scope of the EU regulation on the State aids. It must be noted that not every tax provision likely to produce a potentially harmful tax competition is able to be qualified as a State aid, given the non-recurrence of the necessary requirements established by the art. 107 TFEU.

The amenability of the tax provisions falling within the scope of harmful tax competition in the category of the State aid was then subject to a specific Commission communication (communication C-384 of 12/10/1998), which explicitly affirmed the applicability of the provisions of art. 107 to the measures of fiscal policy.

The use of the procedure for the verification of the compatibility of State aids allows to give a stronger legal significance to the Code of conduct, and permits to evaluate the direct tax systems of the Member States which may distort the competition between the economic agents and encourage the location of the artificial entrepreneurial activities in some privileged territories.

The Commission has thus opened up numerous examination procedures against some Member States with regard to the legality of national tax regimes potentially harmful by virtue of the rules on the State aids. These procedures are in majority concluded with a decision of incompatibility, however without determining an order for recovery of the unlawful State aid because of the formation of a legitimate expectation of the recipient.

The General Principles of the European Law Applicable to the Taxation 12

Contents

12.1 The General Principles of the EU Law 173
12.2 The Principles of Legal Certainty and Legitimate Expectations 175
12.3 The Principle of Effectiveness 176
12.4 The Principle of Proportionality 177
12.4.1 The Principle of Proportionality Within the EU Law 177
12.4.2 The Applications of the Principle of Proportionality in Tax Matters 178
12.5 The Abuse of Law 180
12.5.1 The Abuse of the Law as a General Principle of the EU Law in the Elaboration of the Court of Justice 180
12.5.2 The Abuse of Law in Tax Matters 180
12.6 The Environmental Protection and the Principle "Who Pollutes Pays" 182
12.6.1 The Protection of the Environment as a Primary Value of the EU Legal Order; The Principle "Who Pollutes Pays" 182
12.6.2 The Environmental Taxes 183
12.6.3 The Tax Facilitations with an Environmental Purpose 184
12.6.4 The Principle of Differentiation and the Observation of other European Principles 185

12.1 The General Principles of the EU Law

In addition to the rules and principles explicitly stated in the rules of the Treaty it may be recognised a number of principles with an implicit character—and therefore not formalized and expressed in specific EU rules—which take still a primary importance in the axiological plot of the European legal order.

These principles are determined by the Court of Justice on the basis of an inductive and teleological examination of the EU law (and therefore with reference to the Treaty rules and to the derivate EU law); or because of the recognition of common principles laid down in the national laws of the Member States which may express a homogeneous legal substratum of the European Union; or even by virtue

P. Boria, *Taxation in European Union*, DOI 10.1007/978-3-319-53919-5_12

of an extension within the European legal order to the legal principles established in other regulatory documents of an international character (especially with regard to the European Charter of Human Rights proclaimed in Nice).

Particularly, it may distinguish two categories of principles in the European law:

a. the "*structural principles*", which define the architecture of the European legal order and operate as a guarantee for the legal common space; these principles mark up the competence of EU bodies and Member States and, therefore, contribute to the process of integration; in this category it may be included the principles of subsidiarity, effectiveness, proportionality, fair cooperation among the States;
b. the "*general principles*" (sometime also defined in the ECJ jurisprudence as "fundamental principles"), which promote the protection of the individual rights and freedoms, and are oriented to guarantee the equality, the justice, the liberty; in this category it may be included the principle of legal certainty, the protection of good faith, the principle of the fair trial and the fair administrative proceedings.

Whatever may be the logic of identification, these principles take the nature of "general norms" of the EU law, establishing as the real rules of orientation and limitation of the normative power of the Member States. Consequently, these principles assume a dual legal function: at first, they operate as a parameter for assessing the legitimacy of the exercise of a legislative power, and therefore represent a super-legislative limit with respect to the validity and effectiveness of the rules contained in the Regulations and in the Directives; secondly they assume the function of a guidance in the normative and legislative interpretation, particularly with regard to the decisions of the Court of Justice, such as criteria of selection in the various possible interpretations of the EU law.

As for the effectiveness of the general principles of the EU law it is discussed often if they, although endowed with direct effect because they are binding on Member States, are considered also as directly applicable, thus founding the claim on the part of individual citizens. It seems preferable in this regard to evaluate separately each case, considering that the implementation of the general principle requires an internal discipline to be effectively applied in the legal system (with the consequence that the general principles appear frequently with a direct effect, and also without a direct applicability).

With regard to the area of taxation it is possible to identify a plurality of values that assume the character of the general principles of the EU law. To these values it has been recognized the nature of primary and fundamental aims to the process of European integration as capable to ensure the achievement of the purposes expressed by the Treaty; therefore they should be adequately protected by the EU legal order also with respect to some possible inconsistencies in the national law.

12.2 The Principles of Legal Certainty and Legitimate Expectations

The Court of Justice has repeatedly observed that in the EU legal order a vital role is represented by ensuring the citizens, the Member States and the European institutions to the principles of legal certainty and legitimate expectations. The aim of these principles is to preserve the continuation of existing legal situations, avoiding an unexpected and unpredictable compression of subjective situations as a result of the introduction of some new regulation.

These principles, although not explicitly formulated in the Treaty and in legislative acts (namely in the EU Regulations or Directives) have been deemed applicable peacefully with reference to tax matters, in order to enable the operators to know precisely the extent of the tax obligations imposed by law (case 12/15/1987, *Kingdom of the Netherlands vs. Cee Commission*; case 02/22/1989, C-92/87 and C-93/87, *Commission vs. France and the United Kingdom*).

The EU law may not produce a temporal effect before its publication, and therefore it should be regarded under the principle of non-retroactivity (case 11/22/2001, the *Kingdom of the Netherlands vs. Council the EU*; case 04/29/2004, *Finanzamt Sulingen vs. Sudholz Walter*). Exceptions to this principle are allowed only in some limited cases, where it is necessary for the achievement of the purposes of the regulatory act, and without prejudice to the legitimate expectations of those concerned.

The protection of legitimate expectations should be realized also as a result of interpretative rulings by the Court of Justice that present a reconstruction of the EU provision in a different manner than the previous interpretation (and in any case in a different way than the legal presentation formulated into national law), as the need to safeguard the legal position of the parties affected by the retroactive effects of interpretative rulings by the European Court of Justice have the same axiological background than the recipient of the enactment of the legislation.

However, it should be noted that just in tax matters the Court of Justice has repeatedly exercised the right to limit the temporal effect of its interpretations, recalling in particular the principle of legal certainty, in view of the problems that could be accounted under the judgment in the context of the legal relationships established in good faith in the past.

Another corollary of the above mentioned principles of legal certainty and legitimate expectations can be identified in the requirement of adequate transparency of the activity by the EU institutions in the interests of the recipients of the administrative procedures (case 02/22/1984, *Kloppenburg*; case 06/21/1988, *Commission vs. Italy*); this rule has thus led to the identification of a reasonable deadline with reference to the issuance of rulings of the Commission on the compatibility of the tax reliefs with the State aids regulations.

In particular, it was deemed necessary to protect the good faith and the expectations of the recipient of the tax reliefs subsequently found to be incompatible with the rules on the State aids, where the conduct of the EU institutions has contrarily led to the admission of the favourable tax regulation. At this purpose the Court of Justice assumed a rigorous approach, since it bares the burden of proof on the recipients to ascertain whether the competent State bodies have notified the draft State aid to the Commission and if it has commenced a decision-making procedure in matter; at the same time the Court denies any relevance to the behaviours assumed by the national authorities on the presumed validity of the tax reliefs.

12.3 The Principle of Effectiveness

The principle of effectiveness finds an explicit codification in the Treaty under art. 4 TEU, being expressly provided for the duty of individual States to apply the provisions of the EU law and to carry out all activities aimed to facilitate and not to aggravate the accomplished and effective statement of the rules related to the organization of the EU. The determination of the duty to cooperate also applies to the Member States in order to establish the claim of the EU institutions and citizens to the proper implementation of the EU obligations.

As corollaries of this rule it is identified typically the principle of effectiveness in the narrow sense and the principle of equivalence in the wide sense, both functional to ensure a balance between the procedural autonomy of the legal systems of the Member States and the effective protection of the rights laid down by the EU law (case 12/14/1995, *Van Schijndel*).

The principle of equivalence requires that the recognition and the protection of rights under the EU law is made available to European citizens by the same mechanisms provided by domestic law for the protection of the rights of internal source; in essence the exercise of the EU rights is not placed in deteriorate conditions compared to the national rights. This principle is found at every procedural level and applies to ensure the identification of the legal mechanism and of the procedure used for the protection of subjective legal situations.

The principle of "strict effectiveness" ensures that the provisions of domestic law do not make too difficult or too costly the exercise or the protection of a subjective legal situation determined under the EU law. It is determined on the basis of the suitability of a procedural rule to ensure the protection of some concrete and effective EU rights.

It should be evident that the principle of effectiveness regards typically the area of the implementing of the scope of the EU rights and therefore has a conforming function about the procedural systems of the Member States.

Accordingly, the parameters of effectiveness are to be found mainly in the criteria of good administration and due process. Indeed, it is well established in the ECJ case-law that this principle applies to establish the European regulations of relations between governments and citizens. In particular, with reference to the administrative procedure the Court of Justice has clearly identified these parameters of effectiveness in the principles of legal certainty, good faith, impartiality, efficiency, and transparency of the administration, as well as the principles of cross examination with the counterparty, motivation of the administrative provisions and proportionality with the produced effects. With reference to the process, the Court has instead outlined a series of legal criteria deducted by the logic of a fair trial (also formalized in the art. 6 of the European Convention on Human Rights of Nice), which provides basically the impartiality and fairness of the Court and the reasonable duration of the due process.

It is worth noting that the principle of effectiveness requires by its very nature the abandonment of the formalistic patterns often adopted into national law in favour of legal mechanisms and institutional instruments inspired by a concrete and substantial protection of the EU rights (according to the logic of the "*substantia versus formam*"). It is thus affirmed the belief that the rules of procedure and proceedings may not unreasonably compress the possibility of a legal recognition of the infringed right.

In tax matters the principle of effectiveness has found an application especially with reference to the cases of unfair taxation, permitting to recognize and to protect the actions of tax refund by taxpayers against procedural foreclosures often provided for by the laws of the nation-States.

At this purpose it should be noted that, where a national tax has been considered incompatible with the EU law, the taxpayer is entitled to bring an action for the recovery of the tax in the face of administrative and/or judicial national authorities, in order to obtain a refund of taxes (or public charges) levied in breach of the EU rules (qualifying the legal position of the taxpayer in terms of a perfect subjective right). In accordance with the principle of effectiveness, it was indicated that in each case the terms of prescription and limitation, the terms and conditions of the repetition of undue tax established by the internal discipline may not be adjusted so as to make excessively burdensome the action given to a taxpayer (especially to a resident of another Member State) and in any case these internal rules must be consistent and responsive to the common standards of reasonableness and proportionality.

12.4 The Principle of Proportionality

12.4.1 The Principle of Proportionality Within the EU Law

A further general principle which has developed in the European sensitivity regards the proportionality of regulatory means adopted by Member States to the aims pursued by the European legal system.

In fact, the case law of the Court of Justice adopted frequently the checking about the instrumental and gradual suitability—and thus about the proportionality—of the material scope of domestic law to achieve the goal systematically assigned by the Treaty or by the EU derivate legislation. It is a way of measuring the teleological interpretation of the rule, whose application is entrusted to some probabilistic judgments and to a prognostic analyses on the purpose of the regulatory act within the EU legal order.

The assessment of proportionality is used by the Court of Justice to determine whether the compression of individual rights or of subjective legal rights recognized by the EU law by reason of the pursuit of national public interest is the only possible and reasonable option or if there are other forms of balance between the European order and the national interests which are less costly to the individual positions. The principle of proportionality thus responds to a logic of balancing for the conflicting interests (European and national) according to an assessment of instrumental and gradualist efficiency of the law.

Therefore, the national legislature and the public administration may not impose (by means of legislation or even by administrative measures) obligations or restrictions of individual rights and freedoms to an extent beyond what is strictly necessary to achieve the public purpose to be pursued, making a comparison between the public benefits and the individual disadvantages.

In particular, the proportionality of internal regulations involves the verification of three different standards: suitability, necessity, appropriateness. The suitability is the potential ability to pursue the goal set by the national legislation so as to allow assessment of the adequacy of the means to the aim. The necessity is identified in the lack of an alternative to the legislative choice, given the absence of other equally effective means to achieve the target set by national law. The appropriateness represents the adequacy of the discretionary activity of balancing the involved values (and, especially, the public and the individual interests affected by the regulatory solution chosen).

12.4.2 The Applications of the Principle of Proportionality in Tax Matters

The case law of ECJ has recognized that the principle of proportionality assumes a great importance in the field of taxation, as it is an essential criterion to ensure that the pursuit of the aims of national law produces the least possible detriment to the European purposes (case 07/05/1977, C-114/76, *Bela-Mhle*; case 12/18/1997, C-286/94, C-340/95, C-401/95, *Molenheide*; case 03/21/2000, C-110/98 to C-147/98 *Galbafrisa*).

There are some decisions of the Court of Justice in which it is made explicit recourse to the principle of proportionality in order to criticize certain provisions of the national law which, despite being intended to protect the public interest, generate an evident damage to the individual interest through a measure found not adequately proportional.

So it was considered unlawful a rule that precluded the right to the tax reimbursement in relation to the submission of a duplicate of the original invoice lost for reasons not attributable to the taxpayer, judging unnecessary (and therefore disproportionate and excessive) the foreclosure of the reimbursement compared to the purpose of preventing tax fraud (case 11.6.1998, C-361/96, *Société Generale des grandes sources*).

In another occasion the Court of Justice has ruled against the national regulation which absolutely prevents the taxpayer to provide proof of having actually incurred certain expenses for the purposes of tax deductibility, as disproportionate to the purpose, although abstractly appreciable, of preventing tax avoidance; indeed, there is the possibility to identify alternative rules that oblige the taxpayer to produce documentary evidence enabling the tax authorities to ascertain clearly and precisely the nature and genuineness of the incurred expenses (case 8.7.1999, C-254/97, *Baxter*).

In the mentioned cases the principle of proportionality shows considerable contiguity with respect to the principle of effectiveness, as it expresses the need to secure effective protection to the citizens in respect of the EU rights, ensuring that the national rules pose burdens and obligations not excessively burdensome for the exercise of such rights.

Moreover, the Court of Justice seems to use the principle of proportionality as a decisive criterion for the implementation of the "rule of reason" in order to judge the legitimacy of exceptions coming from the national legislation with respect to the implementation of the EU freedoms and to the non-discrimination of non-residents.

In this regard it can be mentioned, for its high symbolic importance, the decision on the cross-border losses (case 11.7.2002, C-62/00, *Marks & Spencer*) in which it was held to be incompatible with the EU law the domestic legislation that prevented to use the losses of the subsidiary company resident in a Member State to offset the profits of the parent company resident in another Member State, believing that the needs of protection of the tax could be protected with other regulatory mechanisms not disproportionate to the restriction imposed on taxpayers. The Court of Justice held that, if the losses are not used anymore in the State of source (because it may not be offset against profits from previous years or no longer carried forward), it should be allowed to offset against the profits of the parent company resident in another member State as a fair and reasonable rule of balancing the national interests of the State of residence of the parent company and the fundamental principles of the Treaty (and in particular the freedom of establishment).

Thirdly, the Court of Justice has made use of the principle of proportionality in assessing the reasonableness of sanctions and penalties of the national law to combat the tax violations relating to significant operations for the European trade; in particular it was considered disproportionate the extension of penal protection to violations of the intra Community VAT regime, based on a comparison with the milder sanctions imposed for the violations relating to the supply of goods within the State (case 02/25/1988, C-299/86, *Drexl*).

12.5 The Abuse of Law

12.5.1 The Abuse of the Law as a General Principle of the EU Law in the Elaboration of the Court of Justice

In the EU law the concept of "abuse of law" originates from a well-established series of decisions of the Court of Justice where it was stated the general principle that the formal and literal application of regulations may not extend to the abusive practices carried out by economic agents (case 12/11/1977, C-125/76, *Cremer*; case 03/03/1993, C-8/92, *Milk Products*; case 02/05/1996, C-206/94, *Paletta*; case 05/12/1998, C-367/96, *Kefalas*; case 02/09/1999, C-212/97, *Centros*; case 09/30/2003, C-167/01 *Diamantis*; case 03/03/2005, C-32/03, *Fini H.*; case 02/21/2006, C-255/02, *Halifax*; case 04/06/2006, C-456/04, *Agip Petroli*; case 09/12/2006, C-196/04, *Cadbury Schweppes*; case 06/28/2007, C-79/06, *Planzer*; case 07/05/2007, C-321/05 *Kofoed*.).

In essence, the Court recognizes the application of the principle of substance over form, believing that the formal compliance with the literal meaning of the law shall not permit, under any circumstances, to carry on transactions that produce results quite contrary to the purpose which is inspired by the same law and are therefore characterized by a fraudulent intent.

In particular, the Court of Justice has repeatedly stated that "*the fact that there is an abusive practice requires, on the one hand, a set of objective circumstances in which, despite formal observance of the conditions laid down by the EU legislation, the goal pursued by that legislation has not been reached. It requires, however, a subjective element consisting in the intention to obtain an advantage from the EU rules by creating artificially the conditions necessary for its achievement*".

The abuse of the right thus requires two elements:

- the objective circumstances that indicate the lack of a concrete economic basis for the activity carried on;
- the subjective purpose to obtain an undue advantage and especially an illegal benefit not provided for by the EU legislation.

Originally drafted in the areas of EU undergone extensive regulatory legislation (and especially in maritime law, the common agricultural policy, the corporate law), the prohibition of abuse is only recently landed in the area of taxation on the basis of a relevant case law of the Court of Justice (case 02/21/2006, C-255/02, *Halifax*, to be considered a real leading case on the abuse of rights in the field of taxation).

12.5.2 The Abuse of Law in Tax Matters

Although references to the prohibition on abusive transactions in tax matters are found in some rules devoted to combat fraudulent behaviours of taxpayers with respect to the application of EU regulations (see art. 11, no. 1, letter A) of Directive n. 90/434/EEC; art. 1, par. 2, Directive n. 90/435/EEC; art. 5, Directive n. 2003/49/EC), the concept of abuse of law has been formulated only recently by the Court of Justice.

In fact, the Court has identified an autonomous concept of abuse of tax law firstly with reference to the rules of VAT, specifying that the taxpayer is not entitled to deduct the VAT paid on inputs if "*transactions from which derive that right constitute an abusive practice*" (case 02/21/2006, C-255/02 *Halifax*) and then with regard to the direct taxation, stating that the tax restrictive effect on the freedom of establishment of the company is not allowed "*unless it relates only to wholly artificial arrangements intended to escape the normally payable national tax*" (case 09/12/2006, C-196/04, *Cadbury Schweppes*).

In both decisions, the Court of Justice held that the transactions entered into by persons resident in the European Union, although really wanted and immune from surveys of formal validity, which are artificially constructed and show "essentially the purpose of obtaining a tax benefit" in contrast with the purposes pursued by the Treaty, must be qualified as a typical kind of abuse of law.

In this case the behaviour of taxpayer may qualify as an expression of abuse of law if the transactions present the following qualifying elements (case 02/21/2006, C-255/02, *Halifax*):

1. notwithstanding formal application of the rules and conditions laid down by EU law and by transposing national legislation, these transactions are characterised by the "*essential purpose*" to obtain a tax advantage whose grant is contrary to the purpose pursued by the EU regulations;
2. the essential purpose of obtaining a tax advantage must be based on a set of objective factors.

The Court of Justice therefore proposes to include in the tax matters the same ideas already expressed for other legal matters in the elaboration of the general principles, stating that the transaction should be recognized abusive because of a subjective element (the purpose of obtaining a tax advantage contrary to the EU law) to be identified on the basis of a set of objective circumstances.

The Court of Justice also stated that the identification of the tax advantage such as "essential purpose" of the operations is not able to formulate a general condition for the recognition of the abuse, but it identifies a minimum threshold of unacceptability of abuse of rights (case 02/21/2008, C-425/06 *Part Service*).

Given that the taxpayer has the right to choose the form of the management of its business that will reduce the tax liability, the concrete identification of abusive behaviour is considered through the artificial deviation compared to the standard of the market as a decisive index for the recognition of abuse of rights. In this regard, formally distinct measures should be considered as segments of a single unitary transaction, if special circumstances reveal, in a consequential and convergent way, that the correlated acts form functionally a single and indivisible economic chain; in this case the tax treatment of the various acts, which would artificially separate, is that one provided for the principal operation (case 02/21/2008, C-425/06 *Part Service*).

In any case, the assessment of the existence of a fictional and artificial construction by the taxpayer should be made on for each case, basing on the circumstances of the activity actually carried on (case 09/12/2006, C-196/04, *Cadbury Schweppes*).

The same Court of Justice also points out the effect of new regulation of the abusive operation: and indeed, if there is any abusive conduct, it is stated that "*the transactions involved must be redefined so as to re-establish the situation that would have prevailed without the operations carried on through the abusive practice*" (case 02/21/2006, C-255/02, *Halifax*). It determines the failure of the effects produced by the abuse of law, with the consequent regeneration of the transaction according to the standards of behaviour normally applicable.

12.6 The Environmental Protection and the Principle "Who Pollutes Pays"

12.6.1 The Protection of the Environment as a Primary Value of the EU Legal Order; The Principle "Who Pollutes Pays"

In the EU law it is increasingly affirming the value of the environmental protection as a basic rule of coexistence in the European area. Especially, the environment is recognised as a universal value, to be protected e guaranteed in the interest of the whole society e, moreover, in the interest of the future generations.

After a first period where the environmental protection was limited to the market context, assuming a relevance as a precondition for the correct functioning of the commercial flows and of the economic activities, subsequently (since the Single European Act of 1986) it has been developing a process of promotion of the value "environment" as a specific purpose of the European Union, independent with respect to the economic freedoms. So, it has formed the conviction that the development of the European common market is strictly linked to adequate environmental standards, suitable to achieve a sustainable economic growth.

In this perspective, the EU law has promoted several legislative measures devoted not only to dictate incentives in favour of environment-friendly policies, but also to establish forms of punitive damages or otherwise generally disincentive with regard to political or industrial production (often unavoidable, at least in the short time) with a pollutant or anti-ecological content.

Particularly, it has been consolidating the principle "who pollutes pays" (expressly established by the art. 191 TFEU) as the basis for the establishment of environmental legislative measures, typically aimed at penalizing the use of production factors with a potential for pollution and, therefore, to promote the threefold aims of prevention, precaution and correction with respect to pollutants. This principle imposes to attribute a liability towards the community for the person (physical or juridical) who produces damage to the environment, legitimizing the adoption of legislative measures suitable for the recovery of the damage and the environmental protection.

In the area of the legislative measures devoted to the environmental protection are evidently included also the environmental taxes, which are typically suitable to penalize the use of pollutant factors or, on the other side, to stimulate the adoption of environmental factors. So, the environmental tax is addressed to pursue the triple purpose of protection, promotion and correction with regard to the pollutant activities.

The use of fiscal institutions permits to address the economic operations towards a correct purpose under an environmental perspective, so as to favour the reset of the environment damaged by the pollutant factors. In this way tax is utilised as a leverage in order to achieve the best allocation of the economic and social resources within the community, reaching at a balance between the economic growth and the protection of the environment.

Therefore, the principle "who pollutes pays" is suitable to legitimize some legislative measures of fiscal nature as an expression of the "functional finance" in order to promote the protection and the development of the environmental values.

The rule contained in the art. 191 TFEU does not establish an unconditioned obligation for the Member States to adopt in its legal order neither specific environmental measures, nor environmental taxes; this rule establishes the power for the Member States to define and to execute some environmental policies, utilising adequate legislative measures (including the environmental taxation).

So, the decision in order to the concrete adoption of some environmental tax is attributed exclusively to the Member States, being referred typically to the national sovereignty. The EU bodies maintain only a role of coordination and promotion in order to the environmental policy, but not also a legislative function.

The principle "who pollutes pays" represents the juridical basis for the adoption of the environmental taxation, but it does not constitute a binding obligation for the Member States. So, this principle must be considered as well as a programmatic (and not preceptive) principle.

12.6.2 The Environmental Taxes

The provision of an environmental tax identifies a contribution to cover the cost incurred by the civil community for social environmental pollution to be borne by the economic agent who undertakes the polluting behaviours. The logical basis of the ecological tax is identified in the causal relationship that must exist between the production of pollution and the tax levy.

In a legal perspective it is possible to introduce a basic distinction about the environmental taxes:

i. *the environmental tax* (in a strict sense) which shows an assumption characterised by the use of physical elements suitable to produce a damage to the environment (where the physical elements may concern every pollutant substance or natural resources which are consumed); in this case the taxable base is represented by the mentioned physical elements;

ii. *the tax with an environmental purpose*, where the assumption is not directly referred to the environment, but is characterised by the aim to pursue the protection of the environment; particularly this tax may represent an incentive for avoiding the pollutant activities or may produce a redistribution of the resources in order to favour the reset (or the development) of the environment.

In any case, in the literature it has been formulated the unitary classification of the environmental tax whose qualifying feature is identified in the consumption or in the production or in the release in the environment of some physical elements suitable to produce a negative impact for the ecosystem.

Therefore, the concept of tax is expanded with respect to the ordinary model of taxation usually assumed in the national legal systems: the assumption of the tax contribution is not identified in an event suitable to represent the economic attitude to the fiscal contribution (expressive of the personal wealth), but is verified with regard to the social impact over a general interest of the community.

The environmental tax may assume several forms, because it can concern the negative emissions or the pollutant products or the economic activities which can produce a damage to the environment. However, this tax is founded over some monetary performances rendered by the tax payers for which there is not any specific public service; this feature distinguishes the environmental tax from the tariffs for public services.

12.6.3 The Tax Facilitations with an Environmental Purpose

Among the fiscal institutions suitable for the execution of the principle "who pollutes pays", is included certainly the use of tax facilitations with an environmental purpose.

Indeed, it is evident that the legal measures adopted for pursuing a tax facilitation to the tax payers represent an adequate tool in order to stimulate virtuous behaviours by the economic agents with regard to the protection or to the development of the environment. Especially, the tax facilitation may be utilised with the aim to promote the reduction of pollutant activities or to encourage some operations which produce benefit for the environment.

Particularly, the tax facilitations referred to the environment may be distinguished as follows:

a. *Tax facilitations with a structural environmental feature*, which include the environmental benefit inside the assumption or the taxable base; these facilitations determine a tax advantage which is determined on the basis of a calculation of the environmental benefit;

b. *Tax facilitations with a functional environmental feature,* whose purpose consists in the promotion of some virtuous behaviours with reference to the environment, but where the environmental benefit is not included in the assumption or in the taxable basis.

12.6.4 The Principle of Differentiation and the Observation of other European Principles

The Member States may execute the principle "who pollutes pays" through several legal tools with reference to the tax area. This is a choice referred typically to the evaluations of a single State which apply basically a primary principle of the European legal order.

However, the use of the fiscal tools must respect some conditions established by the Treaty:

i. the principle of differentiation;
ii. the observance of other European principles.

The principle of differentiation (established by the art. 191, par. 2 TFEU) envisages the environmental policy to be adopted in consideration of the various territorial situations, so as to the protection of the environment cannot be defined in a unique way in the European Union, but it must be verified through a differentiated logic according to the different characteristics of the various territories. It is outlined, therefore, the link between the environmental purpose and the territory, which attributes a remarkable relevance to the legislative power of the various governments at a sub-State level in order to emphasize the specific needs of the minor communities.

The observance of the other European principles requires to coordinate the use of the fiscal tools with an environmental purpose with the other principles emerging from the European legal order. This rule has been repeatedly enunciated by the jurisprudence of the Court of Justice in order to point out that the environmental purpose cannot represent a justification for avoiding the respect of other European principles and rules. Therefore, the institution of an environmental tax (or of a tax facilitation with an environmental purpose) cannot counteract with the principle of non discrimination or the European freedoms, with the prohibition of national customs or other equivalent levies, with the prohibition of State aids or with other European principles regarding the tax matters.

Part III

The Anti-Sovereign

The Relation Between Sovereignty and Taxation Power Within the European System: The Anti-Sovereign

13

Contents

13.1 The "Negative" Taxation as a Qualifying Feature of the EU Law 189
13.1.1 The Evaporation of the Taxation Power Within the EU Legal System: The "Negative" Taxation 189
13.1.2 The Cultural Background of the Discipline of Fiscal Power Lies in the Economic Doctrine Which Affirms the Principle of Neutrality 193
13.1.3 The Instrumentality of the Taxation Power to the Market in the EU Legal Order: The "Neutral" Taxation 195
13.2 The Anti-Sovereign 198
13.2.1 The Relationship Between Sovereignty and Power of Taxation in the European Union: The Anti-Sovereign 198
13.2.2 The Dangers of the Anti-Sovereign: The Risks of the Assumption of the Idea of "Market" as Paradigm of Taxation Power 199
13.3 The Remedies Against the Risks of the Anti-Sovereign 202
13.3.1 The European Constitution as a (Partial) Antidote to the Anti-Sovereign ... 202
13.3.2 The Formation of a European Financial Administration 203
13.3.3 The EU Taxation Law in the Transition Phase 205

13.1 The "Negative" Taxation as a Qualifying Feature of the EU Law

13.1.1 The Evaporation of the Taxation Power Within the EU Legal System: The "Negative" Taxation

In the modern State the connection between sovereignty and taxation is one of the crucial points of the constellation of values defined at the constitutional level. The sovereignty, which is expressed in constitutional and pluralist democracies using the regulatory powers related to the primary interests and needs of community life according to a logic of balancing and weighting of the conflicts of interest, involves the management of the necessary financial resources as an essential tool for the realization of the general aims. The taxation, which is the key stage of the formation

P. Boria, *Taxation in European Union*, DOI 10.1007/978-3-319-53919-5_13

of public financial resources, is presented as well as a basic element of the institutional organization of the social community, as an indispensable condition for achieving the basic collective purposes, including the protection and the development of primary individual rights. In this perspective, taxation can be represented as a kind of transcendental condition of common life, not only aimed at the achievement of the overarching goals of freedom, security and development defined in the constitutional table, but also directly instrumental to the self-realization of the personality of each individual in the social community.

The declination of the link between sovereignty and taxation assume different connotations depending on the inclination of the axiological framework either towards the State or rather in the direction of the civil society (considering the rights and freedoms of individuals). In the diachronic modern constitutional history it has indeed found a significant correlation between the idea of sovereignty, widespread and accepted in the Constitution, and the general taxation.

In the English constitutionalism of seventeenth century the tax interest is presented firstly as a specific interest of the sovereign, focused mainly in his individual position of monarch, owner of an estate, which stands in the dialectical confrontation and often in conflict with the interest of the singular citizens to safeguard their own sphere of freedom and wealth; then, with regard to the developments of the bourgeois revolution, the relation of taxation with the general purposes of the economic and social community begins to emerge, although in a recessive position with respect to the fundamental rights of property and freedom recognised to the individual sphere.

French Enlightenment develops the connection between the sovereignty and the fiscal interest, being accentuated the instrumental role of the tax power with respect to the general purposes of the social community; in comparison with the tax interest, the individual rights fade significantly, going to occupy a subordinate and marginal role.

Even in the era of German Idealism the fiscal interest is presented as a fundamental value of the community, such as to establish the attribution of strong public powers to the State with respect to which the individual citizens stand in a totally subordinate position: thus it becomes definitively surpassed the thesis which identified the power to tax as an personal attribute of the monarch-sovereign, with consequent fixation of the relation between taxation and sovereignty at a primary axiological level.

Finally, in modern Constitutions it is peacefully implemented the reconciliation between the tax authority and the sovereignty: in particular, it is explicitly stated in any Constitution that the exercise of regulatory powers in tax matters is to be reserved primarily to the Parliament, indicating a clear connection between the democratic and popular sovereignty and the regulation of the phenomenon of taxation; it was also recalled, in this regard, how the recognition of Parliamentary competence essentially brings the debate about making law to the constitutional organ that, in line with the needs of a pluralistic society, seems better able to proceed to the balancing of the values involved in a complex and delicate matter like taxation.

Now, the advent of European law has placed a question of considerable consistency in order to the actual axiological dimension of taxation: in fact, if it is indisputable that the European Union has led to a significant restriction on the exercise of legislative powers of nation-States, it must be checked what is the role played by the power of taxation in this institutional context.

The examination effectuated in the previous chapters revealed in principle how the so-called "fiscal sovereignty" (namely the complex of powers relevant to the needs of the tax regulation) has remained a core competence of the Member States. The legal system coming from the EU sources is in fact marked by the principle of "negative taxation": the values of the Treaty and the provisions established by the Directives (and sometime by the Regulations) are clearly indicating that the primary aim set at the European level is represented by the identification of constraints and conditions, and more generally by the definition of "limits" to the exercise of legislative power by the Member States; therefore, it emerges the need to contain and to "limit" the taxation power outsourced at peripheral level (of the Member States) and not to assume that regulatory power at the central level (of the European Union). The "negative taxation" therefore expresses the purpose of limiting the fiscal sovereignty of another counterparty, which is still acknowledged to the individual Member States, excluding a main process of "positive taxation", through which the supranational organization (the European Union) independently establishes and implements a plan of legal values, as a result of the transfer of fiscal sovereignty from the national States.

It is to point out that even from a procedural and formal point of view the framework of "negative taxation" finds an evident confirmation. Indeed, the legal tool to be most commonly used to adjust the tax matters at EU level is undoubtedly represented by the Directives, being relegated to a very sporadic and marginal use the role of Regulations; in addition, the field of direct taxation—which is crucial to any modern tax system—is largely defined through the tools of the *soft law* (namely, recommendations, guidelines and opinions by the EU institutions); this is clearly indicating that the European Union operates basically as an institution of orientation and legal suasion, that is called to promote adherence to certain lines of regulation, but basically unfit to directly adjust the tax matter with strict and rigorous effects, especially when compared to the measurably relevance of the financial measures of the nation-States. It should be added that the principle of unanimity, that apply to the deliberations of the Council with regard to decisions on tax matters, is another significant indication of the unsuitability of the EU to intervene promptly and extensively to the definition of the tax regulations, expressing on the contrary the permanence of a role essentially limited to the identification of general principles that can detect the unanimous consent of each Member State.

A confirmation of the conceptual background shown here arises also from the position taken by the Court of Justice; in accordance with a framework of "negative taxation", it emerges a clear inclination towards specific treatment of the peculiarities of the case, which is typical of a jurisprudence oriented to the case law, which is essentially to express a certain lack of connective tissue of legal values. With regard to indirect taxes—known as the most regulated area of taxation in the European legal order—the Court assumes a recognitive attitude about the rules established in the primary and secondary EU law, refusing to put in critical discussion, or at least to develop an "evolutionary" interpretation, about the normative postulates expressed by the European legislature; only with regard to the area of direct taxes, considering the lack of adequate legislation regulating the matter, the case law focuses on the identification of general principles, related primarily to the protection of the four freedoms of the Treaty and to the affirmation of the principle of non-discrimination. In any case, the Court of Justice shows a highly pragmatic approach, aimed primarily at the declination of the obstructive rules formalized under the EU law (and firstly, of the principle of non-discrimination in its various forms and methods), without showing the axiological impulses which characterize the judicial construction of the law in the legal systems with "positive" content.

It should also be noted that the structure of fiscal powers as regulated under EU legal order appears to be completely upside down compared to the usual distribution of powers in the constitutional orders inspired by a federalist logic; indeed, the bodies of the European Union are holders of a regulatory power (although limited) with particular regard to the field of indirect taxes, while direct taxes are attributed to the exclusive competence of the individual Member States (except the guiding role of the EU institutions for some matters); on the contrary in the federal systems it is attributed to the central organs typically the power to regulate the direct taxation, and it is recognized a limited (and non-exhaustive) competence with regard to the indirect taxes and to the minor tributes. Even from this perspective it emerges the clear distinction of the European Union with respect to the federal organizations, confirming the lack of an incisive power to tax in the hands of the European bodies.

Therefore it is possible to argue that the "negative taxation" denotes the delimiting function of the European regulations with respect to the exercise of the tax powers by the nation-States, fragmenting (if not pulverizing) the constellation of values expressed around the phenomenon of taxation in individual particles with a precisely negative content.

The power of taxation, as an engine for development of the idea of sovereignty, from the centre of propulsion for the theoretical configuration of the primary relationships between the governed subjects and the governors, inescapable as a hub for the reconstruction of the balance between the interests of the social community and the rights and freedoms of the individual, which has been spreading in pluralistic democracies of the twentieth century, is transformed into the European framework in a mere regulatory mechanism to be contained and circumscribed. The European taxation thus becomes essentially a matter related to the research of "limits" and to the definition of the areas of national competence.

From this point of view, it seems possible to formulate an answer to the first reported question: the affirmation of the European Union is considered to indicate an evaporation of the power of taxation, at least when compared with the general lines of evolution in modern constitutional history. It is completely abandoned the axiological core of the taxation interest which has emerged in the current Constitutions, in favour of a minimal position oriented towards the negative logic of non-discrimination.

13.1.2 The Cultural Background of the Discipline of Fiscal Power Lies in the Economic Doctrine Which Affirms the Principle of Neutrality

One element that contributes substantially to the configuration of the European taxation in "negative" terms must be found in the power of suggestion exerted on the EU institutions by the economic doctrine that affirms the importance of the principle of neutrality in international transactions.

In fact, the concept of "common market" has been interpreted in the literature as a concept of efficiency in the allocation of resources and factors of production, and thus according to a typically economic perspective. So, the allocative efficiency is determined crucially on the basis of the phenomenon of taxation, given that the tax levy is likely to affect the flows of goods and capital towards the most productive locations, thereby distorting the functioning of the common market. In this context it is defining the principle of "fiscal neutrality" as the value for the purpose of establishing a common market of an international nature.

The neutrality assumes, however, several aspects, being able to configure as a criterion for the adjustment of fiscal policies related to the commercial or financial transactions for inbound or for outbound. Therefore it emerges the concept of "capital export neutrality" in order to indicate that the tax factor may not take the character of a distorting disincentive with respect to the conduct of cross-border investments, having rather to generate the equalization of the tax treatment of income produced abroad compared to the national income earned in the country. Moreover, it has been identified the concept of "capital import neutrality" in order to define the equality of tax treatment of capital arriving at the financial market of a State, regardless of the national or foreign origin, according to a perspective of "competitive neutrality".

The economic doctrine (R. A. Musgrave) pointed out that these two forms of neutrality can be adopted jointly when the tax systems of the nation-State show a fundamental identity, which may be judged as a mere theoretical abstraction, almost unworkable on a concrete plan. Thus it appears preferable to identify the priority form of neutrality to be taken as a reference point in the construction of a common fiscal policy by a supranational organization: in this regard it has been identified the criterion of "capital export neutrality" as the principle prevailing at an axiological level, since it is considered more functional in achieving an efficient allocation of capital on the global (supranational) market.

In fact, the capital export neutrality favours the outflow of capital to the locations with intrinsically greater capacity on the basis of the mere elimination of distortionary tax factors: capital and economic activities are thus oriented towards the production sites on the basis of evaluations linked exclusively to the degree of effectiveness and efficiency in the combination of production factors, and therefore according to an essentially economic judgment.

On the contrary, the "capital import neutrality" creates a flow of capital in the domestic market because of an equality of tax treatment; so if the tax rates (or generally the taxation) in the domestic market seem to be more attractive than those of the foreign States, capitals flow into the market of the importing State on the basis of assessments of fiscal convenience and not of economic opportunity.

The capital import neutrality poses therefore a typically "domestic" criterion, showing the features of its "internal neutrality" as dependent on the fiscal policy adopted exclusively by the importing State; otherwise, the capital export neutrality is presented as an "external neutrality" which is related to the policy of several States (namely the State of the source and the State of the residence), requiring the coordination and the adaptation of the national taxation laws.

Only the capital export neutrality must therefore be considered as an appropriate criterion to ensure the effective tax neutrality with respect to the allocation of factors of production within the common market and as such it represents the concept of neutrality to be taken in the definition of the fiscal policy to the supranational unions.

Moreover, the criterion of capital export neutrality has the added advantage of leaving almost unchanged the tax sovereignty of the individual States, because each of them is able to maintain the full capacity to establish the system of taxation applicable to the economic agents, without interfering with the efficient allocation of productive resources at the international level: it is sufficient, in the implementation of the aforementioned criterion of "external neutrality", to ensure the full deduction of the tax paid by an economic agent in other EU countries on the basis of multilateral agreements, to achieve the full equality of tax treatment of the foreign income compared to the income generated in the country.

Therefore it is clear that the taxation is considered in predominantly negative terms, as a factor likely to lead to distortions than the "natural ability" of the market operations, and therefore as an element to circumscribe (if not even to delete).

This theoretical approach was clearly taken as the basis of the decisions of EU institutions in order to regulate the phenomenon of taxation, formulating a clear option for the reconstruction of the power of taxation as a specific and typifying attribute of the nation-State to be contained and restrained where appropriate to avoid interference with the structure of the common market.

In this regard it must be cited the Ruding Report where it is clearly stated the belief that the primary aim of the European Union in the field of taxation consists in the elimination of distortions and inefficiencies determined by the national tax systems about the full allocative efficiency of productive resources. According to a careful investigation carried out on the economies of EU countries, it was found that taxation is likely to influence sensitively the choice of location of productive investment and, consequently, the conformation of the legal and financial structures of economic agents; it produces, therefore, the opportunity to establish appropriate criteria of "external neutrality" capable to ensure precisely the elimination of tax barriers that may interfere with the pursuit of an optimal structure of the common market, at least in terms of allocative efficiency.

13.1.3 The Instrumentality of the Taxation Power to the Market in the EU Legal Order: The "Neutral" Taxation

The "negative" taxation of the EU legal order reconnects to the axiological liberal system which has typically denoted the development of the European Union. As already observed, the principle of tax non-discrimination constitutes one of the most significant corollaries of the four fundamental freedoms of the Treaty, expressing one of the most robust safeguards for the protection of a competitive structure of the market.

However, it is known that the promotion of economic freedom was the driving force for the development of the common market, featuring not only the rules of the Treaty, but also the rules developed in the derivate legislation. This is an assessment easily understandable, considering that the conviction of the Member States about the economic integration was seen as the first, indispensable step towards the political and social integration.

By the approval of the Treaty of Maastricht some additional values, not of an economic nature—and in particular the security policy and the development of international policies—have been considered in the EU constitutional framework in order to express an enlargement of the European purposes. However, it still seems to be limited to a primordial stage the practical and operational implementation of such values, remaining the EU integration process basically related to typically economic purposes.

The dominant idea of the EU law is so yet to be identified in the protection and promotion of competition and connected freedoms, avoiding obstacles and barriers that could restrict the free economic action of the individual agents resident in the Member States. The "negative" taxation is presented as the legal instrument to prevent tax regulations that can take an obstructive connotation about the free development of the common market.

It is evident that the cardinal point of reference regarding the evolution of the EU legal order about taxation matters can be identified in the concept of "market", or rather in the conviction that the protection of the market—understood as the metaphoric place where the commercial transactions and the entrepreneurial initiatives are carried out—represents the primary goal of the process of European integration.

This ideological background appears consentaneous to a general climate, more and more widespread in European democracies, which seems to reproduce patterns strongly inclined towards political and institutional structures of liberal type, in which the decisions on the redistribution system of general income are assigned precisely to the natural composition of the "market", as a consequence of the crisis of the Welfare State. The market is thus seen as a kind of regulatory mechanism of social and economic balances, to serve as a parameter of the allocative efficiency only on the basis of individual capacities and not on the basis of general assessments previously determined by the State.

Therefore, also the fiscal phenomenon is adjusted accordingly: the European order comes to reducing the weight of the tax measures, while necessary for the achievement of essential resources for public expenditures, in order to avoid that taxes can result in impediments that alter the ability of the natural functioning of the market. "Negative" taxation is presented as well as the corollary of "neutral" taxation, which assumes the character of the postulated theoretical background around which is developed the legal system. In this perspective, there is a clear understanding in the EU institutions about the implementation of economic theories that face the model of "neutral" taxation for the configuration of the systems of public finance in supranational unions.

Moreover, the formulation and the development of the concept of "harmful tax competition" as an emerging value of EU legal order aligns conceptually the "negative" taxation, connecting to the same axiological liberal system. This idea denotes the opening to the "market" as a reference point of the fiscal choices, clearly showing the failure of national fiscal sovereignty with regard to the logic of full competition of economic agents.

It should be noted, however, that the assumption of the "market" as the reference value of the EU legal order contrasts sharply with the choices adopted in the Constitutions of the nation-States, where the taxation is generally recognized to have an important propulsive function with respect to the process of social transformation. The implementation of an efficient and balanced tax system, in fact, performs a crucial role in the social development programs in line with the fundamental rule of substantial equality formally implemented in many constitutions and in any case received in the material Constitution of each democratic country. The involvement of all citizens in the payment of taxes, eliminating spaces of impunity and privilege, as well as reducing the specific weight of the categories favoured by reasons of timocratical prevalence, more than any other social mechanism allows to operate a distribution of resources between the unequal people which is capable to produce a reduction of economic inequalities and an elevation of weaker social classes. The adjustment of taxation—*rectius*, the taxation interest—connects closely to the protection of values far from the neutrality of the market, to identify otherwise in the promotion of social integration through the establishment of appropriate "chances of life" that enables people effectively to achieve the implementation process of social freedom. The fiscal interest in national Constitutions thus appears as a principle of "freedom from deprivation", under which a pulse is output to correct imbalances in the distribution of natural resources so as to facilitate the process of social transformation.

In this perspective it is clear that the line of demarcation between the EU law and the national Constitutions is typically due to a different presentation of the criterion of equality as founding principle of the taxation. In the EU law it has been imposed the logic related to the principle of "formal equality", whereby the position of the taxpayers—essentially concerned to as *homines oeconomici* (so as agents of the production system)—is assessed on the basis of a "horizontal" equality of treatment: taxation should not alter in any way the opportunity to enter the market, so as to ensure a levelling of the tax burdens for homogeneous categories of subjects, regardless of timocratic importance or productive force; the individuals are therefore equalized as to the taxation in relation to the formal aspect of the production of a single event economically significant (act or activity) and not further discriminated with reference to the subjective position overall. The national Constitutions shows, otherwise, the acceptance of a criterion of taxation regulated on the redistribution of national income for social purposes; it determines the transposition of the principle of "substantial" equality, according to which the taxation should be joined to the purpose of promoting the equality of *chances* between consociates, and thus should overcome the differences (especially economic and social) of the starting positions in order to seek equal treatment of "vertical" type; in this context, the levelling of taxes is not identified with regard to the single economic act or activity, but rather to the overall situation of the taxpayer—regarded not as an economic agent, but essentially as a "personality" whose development and self-determination is to be encouraged—and therefore by reference to the figure of the substantial economic capacity of the subject.

Accordingly, the principle of non-discrimination is a natural application of the principle of formal equality within the EU, used to preserve the maintenance of liberal opportunities typically belonging to the system of the European Union (namely the equal access to the market). In contrast, the tax interest and the ability to pay are the axiological corollaries of the substantial equality spread in the national Constitutions, devoted to promote the social development programs and the redistribution of national income among the consociates.

This is a clear axiological demarcation also reflected in terms of tax system. Indeed, in the context of the EU legal order there is no place for some regulations completely metabolized into national legislation (such as the progressivity of taxation or the use of tax benefits in order to permit a social configuration of the economic structure, or the protection from the tax evasion or elusion and the general promotion of efficiency measures, which are clearly linked to the tax interest to ensure the effective collection of tax revenues to be used for the pursuit of collective utility).

The "neutral" finance towards which the EU legal order is oriented appears, therefore, significantly different, in axiological terms, from the national tax legislation, which on the contrary is inspired by models of "functional" finance. The idea of "market" is worth so to mark a remarkable distance between the regulatory system of the taxation power granted within the EU and the legal framework widespread in the individual States.

13.2 The Anti-Sovereign

13.2.1 The Relationship Between Sovereignty and Power of Taxation in the European Union: The Anti-Sovereign

The "negative" taxation, expression of an ideological option oriented towards the concept of market and the neutrality of the public finance, clearly indicates how the EU legal system is characterised by a subtractive but not substitutive function with regard to the tax power exercised by individual Member States.

In other words, the European Union assumes directly the power to regulate some tax matters to be subtracted to the competence of the nation-States, and thus reducing the national fiscal sovereignty; otherwise, the EU legislation shall not determine basically a positive regulation of taxation, and therefore a substitution of a new fiscal power to the power originally conferred to the nation-States, but rather shall produce a restriction on the national tax power, aimed at preventing that it can be addressed in certain directions, and in particular that might result as an obstructive factor to the freedom of the market and to the structure of competitive business.

The "negative" taxation typically marks the limitation of the national sovereignty in tax matters, without leading to a replacement of the same through a European fiscal sovereignty. In this perspective it can be argued—echoing the intuition of relevant constitutional doctrine—that the European Union represents the "anti-sovereign", in opposition to the national power in order not to introduce a new sovereignty, but to contain and sometimes to exclude the sovereignty of nation-States.

Indeed, it is known that the European Union shows some institutional features that are not easily reconcilable (at least in the version currently regulated by the Treaties) with the modern concept of sovereignty. Especially the EU lacks the two fundamental preconditions of sovereignty: the conception of the ascending power (determined by the popular representativeness) and the connection with a nation of people. Furthermore, it seems doubtful the uniqueness of a political subject, appearing often the EU initiative distributed in a plurality of organs and institutions with an highly differentiated statute, which basically express the inability to assume a monopolistic control of the sovereign power. The same institutional organization, spoiled by the lack of democratic legitimacy, is often an expression of the interests of social and economic forces not ordered according to the usual criteria of the political competition, but rather through extemporary and uneven agreements.

Therefore, it produces naturally the attribution to the European Union of a regulatory function that does not respond to a logical ordering with a positive content, according to the directions made by the holder of the sovereign power, but rather it is aimed at annihilating the national sovereign power, so to remit the composition of the interests at stake to the trans-national judgment of the market.

The process of erosion of national sovereignty does not respond to the establishment of a new order of values adjusted according to the feedback of a different and superior holder of sovereign power, but on the contrary is the premise of the spread of a self-referential and self-regulated order, which is formed as a result of commercial transactions and by the meeting of supply and demand and is not imposed by a democratic force representative of the interests of the social community; an order that is typically responsive to the logic of the market competition in the global society, which misses any constellation of collective values, and where it emerges and self-protects the freedom to act for the pursuit of economic goals.

Therefore it also changes the traditional correlation between freedom and public power: in the democratic systems the scope of the individual freedom has to be compared and weighted with the general interests of the social community which are guaranteed by the law and therefore represented and collected by the sovereign power; within the European framework the freedom to act is presented essentially as a freedom of fact, whose implementation appears as a space not governed by the law or at least (if it is accepted the idea that the market is an order of relations *always* governed by a norm of law) subtracted from the control of the public power, being referred directly to itself and therefore disconnected from any relationship with respect to the general interests and to the social purposes.

In this scenario it coherently emerges the "negative" taxation of the EU legal order, bringing out a set of rules that cancel out the national sovereignty and thus undermine the reasons of legitimacy of the tax power and, at the same time, bring to the market the ability of self-regulation of the economic phenomena. The power of taxation thus loses all social elements, waives the progressive aspirations to the income redistribution and the promotion of a process of transformation of society in line with the needs of removing the material obstacles to the full development of the personality of all citizens, and becomes a mere instrument for raising financial resources for the performance of public tasks, to be carried out without further social connotations, as neutral as possible with respect to the productive ambitions of the economic agents.

The plot developed in the tax legislation so provides a significant conceptual contribution to the reconstruction of the relations between centre and periphery in the European framework, contributing to the configuration of the European Union as an anti-sovereign which limits and weakens the sovereignty of the nation-States, but does not replace it with a different sovereignty, capable of a discretionary assessment about the general interests, considering instead that the assessment must be remitted to the market evaluations.

13.2.2 The Dangers of the Anti-Sovereign: The Risks of the Assumption of the Idea of "Market" as Paradigm of Taxation Power

In the anti-sovereign perspective it further increases the tension of the relationship between the EU law and the national law, being emphasized a contrast between the European system decisions, due to the market, and the complex of values with a social connotation, metabolized in the national Constitutions.

In this regard, according to a recurring trait of the democratic systems of the twentieth century, the social structure and the balance of interests are realized through the regulation of the relationship between the political power and the economic power. The globalization of the economy and the development of productive entities with a multinational character, connected to a spatial context which is not circumscribed and limited to the national territory, have changed the logic of the national adjustment of economic phenomena. The international market does not coincide with the territory of one or more States, it is not marked or divided by material borders and even does not show the physicality of the territory; the space of the globalized economy (more correctly the plurality of international economic spaces) is marked from the network of trade and contractual relationships, often virtual and managed by remote, and therefore it is de-materialized or rather *de-territorialized*. The abandonment of reference to the territory is to indicate the decline of the national political power, inappropriate with respect to the regulation of phenomena that develop over the spatial area of competence, in an axiological dimension that escapes, often completely, the regulatory capacity of the national sovereignty.

The split between political and economic space is so recorded in the European treaties through the abandonment of the national sovereignty—as in tax matters—and emphasized by setting an order of freedom that recognizes the capacity for the self-regulation of the globalized market. In this perspective, it is argued, not unreasonably, that the EU legal order presents itself as an *a-political* framework, namely disengaged from the fabric of social values that characterize the democratic Constitutions and orient the political action, rather having to be brought to the spontaneity of the market interests, as a kind of natural and neutral regulation about the production and the commercial exchange.

The crisis of the traditional concept of absolute sovereignty of the nation-States thus leads to put the control of the economic resources from the political class to the forces that direct the unified market. There is thus a kind of reverse logic than the traditional relationship between State and market: the Member States begin to become functional to the markets, and adhere to the decisions and the linkages emerging from the market about the economic and social reasons, moving away from the traditional concept of sovereignty. It determines a clear reversal of the relationship between economic power and political power: the plan of the choices and decisions made by the State is often subordinated and controlled by the international finance and the supranational economy. So the control of social changes tends to escape from the political and institutional governance of the States to flow naturally towards the centres of power that determine, more or less unconsciously, the economic relations which combine and dissolve time after time in the market.

The national State, in this context, becomes a regulatory centre of the market, the holder of a power of mediation about the economic resources between the social partners and the productive forces multinationals. In essence, it emerges an "administrative" function of the State instead of the social function which denoted the development of pluralist democracies and which has been widely absorbed in the democratic Constitutions.

It may be obvious what the major threat is looming with the consolidation of such a weakening of the national sovereignty: bringing the decisions of general interest to the natural composition of demand and supply and relying on the capacities of self-regulation of the market attribute the power to define the set of conflicting interests to the international economic community, where—as well know—there is not a stable hierarchy of powers and it totally lacks an institutional organization, but rather it comes to appear the dominant economic forces of large multinational corporations, trade unions and productive organizations, centres of cross power and groups of interest, even transient and temporary.

The market, in its most "wild" and aggressive profile, where the "strong agents" also ruthlessly impose themselves on the "weak agents" favouring the expulsion from the production cycle or otherwise confining them to narrow areas, is the true core of the decisions that are taken in a globalized society. The marginalization of the political power and the downsizing of the national sovereignty behave like the emergence of a class of indefinite and indefinable holders of the new sovereign power (often even causally), which is called upon to make the decisions regarding the allocation of resources and wealth flows.

The danger of the anti-sovereign, therefore, is the abandonment of the idea of the social function in the establishment of a market order which may produce a balance between the different interests of the social community, according to a plan of progressive transformation of the society fostered and promoted by the set of values assumed in the constitutional charters; on the contrary, it is determined a structure of economic relations uncontrollably generated by the market forces and related to the ungovernable and casual composition of the interests through the trading transactions, which shows the progressive strengthening of the "strong and rich agents" to the detriment of the "weak and poor agents". In addition, the democracy of the market that is going to replace in concrete terms the democracy of the Constitutions appears unfair and socially disharmonious, calling to the effective participation in the competitive game—and thus to the allocative decisions—only a few subjects and excluding the majority of associates (considered only as passive consumers).

In this light, the assumption of the "negative" taxation as paradigm of the taxation power stresses the risks of the anti-sovereign: the abandonment of any social connotation about the redistribution of the tax burden, which is considered only as a mere financial instrument for the coverage of the public debt, steadily promote the primacy of the market compared to any function of the State in order to conform the regulatory and public power; it establishes the axiological interests of the competitiveness compared to the general interests of the social community; it determines the decay of the fabric of the values established by the democratic Constitutions in comparison with the need for the self-adjustment of the economic forces.

The tax interest and the ability to pay, the general needs of the community and the individual liberties, which have traditionally made up the constitutional dialectic of the tax law, lose this role in the EU legal order, assuming the hazy outlines of a distant luminescence, which is basically unable to address the regulatory action.

On the contrary, the principle of non-discrimination—which is the cardinal point of reference of the tax legislation in the European legal system—creates a new framework based on the free competition, which is the natural balance of the market interests, for the choices on the allocative and redistributive structures.

The "negative" taxation provides, therefore, a further impulse to the spontaneous order of the market, to the *cosmos* (in the sense proposed by Von Hayek) of the economic forces, in which the composition of the interests happens according to an a-causal and indeterminate logic, to the detriment of the less protected parties of the social community.

13.3 The Remedies Against the Risks of the Anti-Sovereign

13.3.1 The European Constitution as a (Partial) Antidote to the Anti-Sovereign

A remedy to contain the risks of the anti-sovereign seems to be visible in the promulgation of the (future and hopeful) European constitution, which can be defined as a pattern of the values that serves to trace the path of the EU legislation.

In particular, hopefully the European Constitution could resume in its plot legislation the principles formulated in the constitutional traditions of the Member States.

At first, as part of a general review of the mechanisms of formation of the EU rules about taxation matters, it should be accepted and formalised the principle of "the consent to the imposition" which implies the popular representativeness as a source of legitimation of the taxation power. This would obviously reassemble the split between the exercise of the power of taxation and the lack of democratic legitimacy that seems to be one of the main critical factors in the process of adjusting the fiscal phenomenon at the European level.

In addition, and more importantly, the European Constitution should pick up the fundamental principles of the ability to pay and of the tax interest as unavoidable moments of the dialectic of the constitutional tax law.

On the one hand, it seems so appropriate that in the European Constitution it is formalised the interest of the general community corresponding to all the citizens and residents of the Member States (to be called as a real *European taxation interest*) to the collection of the financial resources necessary for the development and the promotion of the process of social transformation and the removal of the material obstacles to pursue the substantial equality of the consociates.

On the other hand, it should also be highlighted the principle of allocation of tax burdens among the citizens that connects to the principle of equality, always understood in a substantial way, aimed at encouraging the pursuit of a genuine equality of chances of the individuals.

Both principles may be expressed in an explicit form, as in the most recent European constitutions (Italy, Spain, Portugal), or be implicitly inferred through an exegetical interpretation endorsed by the parliamentary work and the reconstruction of doctrine and jurisprudence. In any case, regardless of the option granted, the presence of these principles into the structure of constitutional values undoubtedly gives an innovated axiological impetus to the normative regulation of the phenomenon of taxation, taking it away from the exclusive conditioning pulse of the market and bringing it to a controlled environment, governed by the political class in adherence to a system of values which is socially shared.

Certainly, the highlighting of the constitutional principles that innervate the tax laws is not enough to exclude definitively the permanent role of the anti-sovereign: the tax regulations of the Treaty and the maintenance of the regulations of the derivate tax law always remain oriented in the direction of the "negative" taxation and therefore would leave unchanged the normative assumption for the attribution of the allocative decisions to the market, resulting in a relevant limit to the national sovereignty without actually replacing it with a European sovereignty.

In any case, the claim in the European Constitution of the basic values of the fiscal dialectic introduces a fundamental element of impulse in order to initiate a regulatory process in a counter-direction compared to the anti-sovereign, that is suitable to trigger progressively the formation of tax rules with a positive content (and not only with a limited and negative function), orienting the tax function towards a social and redistributive task that fits with the modern concept of sovereignty.

In this context, the approval of the European Constitution, without representing a *panacea* that removes any risk of the assumption of the market as a paradigm of the power of taxation, may undoubtedly be considered as a fundamental step forward in the construction of a European sovereignty and, in the meanwhile, in the substantial regulation of the phenomenon of taxation according to the logic of a federal State which is worth to partially and progressively overcome the anti-sovereign.

13.3.2 The Formation of a European Financial Administration

Alongside the development of the European Constitution a second element seems to provide a significant boost to overcome the logic of the anti-sovereign, namely the formation of a real European financial administration.

In particular, it consists in initiating a process of setting-up a force of control which is relevant for tax purposes within the territory of the entire European Union, with the means and powers typically granted to the tax authorities, but that is dropped by the national executive and which is placed at the service of the EU institutions (according to a model to some extent prefigured in the *Fiscalis* program). The presence of administrative offices typically dedicated to the achievement of fiscal targets of the European Union, independent from the national forces, is to ensure an instrument capable of actually allowing the concrete implementation of a European tax policy, without having to depend on the degree of adhesion and cooperation of the Member States. Indeed, the establishment of an independent administrative force allows the European Union to act directly for the protection and implementation of the EU regulatory requirements, through a complex of offices that receive instructions and directives by the EU institutions and answer for their actions only to the same institutions.

Following the general guidelines presented by relevant doctrine on the interesting hypothesis to establish a world tax organization, it can imagine that such a European administrative force entrusted with a wide range of functions and in particular:

- *cognitive functions*, relating to the acquisition of specific information on tax-relevant behaviours of residents in the European Union, including electronic tax declaration (it can even think about the preparation of *tax return* models according to the needs and characteristics defined at EU level that each taxpayer could send annually);
- *control functions*, relating to the monitoring and to the control of the economic agents residing in EU territory, to be achieved through the so-called "knowledge management" (and thus through desk checks, with examination of databases and telematics verification of the facts), and, where appropriate, through checks "on the ground", with access and inspections of the places where economic activities take place;
- *conciliatory functions*, to be achieved through the establishment of offices and conciliation procedures of the tax disputes out of court, both with reference to the possible disputes between States and the European Union, and (in further perspective) with regard to the claims of individuals residing in the EU territory with respect to the rules of EU origin;
- *functions of study*, such as the analysis of the trends of national tax systems and the problems of international taxation (and particularly of harmful tax competition) with the main task of compiling statistics and details of general economic and fiscal policy, which should become the common reference point for the legislative activity in the field of taxation (in that respect it can think about the preparation of an annual tax report of the EU);
- *advisory functions*, consisting of the technical assistance to the legislative and parliamentary institutions and to the national tax administrations, in order to facilitate the coordination and harmonization of regulations and procedures with respect to the models highlighted in the EU legal order.

In essence, these functions are recognized, almost everywhere, to the national tax authorities and are a necessary counterpart of the fiscal sovereignty as they allow to concretely implement the rules developed in the abstract into legislation.

On the other hand, it can be considered as acquired into the democratic constitutional system the recognition of the public function of the administrative apparatus, as an essential tool for the achievement of the general purposes of the social community through procedural modules which allow to compose the inevitable tensions between the individual freedoms and the administrative efficiency. In particular, in the dialectic between the interests and values involved in the tax matters, the administrative operation is teleologically coordinated with the balance achieved by the taxation legal system in order to facilitate the solution of weighting of individual rights with the taxation interest. The organizational dimension, and especially the regulation of the financial administration, thus assumes a clear instrumental connotation to the definition of the tax laws.

In this perspective, it should be evident that the formation of a European administration constitutes an essential moment in the process of establishing a EU taxation sovereignty, as an essential step to make concrete and operational the regulatory provisions enacted into the EU law.

This should facilitate the effective dissemination and stabilization of normative values developed at the EU level, in line with the principles accepted in the European Constitution, thus helping to overcome the phase of the "negative taxation" and, however, accentuating the sensitivity of the EU institutions to consider the power of taxation not as a mere tool of the market liberalization, but also as an effective means to implement directly the social and redistributive policies that represent assets of an irrevocable and pluralist democratic Constitution of our time.

13.3.3 The EU Taxation Law in the Transition Phase

At the current stage the EU institutions show to be taking a typically transient historic step, going to overcome the initial design of a confederation of States devoted to satisfy only the purpose of an economic cooperation and moving in the direction of an institutional organization with the consistency of a federation which has an effective and overt power of sovereignty.

Even the legal system suffers from this stage presenting as a transitional law, which characterizes the legal categories of flowing and mutable meanings.

Therefore, the "negative" taxation, despite having been the original paradigm of the power of taxation, currently assumes the character of a transitory discipline, which is destined to be overcome by the progressive changes resulting from the European constitution and from the still incipient "federalization" of the European Union.

At least, at this stage, the defensiveness of the fiscal sovereignty constantly sought by the individual Member States can be covered under a different point of view: it does not seem to indicate the entrenchment of the States on selfish positions, aimed at combating the centripetal logic of the European aggregation; indeed, this would conflict not only with the popular European motion which has continually been raised in the policy statements of several governments, but it also appears purposively unjustified considering that none of the major Western countries intend to carry out international tax competition to the detriment of other countries.

Rather, it is to be assumed that the defence of the fiscal sovereignty on significant portions of the national taxation is due to an axiological choice: through the proper taxation, the States choose to preserve the constellation of values consecrated in the constitutional Charters by the attacks of the anti-sovereign, thus avoiding to give up in the regulation of the phenomenon of taxation the fundamental values of equality and freedom, protection of the social community and promotion of the civil transformation, fighting back with the strong impetus of the market towards the definition of the values and interests according purely to the expectations and the decisions of the economic forces.

The tightness of the national fiscal sovereignty can thus be understood not as an obstructive or protective attitude of the nation-States, but as the defence of the Constitutions from the attack of the anti-sovereign, waiting for the completion of institutional processes that have as their goal the formation of a federal European State.

In essence, the maintenance of the strong core of the national taxation power is one of the last gasps of the democratic Constitutions, perhaps a bridge for the transition to a new higher constitutional Charter of supranational and European dimension, which is in any case symptom of the vitality of the constitutional values in the democratic society and expression of the ability to resist to the urges coming from the market and its economic forces.

Bibliography

AA.VV. (2007) *Aiuti di Stato in materia fiscale*, a cura di L. Salvini, Padova.

AA.VV. (2008) *Per una costituzione fiscale europea*, a cura di A. Di Pietro, Padova.

AA.VV. (2009) *Agevolazioni fiscali e aiuti di Stato*, a cura di M. Ingrosso, Napoli.

AA.VV. (2012) *Diritto tributario internazionale*, a cura di R. Cordeiro Guerra, Padova.

AA.VV. (2013) *I principi europei nel diritto tributario*, a cura di A. Di Pietro, Padova.

Ardizzone (1988) *Comunità economica europea (disciplina tributaria e valutaria)*, in *Enc. Giur. Treccani*, VII, Roma.

Ballarino, Bellodi (1997) *Gli aiuti di Stato nel diritto comunitario*, Napoli.

Basilavecchia (2009) *L'evoluzione della politica fiscale dell'Unione europea*, in *Riv. Dir. Trib.*, I, 361.

Berlin (1988) *Droit fiscal communautaire*, Paris.

Boria (2004) *L'anti-sovrano*, Torino.

Boria (2010) *Diritto tributario europeo*, Milano.

Brennan, Buchanan (1980) *The power to tax: analytical foundations of a fiscal constitution*, Cambridge.

Carinci (2006) *Autonomia impositiva degli enti sub statali e divieto di aiuti di Stato*, in *Rass. Trib.*, 1783.

Carpentieri, Lupi, Stevanato (2003) *Il diritto tributario nei rapporti internazionali*, Milano.

Comelli (2000) *Iva comunitaria e Iva nazionale*, Padova.

Cosciani (1958) *Problemi fiscali del mercato comune*, Milano.

Del Federico (2006) *Agevolazioni fiscali nazionali ed aiuti di Stato tra principi costituzionali ed ordinamento comunitario*, in *Riv. Dir. Trib. Int.*, 3.

Devereux, Pearson (1989) *Corporate tax harmonisation and economic efficiency*, Londra.

Fantozzi (2003) *Problemi di adeguamento dell'ordinamento fiscale nazionale alle sentenze della Corte di giustizia europea e alle decisioni della Commissione CE*, in *Rass. Trib.*, 2262.

Fantozzi (2007) *L'armonizzazione comunitaria degli ordinamenti tributari, tra autorità e consenso*, relazione al convegno di Catania del 14.9.2007.

Ficari (2007) *Aiuti fiscali regionali, selettività e insularità: dalle Azzorre agli enti locali italiani*, in *Dir. Prat. Trib. Int.*, 319.

Fichera (1992) *Le agevolazioni fiscali*, Padova.

Fichera (1997) *L'armonizzazione delle accise*, in *Riv. Dir. Fin.*, I, 219.

Fransoni (2007) *Profili fiscali della disciplina comunitaria degli aiuti di Stato*, Ospedaletto – Pisa.

Gallo (2000) *Mercato unico e fiscalità: aspetti giuridici del coordinamento fiscale*, in *Rass. Trib.*, 725.

Gallo (2003) *L'inosservanza delle norme comunitarie sugli aiuti di Stato e sue conseguenze sull'ordinamento fiscale interno*, in *Rass. Trib.*, 2282.

La Scala (2005) *I principi fondamentali in materia tributaria in seno alla Costituzione dell'Unione europea*, Milano.

P. Boria, *Taxation in European Union*, DOI 10.1007/978-3-319-53919-5

Lupi (2004) *Concorrenza tra ordinamenti, comunità europee e prelievo tributario*, in *Rass. Trib.*, 989.

Melis (2008) *Coordinamento fiscale nell'Unione europea*, in *Enc. Dir. Annali I*, Milano, 406.

Melis (2009) *La delega sul federalismo fiscale e la cosiddetta fiscalità di vantaggio: profili comunitari*, in *Rass. Trib.*, 997.

Miceli (2009) *Indebito comunitario e sistema tributario interno*, Milano.

Miceli (2014) *Federalismo fiscale e principi europei*, Milano.

Musgrave R. (1969) *Fiscal systems*, Yale university press, New Haven.

Nicolaides (2004) *Fiscal aid in the EU: the limits of tax autonomy, World competition.*

Ocse (1998) *Harmful tax competition: an emerging global issue.*

Ocse (2000) *Progress in identifying and elimination harmful tax competition practices.*

Orlandi (1995) *Gli aiuti di Stato nel diritto comunitario*, Napoli.

Perrone (2006) *L'armonizzazione dell'Iva: il ruolo della Corte di giustizia, gli effetti verticali delle direttive e l'affidamento del contribuente*, in *Rass. Trib.*, 432.

Perrone (2007) *Diritto tributario e convenzione europea dei diritti dell'uomo*, in *Rass. Trib.*, 675.

Pontolillo (1999) *Il ruolo della fiscalità nella UE*, in *Rass. Trib.*, 23 ss.

Roberti (1997) *Gli aiuti di Stato nel diritto comunitario*, Padova.

Russo (1990) *L'armonizzazione fiscale nella Comunità europea*, in *Rass. Trib.*, 628 ss.

Sacchetto (1994) *Armonizzazione fiscale nella comunità europea*, in *Enc. Giur. Treccani*, Roma.

Schiavolin (2000) *Accise*, in *Enc. Dir., Aggiornamento* IV, Milano, 23 s.

Tridimas (2006) *The general principles of the EU law*, New York.

The manufacturer's authorised representative in the EU is Springer Nature Customer Service Centre GmbH, Europaplatz 3, 69115 Heidelberg, Germany. If you have any concerns regarding our products, please contact ProductSafety@springernature.com

Printed and bound by CPI Group (UK) Ltd, Croydon, CR0 4YY
01/10/2026
02225968-0003